Moral Responsibility
in the Holocaust

Moral Responsibility in the Holocaust

A Study in the Ethics of Character

David H. Jones

ROWMAN & LITTLEFIELD PUBLISHERS, INC.
Lanham • Boulder • New York • Oxford

10/99   #40200356

ROWMAN & LITTLEFIELD PUBLISHERS, INC.

Published in the United States of America
by Rowman & Littlefield Publishers, Inc.
4720 Boston Way, Lanham, Maryland 20706

12 Hid's Copse Road
Cumnor Hill, Oxford OX2 9JJ, England

British Library Cataloguing in Publication Information Available

Library of Congress Cataloging-in-Publication Data

Jones, David H., 1930–
    Moral responsibility in the Holocaust : a study in the ethics of
character / David H. Jones
        p.   cm.
    Includes bibliographical references and index.
    ISBN 0-8476-9266-3 (cloth : alk. paper). — ISBN 0-8476-9267-1
(pbk. : alk. paper)
    1. Holocaust, Jewish (1939–1945)—Moral and ethical aspects.
I. Title.
D804.3.J66   1999
940.53'18—dc21   98-48271
                                                            CIP

Printed in the United States of America

♾ ™ The paper used in this publication meets the minimum requirements of American National Standard for Information Sciences—Permanence of Paper for Printed
Library Materials, ANSI Z39.48-1984.

For Virginia

Contents

Preface

The idea for writing a book about moral responsibility in the Holocaust grew out of my experience teaching a philosophy course on the Holocaust for over a decade at The College of William and Mary. The course focuses on issues of responsibility raised by what people did or failed to do in the course of the implementation of the "final solution of the Jewish question" in Germany and throughout German-occupied Europe. The very first time I taught the course, I realized that the relevant philosophic materials on responsibility were widely scattered in the literature in various disciplines such as ethics, philosophy of law, and psychology. Not only was it difficult to bring these diverse materials together and synthesize them into a coherent theory of responsibility, only a few of them were addressed to the particular problems raised by the Holocaust. Consequently, in order to provide my students with a workable theory of moral responsibility that they could apply directly to these problems, I found myself writing longer and longer handouts on topics such as the basic concepts of responsibility (praise, blame, excuses, justifications, liability to punishment, etc.), virtues and vices, and self-deception, illustrating how these concepts are applied by using examples drawn from the Holocaust. These handouts evolved into the chapters in part 1 of this book.

I finally started writing this book as a result of prodding and encouragement from my colleague Larry Becker. As I shared my continuing frustration over not being able to find a philosophy text that covered the ethics of responsibility for the Holocaust course, Larry suggested that I write the book I had in mind myself. In addition to suggesting the idea, Larry also provided encouragement while I was writing the book and gave me the opportunity to share early drafts of a couple of chapters with members of the social and political philosophy discussion group at William and Mary.

My principal aim in writing this book is to help readers (whether or not they are students in a Holocaust course) think more clearly and systematically about questions of individual moral responsibility raised by the Holocaust. This aim can be achieved, I believe, by using the considerable resources already at our disposal in such disciplines as ethics, law, and psychology (to name only a few). I make no attempt to present an original or comprehensive theory of responsibility. Indeed, the theory I present and defend in part 1 is parsimonious; it contains only those elements that I believe are needed to address the flagrant violations of basic moral principles that constitute the essence of the Holocaust, especially the unjustified mass killing of defenseless Jewish men, women, and children, with the aim of permanently destroying the Jewish people. Although I make a number of moral judgments (on the basis of explicit reasons and arguments) about the blameworthiness and praiseworthiness of certain kinds of perpetrators, accomplices, bystanders, victims, helpers, and rescuers (including some particular individuals), I do not present these judgments as being definitive or beyond dispute. However, I hope that attentive readers may profit from following the reasoning by which I come to those conclusions, even if (as is very likely to be the case) they do not always agree with them.

Acknowledgments

The author and publisher gratefully acknowledge permission to quote material from Raul Hilberg, *The Destruction of the European Jews,* rev. and definitive ed. (Holmes & Meier, 1985).

Introduction

Studying the ethics of the genocide that has become known as the Holocaust is fundamentally different from studying other issues of life and death such as abortion and capital punishment. Leaving aside a considerable number of dogmatists, there are many people who recognize that the ethical issues raised by abortion and capital punishment are complex. Consequently, they do not find it unusual that some people, even those who have given the issues careful thought, hold conflicting opinions about them. In sharp contrast, there is virtually universal agreement that the genocide at the heart of the Holocaust was deeply immoral; there simply is no public controversy on this issue. In this respect, genocide has come to occupy a place in popular moral opinion rather like that held by slavery. Not only is there no popular debate on the question of whether the Holocaust was right or wrong — no one since the Nazis has attempted to give it a philosophical justification or ethical defense. Even anti-Semites have had to settle for Holocaust denial. Of course, this is as it should be. In chapter 2 I provide a justification for the correctness of the popular consensus that genocide is immoral, since this moral judgment cannot be justified merely by pointing to the consensus. The fact of consensus alone is not sufficient to establish an opinion as morally correct.

Nonetheless, despite the consensus on the profound evil and immorality of the Holocaust, there is a great deal of confusion about other closely related, and equally fundamental, ethical questions. First, there are basic questions about human nature and moral psychology. If genocide is so obviously immoral, how were people able to participate in mass slaughter, seemingly with a clear conscience? Why did so few people help or rescue Jews? Second, there are questions about responsibility. Were the perpetrators to blame for killing? Did they realize the immorality of what they were doing? If they were ignorant of the immorality of their acts, was their ignorance culpable? Were they coerced, or did they kill willingly? Did bystanders know about the genocide? If not, were they to blame for not knowing and for not helping? Third, there are questions about how to prevent future genocides, for example, would an increase in the general level of altruism in society be the best way to prevent genocide? Are better political institutions needed? Or is outside intervention necessary?

One main reason for writing this study of moral responsibility in the Holocaust is very simple: Most of the literature on the Holocaust has not been generated by moral philosophers but by historians, psychologists, theologians, experts in Jewish studies, journalists, and survivors. Consequently, although the writers in these various disciplines have done an enormous amount of extremely valuable and essential work, there has been relatively little sustained and probing ethical analysis of these kinds of fundamental ethical questions about human nature and responsibility.

It is not that these writers are unaware of ethical questions. Historians, psychologists, and others often give seemingly obligatory assurances that they too assume that individual human beings have to make choices and are responsible for them. Here is a sample culled from works on the Holocaust by a variety of professionals.

> How did the German bureaucrat cope with his moral inhibitions [against killing the Jews]? He did so in an inner struggle, recognizing the basic truth that he had a choice. He knew that at crucial junctures every individual makes decisions, and that every decision is individual. He knew this as he faced his own involvement while he went on and on. (Raul Hilberg, historian)[1]

> Some of these conventional explanations also caricature the perpetrators, and Germans in general. The explanations treat them as if they had been people lacking a moral sense, lacking the ability to make decisions and take stances. They do not conceive of the actors as human agents, as people with wills, but as beings moved solely by external forces or by transhistorical and invariant psychological propensities, such as the slavish following of narrow "self-interest." (Daniel Jonah Goldhagen, political scientist)[2]

> The thrust of this chapter has been to bring the phenomena of the camps closer to home, to see how this horror, this inhumanity, could have been the product not only of deranged individuals but of "normal" people placed in deranged circumstances. . . . There is a danger in this . . . a tendency to slide from understanding to excusing. . . . But no matter how well we understand, no matter how clearly we see the behavior as an expression of something basic to human nature, we cannot alter our moral judgments of these actions or of the actors who performed them. (John Sabini and Maury Silver, psychologists)[3]

> I also fear that some readers may see me as exculpating killers; I have no such intention. Understanding the motives of those who perpetrate genocide may seem to blunt outrage because the individual and group changes that lead to increasingly vicious acts may become not only more comprehensible, but even seemingly natural. Although outrage is easier to feel in the face of uncomprehended evil, to understand is not necessarily to forgive. In fact, understanding can *increase* our

awareness of the culpability of perpetrators of great evil because we can see them as human beings, not beasts without moral capacity. (Ervin Staub, psychologist)[4]

The Holocaust was not the result of the machinations of a few people at the top but required over its twelve-year history the active participation and toleration of hundreds of thousands of people in every walk of life. These people were not unintelligent, amoral, or insensitive. They acted consciously, conscientiously, and in good faith in pursuit of what they understood to be good. What is unique about the Holocaust in not that its ethic operated with such force but that it allows us to achieve an insight into just how greatly an ethic does condition what we see as we relate to other people. It is just this power of an ethic to shape conceptions that the preceding pages have, I hope, begun to define. (Peter Haas, professor of religious studies)[5]

Each quotation reflects some degree of unease with the fact that historical, social, and psychological explanations of the perpetration of the Holocaust tend to ignore the role of individual choice and responsibility. For example, Raul Hilberg's own historical explanation focuses almost entirely on institutional events and processes; he gives a masterful account of the way in which German bureaucracies, manned by functionaries with strong authoritarian and anti-Semitic traditions, met the challenge of implementing the "final solution of the Jewish question" with creative improvisation and unflagging efficiency. In addition, he defends the controversial thesis that eastern ghetto Jews, trapped by their own cultural traditions of accommodation and passivity, were complicitous with the Germans in bringing about their doom. The overall picture drawn by Hilberg is decidedly fatalistic. He concludes that there was no way the Germans could have failed to overwhelm the Jews and succeed in killing most of them. Here is Hilberg himself summing up his view: "The destruction of the Jews was thus no accident. When in the early days of 1933 the first civil servant wrote the first definition of "non-Aryan" into a civil service ordinance, the fate of European Jewry was sealed."[6]

What is left out of Hilberg's explanation, of course, is the literally millions of choices that individual Germans and Jews made that, taken together, constitute the large-scale institutional events and processes he seeks to explain. It is not that Hilberg is failing to do something that he ought to do. Historians often, and quite properly, deal with human events at the level of whole societies, states, armies, and other institutions and groups, largely ignoring the individual human beings who compose them. However, when one is explaining something as dreadful and morally disturbing as the Holocaust, the need to look more deeply into the behavior of individuals and the choices they made becomes undeniable. This helps explain why Hilberg interjects a few comments about German bureaucrats' realization that they had their own individual choices to make. At the same time, his explanation of how they made those choices is devoted almost entirely to citing institutional measures of "repression" and ideological justifications.[7] Similar observations can be made about psychological explanations of the behavior of perpetrators based on analogies with how experimental subjects have been found to behave in scientifically controlled settings. For example, Sabini and Silver use findings from Milgram's well-known obedience studies and from Zimbardo's prison simulation study to explain the behavior of perpetrators of the Holocaust. Of course, neither Milgram nor Zimbardo attempted to ethically evaluate the behavior that their experiments elicited (in Milgram's study, intentionally subjecting a "learner" to what was believed to be painful and dangerous levels of electric shock; in Zimbardo's study, subjecting volunteer "prisoners" to verbal abuse, physical abuse, and humiliation); neither did they attempt to assess the blameworthiness of their subjects. However, after using these findings to explain the behavior of actual perpetrators in the Holocaust, Sabini and Silver have last-minute worries about being misunderstood. This helps explain why they add a coda from which the quotation above is taken.

The statement by Goldhagen is a quotation from his book *Hitler's Willing Executioners,* one of several recent studies that mark a departure from the institutional focus that pervades so much historical research on the Holocaust. Goldhagen insists that we will not understand how the Holocaust happened until we understand the thinking and motivation of the individual perpetrators.[8] Goldhagen's focus on individual perpetrators, and especially his searching inquiry into their motives, brings us much closer to the ethical questions that I want to investigate, but it stops short of ethics and moral judgment. Goldhagen is explicit about his reasons for refraining from making moral judgments.

> It is because the task of this investigation is historical explanation, not moral evaluation, that issues of guilt and responsibility are never directly addressed. The book explains why and how people thought and acted as they did, not how we should judge them. . . . I also have no particular professional competence for writing about these issues, so I was eager to leave them, on the one hand, to those with greater expertise—such as moral philosophers—and, on the other hand, to each reader to judge for himself or herself according to each one's own moral framework.[9]

Ervin Staub's book *The Roots of Evil* is one of the best attempts made so far to find an adequate explanation of how genocide occurs. It is especially fine in its sophisticated use of psychological theory and experimental findings to explain how genocide emerges from a process of gradual escalation of violence that he calls "a continuum of destruction."[10] However, Staub also defends a version of cultural determinism according to which individuals who are completely socialized to have unquestioning loyalty to the group and obedience to authority, and consequently regard these values as overriding individual moral autonomy, cannot reasonably be held accountable for their resulting misdeeds. Moreover, he clearly thinks that socialization into German culture at the time of the Holocaust had these characteristics.[11] This view appears to be inconsistent with Staub's claim (quoted above) that he does not wish to exculpate perpetrators of genocide. This is another example of a fundamental ethical issue left unresolved, one that I address in chapter 5.

Peter Haas's book *Morality after Auschwitz,* from which the quotation above is taken, is similar to Staub's in defending a complex (and in my view insightful) explanation for the fact that so many Germans came to believe that killing the Jews was at least morally permissible, if not required. In Haas's view, each society creates and adopts an ethical system that provides justifications for acting one way or the other; German society under the Nazi regime had such an ethical system, which had evolved out of traditional morality. Consequently, he argues, many (most?) individual Germans sincerely believed that killing Jews was not immoral. This explains why they did not feel guilty or responsible. However, Haas never raises the question whether individual Germans might be blameworthy for accepting the bizarre and empirically false beliefs about Jews that "justified" the killing. In other words, he never asks whether their ignorance was culpable.

If historians, psychologists, and other writers on the Holocaust have dealt in a less than satisfactory manner with important ethical questions of responsibility, professional moral philosophers have not done much better. It should be mentioned immediately, of course, that there is a relatively small group of philosophers who have published work on the ethical questions raised by the Holocaust, some of it quite distinguished. Karl Jaspers's classic essay, *The Question of German Guilt,* was first published in Germany in 1947. In it Jaspers touches on several of the topics in this study.[12] However, in contemporary mainstream philosophy, especially in the Anglo-American scholarly community, only a few people have given the Holocaust and the ethical issues it raises the kind of attention they deserve, including (without attempting to be exhaustive) Lawrence Blum, Berel Lang, Gerald E. Myers, Alan Rosenberg, John K. Roth, and Laurence Thomas.[13] In particular, moral philosophers (with the notable exception of a few individuals like those mentioned) have not used their much-needed professional skills on the fundamental ethical questions about individual responsibility in the Holocaust. The most directly relevant effect of this neglect is the need for a systematic application of philosophical ethics to these issues; this study is intended to address that need.

Recent years have witnessed an increasing number of "fine-grained" historical and sociological studies of categories of individuals involved in the Holocaust. In-depth studies of perpetrators, victims, and rescuers have provided a wealth of pertinent examples and detailed relevant information that can be used to illustrate the moral problems that people encountered and identify the principal difficulties in trying to make assessments of moral responsibility. Goldhagen's *Hitler's Willing Executioners* (1996), which takes a look at the men who served in police battalions (among others), was preceded by Christopher

Browning's *Ordinary Men* (1992) on the same topic.[14] Ernst Klee and others
wrote "*The Good Old Days*" (1988), first published in Germany and also devoted to perpetrators.[15] Among a number of studies of victims of the Holocaust
are Marion Kaplan's *Between Dignity and Despair* (1998) on German Jews;[16]
A Mosaic of Victims (1990), edited by Michael Berenbaum;[17] and Raul
Hilberg's *Perpetrators Victims Bystanders* (1992).[18] Rescuers have long received attention with books like Thomas Keneally's *Schindler's List* (1982)
and Philip Hallie's *Lest Innocent Blood Be Shed* (1979).[19] Now we also have
Nechama Tec's *When Light Pierced the Darkness* (1986), Gay Block and
Malka Druker's *Rescuers* (1992), and Eva Fogelman's *Conscience and
Courage* (1994).[20]

A Brief Overview of the Content of This Study

This study is presented in two parts. The first part discusses the ethics of responsibility, and the second part deals with substantive problems raised by the
Holocaust. Readers who are unfamiliar with ethics should definitely read the
first part. For other readers this will not be necessary. Readers who are already
familiar with ethics, particularly with the concepts and distinctions used in the
ethics of responsibility (e.g., praise and blame, excuses, and liability to punishment) and topics in the psychology of morals (e.g., character, virtues, vices,
and self-deception) may want to skip part 1, "The Ethics of Responsibility,"
and go directly to part 2, "Application of the Ethics of Responsibility to Problems Raised by the Holocaust," which begins with chapter 5, "Political Culture,
Socialization, and Responsibility."

Part 1: The Ethics of Responsibility

The first part of the study (1) provides a set of concepts and distinctions that are
intended to serve as a philosophical tool kit to be used in the remainder of the
study and (2) introduces some of the main problems to be studied, using examples from the Holocaust. Each of the four chapters deals with a principal
concept (or set of concepts) in the theory of moral responsibility. Throughout
this study we will be concerned with *individual* moral responsibility, with an
emphasis on personal blameworthiness and praiseworthiness for one's actions.
Chapter 1 is devoted primarily to defining and explaining these basic concepts
of moral responsibility and contrasting them with legal responsibility. Chapter
2 addresses two basic ethical questions. The first basic question is, What makes
the actions of perpetrators of the Holocaust morally wrong? As I mentioned,
the nearly universal consensus that they were wrong does not suffice to show
that they were. The answer I defend, put simply, is that those actions violated
basic rules at the core of morality, for example, the prima facie duty not to harm

others. I do not attempt to provide the kind of comprehensive theory of ethics that would be needed to address a wide range of problems in ethics; the basic rules of prima facie duty cover the vast majority of actions (right and wrong, good and bad) that constitute the morally relevant set of actions addressed in this study. The second basic question is, What makes good moral character? The answer I give, again put simply, is that good character consists in having certain traits, or moral virtues, among which are benevolence, conscientiousness, courage and self-control, self-knowledge, and practical wisdom. Correspondingly, bad character consists in the absence of virtues or the presence of vices, traits such as cruelty, untrustworthiness, cowardice, self-deception, and culpable ignorance. These virtues and vices are described, explained, and justified in considerable detail.

Another important aspect of responsibility, moral excuses, is introduced in chapter 3. The main purpose of the chapter is to identify the principal excuses recognized in commonsense morality and to gain an understanding of why they are properly recognized as providing exculpation for wrongdoing and blocking blame. For example, an excuse that one acted under coercion (assuming that the facts that are alleged are indeed true) acts to block the blame that one might otherwise deserve by showing that one's action did not result from some bad motive or trait in one's character. This brings out an interrelationship between the concept of excuse, on the one hand, and both the concepts of blameworthiness and of good character, on the other. I take great pains to distinguish between the justified social activity of giving and accepting valid excuses, and the parasitic activity of making (bogus) excuses.

Because so many people caught up in the Holocaust were motivated to avoid taking responsibility for what they were doing (or not doing), they often engaged in self-deception in order to avoid feelings of bad conscience. Consequently, I devote chapter 4 to the psychology and ethics of self-deception. The discussion is restricted to garden varieties of self-deception that could almost be called normal because they are so pervasive in human thinking. That does not mean that all self-deception is morally acceptable, far from it; some of the worst atrocities were perpetrated because people deluded themselves. I largely ignore pathological forms of self-deception such as unconsciously determined denial and psychotic delusions, since they play at most a very marginal role in explaining the actions of perpetrators and others involved in the Holocaust.

Part 2: Application of the Ethics of Responsibility to Problems Raised by the Holocaust

In part 2 of the study I use a set of distinctions among the various roles that people played in the Holocaust that has been widely adopted in the literature: perpetrators, accomplices, victims, helpers and rescuers, and bystanders. This scheme for organizing the discussion into five chapters allows me to address the different ethical problems that arise for each of these groups of individuals. Of course, there are some problems that cut across this classification; for example, many individuals in each category were highly motivated to "make excuses" and engage in self-deception, but the motives tended to be different from one category to the next.

In general, my aim is not to make judgments about the blameworthiness or praiseworthiness of particular individuals. The main reason is that in most cases hardly anything is known about individuals. Information that does exist about particular persons is often either not directly relevant or not sufficiently detailed to justify a moral judgment. Instead, I try to identify the principal moral issues faced by a typical person in each category, discuss the relevant evidence about the various ways in which many people actually behaved, and then draw what seem to be reasonable conclusions about what the relative degree of blameworthiness or praiseworthiness of a person would most likely be for having acted, or failed to act, in these various ways. There are three principal exceptions to this approach. In chapter 4 I scrutinize Albert Speer's claim that he was to blame for having engaged in self-deception about the nature of the Final Solution; in chapter 6 I discuss the moral blameworthiness of Adolf Hitler in some detail, both because he was the principal perpetrator and because there is a lot of relevant information about him; and in chapter 9 I discuss in some detail the moral praiseworthiness of several individual rescuers about whom we have a good deal of information.

In chapter 5 I critically evaluate and reject a particular thesis of cultural determinism that, if it were true, would seriously challenge the viability of the project in the second part of this study. This is the thesis mentioned previously in connection with the work of Ervin Staub, namely, that people who were socialized in the bad political culture that existed in Germany before and during the Holocaust ended up lacking the capacity to realize that it was immoral to kill Jews and thus suffered from a form of diminished responsibility that rendered them not blameworthy (or at least not as blameworthy) for their participation in the Holocaust as they would otherwise have been.

As I have already indicated, the subject of chapter 6 is the actions and moral character of Adolf Hitler. Chapter 7 deals with the actions of ordinary Germans who served in police battalions that had a central role in perpetrating the genocide against the Jews. The central factual question addressed concerns the motives of these men: Did they kill willingly, or were they coerced or in some other way caused to participate by the situation in which they found themselves? The assessment one makes of their blameworthiness clearly depends on what one judges to be the correct answer to this basic question. In contrast with the topic of perpetrators, it might seem that there is no need for a chapter on the responsibility of the victims. This attitude is mistaken. First, it is important to remember that responsibility does not always involve blameworthiness; there is also the positive aspect of responsibility, namely, praiseworthiness. In chapter

8 I discuss various ways in which the behavior of victims was exemplary, even in some of the most horrendous conditions. I also evaluate some criticisms of the behavior of some of the Jewish councils that governed the eastern ghettos for the Germans, as well as the Jewish police who carried out German policies, including rounding up their fellow Jews for deportation to death camps.

In chapter 9 I look at three categories of people: helpers, rescuers, and by-standers. The discussion is designed to establish three conclusions, first, that many helpers and rescuers acted in ways that were clearly supererogatory, that is, above and beyond duty; second, the first conclusion notwithstanding, many helpers and rescuers only did what they had a duty to do (though they were nonetheless praiseworthy for doing so, since it is often difficult to do one's duty); and third, that many (perhaps most) people who were bystanders were blameworthy for failing to do what was clearly their duty, namely, to give help and to rescue Jewish victims whose lives were in jeopardy when they had opportunities to do so.

This study does not discuss how the Nazis came to power in Germany or who was responsible for that calamity; my sense is that there is more than enough blame to go around.[21] Neither do I discuss the Nuremberg trials or other war crimes trials, since that topic alone would require another book. Furthermore, legal responsibility, especially liability to criminal punishment, raises a whole host of other ethical issues that would take us far afield from moral responsibility. However, I briefly discuss the relationship between moral responsibility and legal liability in chapter 1.

Suggestions for Complementary Readings for Courses on the Holocaust

This study was written with the hope that it would be both of interest to a general audience and useful as a text in courses on the Holocaust at the college and university level. Each of the chapters in part 2 contains a great deal of relevant information derived from historical and psychological studies on which much of the ethical analysis is based; therefore, it is feasible to use this study without collateral readings if an instructor so desires. However, it has been my experience that most students profit greatly from reading works on the Holocaust from other disciplines, particularly history and psychology, as well as original sources such as memoirs by survivors. The works listed below are suggested because they complement this study by providing greater historical depth, alternative psychological perspectives, and firsthand accounts by survivors. Some of these works are also listed along with others in the bibliography, "Suggestions for Further Reading," provided at the end of each chapter. Needless to say, the list below is highly selective; it is meant only as a helpful tool for instructors and interested readers.

History Texts

Raul Hilberg. *The Destruction of the European Jews*. Student ed. New York: Holmes &
   Meier, 1985. Contains extensive excerpts from the complete three-volume work
   listed below; both were published in 1985. Excellent on the German planning, implementation, and execution of the "final solution to the Jewish question." Paperback.
————.. *The Destruction of the European Jews*. Rev. and definitive ed. 3 vols. New
   York: Holmes & Meier, 1985. Page references in this study are to this edition. The
   complete edition is not suitable for classroom use.
Jackson J. Spielvogel. *Hitler and Nazi Germany*. 2nd ed. Englewood Cliffs, N.J.: Prentice-Hall, 1996. Excellent text with a wealth of background on German culture, a biographical and psychological study of Hitler, and perhaps the best thirty-page ac-
   count of the Holocaust currently available. Paperback.
Lucy S. Dawidowicz. *The War against the Jews*. New York: Bantam Doubleday, 1991.
   A defense of the "intentionalist" view that the Final Solution was the result of Hitler's
   long-held and deliberate plan to kill all Jews. Paperback.
Martin Gilbert. *The Holocaust*. New York: Holt, 1987. A very readable history. Paperback.

An Anthology of Historical Documents

Lucy S. Dawidowicz, ed. *A Holocaust Reader*. New York: Behrman, 1976. Covers both
   German and Jewish perspectives using primary sources translated into English. Paperback.

Psychology

John Sabini and Maury Silver. "On Destroying the Innocent with a Clear Conscience:
   A Sociopsychology of the Holocaust." In *Moralities of Everyday Life*. Oxford: Ox-
   ford University Press, 1982. Paperback.
Mark P. Zanna et al. *The Psychology of Prejudice: The Ontario Symposium*. Hillsdale,
   N.J.: Erlbaum, 1994. Recent work on stereotypes, racism, and authoritarianism.

Survivors' Memoirs

Jean Amery. *At the Mind's Limits: Contemplation by a Survivor on Auschwitz and Its
   Realities*. Bloomington: Indiana University Press, 1998. The author, the son of a
   Catholic mother and a Jewish father, was born Hans Meier in Vienna, Austria.
Primo Levi. *Survival in Auschwitz*. New York: Collier, 1993. Widely regarded as among
   the most penetrating and acute memoirs by a survivor. Paperback.
Elie Wiesel. *Night*. New York: Bantam, 1982. A haunting account of imprisonment in
   Auschwitz and Buchenwald. Paperback.

A Comprehensive Holocaust Anthology

John K. Roth and Michael Berenbaum, eds. *Holocaust: Religious and Philosophical Implications*. New York: Paragon, 1989. An excellent anthology of reflections on the
   nature and meaning of the Holocaust. Paperback.

Notes

1. Raul Hilberg, *The Destruction of the European Jews* (New York: Holmes & Meier, 1985), 3:1012.

2. Daniel Jonah Goldhagen, *Hitler's Willing Executioners: Ordinary Germans and the Holocaust* (New York: Knopf, 1996), 13.

3. John Sabini and Maury Silver, *Moralities of Everyday Life* (New York: Oxford University Press, 1982), 86–87.

4. Ervin Staub, *The Root of Evil: The Origins of Genocide and Other Group Violence* (New York: Cambridge University Press, 1989), xiii–xiv.

5. Peter J. Haas, *Morality after Auschwitz: The Radical Challenge of the Nazi Ethic* (Philadelphia: Fortress, 1988).

6. Hilberg, *Destruction of the European Jews,* 3:1044.

7. Hilberg, *Destruction of the European Jews,* 3:1010–1029.

8. Goldhagen, *Hitler's Willing Executioners,* introduction and chap. 1.

9. Goldhagen, *Hitler's Willing Executioners,* 481, paperback edition published by Vintage Books.

10. Staub, *Root,* chap. 6

11. Staub, *Root,* 148.

12. Karl Jaspers, *The Question of German Guilt* (New York: Capricorn Books, 1947).

13. Lawrence A. Blum, "Moral Exemplars," in *Midwest Studies in Philosophy,* vol. 13, *Ethical Theory: Character and Virtue,* ed. Peter A. French, Theodore E. Uehling Jr., and Howard K. Wettstein (Notre Dame, Ind.: University of Notre Dame Press, 1988), 196–221; Lawrence A. Blum, "Altruism and the Moral Value of Rescue: Resisting Persecution, Racism, and Genocide," in *Embracing the Other,* ed. Pearl M. Oliner (New York: New York University Press, 1992), 30–47; Berel Lang, *Act and Idea in the Nazi Genocide* (Chicago: University of Chicago Press, 1990); *Echoes from the Holocaust,* ed. Alan Rosenberg and Gerald E. Myers (Philadelphia: Temple University Press, 1988); John K. Roth, *Approaches to Auschwitz: The Holocaust and Its Legacy* (Atlanta: John Knox, 1987); Laurence M. Thomas, *Vessels of Evil: American Slavery and the Holocaust* (Philadelphia: Temple University Press, 1993).

14. Christopher Browning, *Ordinary Men: Reserve Police Battalion 101 and the Final Solution in Poland* (New York: HarperCollins, 1992).

15. Ernst Klee, Willi Dressen, and Volker Riess, *"The Good Old Days": The Holocaust as Seen by Its Perpetrators and Bystanders* (New York: Free Press, 1988).

16. Marion Kaplan, *Between Dignity and Despair: Jewish Life in Nazi Germany* (New York: Oxford University Press, 1998).

17. Michael Berenbaum, *A Mosaic of Victims: Non-Jews Persecuted and Murdered by the Nazis* (New York: New York University Press, 1990).

18. Raul Hilberg, *Perpetrators, Victims, Bystanders: The Jewish Catastrophe, 1933–1945* (New York: HarperCollins, 1992).

19. Thomas Keneally, *Schindler's List* (New York: Simon & Schuster, 1982); Phillip Hallie, *Lest Innocent Blood Be Shed* (New York: Harper & Row, 1979).

20. Nechama Tec, *When Light Pierced the Darkness: Christian Rescue of Jews in Nazi-Occupied Poland* (New York: Oxford University Press, 1986); *Rescuers: Portraits*

of Moral Courage in the Holocaust, ed. Gay Block and Malka Drucker (New York: Holmes & Meier, 1992); Eva Fogelman, *Conscience and Courage: Rescuers of Jews During the Holocaust* (New York: Doubleday-Anchor, 1994).

21. Jackson J. Spielvogel, *Hitler and Nazi Germany: A History* (Englewood Cliffs, N.J.: Prentice-Hall, 1992), 53–81, for a succinct account.

PART 1

THE ETHICS OF RESPONSIBILITY

Chapter 1

Moral Responsibility

A Theory of Moral Responsibility

Beginning in this chapter and continuing into the next three chapters, I present and defend a theory of individual moral responsibility. In part 2 I apply that theory to a number of problems raised in the study of the Holocaust. The theory is parsimonious in the sense that it provides only the basic elements of moral responsibility that are needed to think reflectively about those problems. The basic features of this theory can be introduced through a simple example. Suppose that in 1942 a German man living in Berlin informed the Gestapo that a Jewish woman and her child were hiding with another German family in an apartment next door; as a result, the Jewish woman and her child were arrested and sent to Auschwitz, and the members of the German family sheltering them were also arrested and their apartment was confiscated by the informer and his family. I assume that this is a *morally wrong act,* all things considered.[1] The German informer was not an anti-Semite and he knew that what he was doing was wrong, but he did it anyway in order to get his neighbors' apartment. He acted *intentionally* and *knowingly.* Moreover, the informer did not have to tell the Gestapo about the hidden Jews; no one else knew that they were being hidden by the family next door. So even if the Gestapo had found out about the hidden Jews, the informer would not have been implicated; he and his family had not been involved in any way. So the informer's act was completely *voluntary;* he had a choice; he could easily have kept quiet. Finally, the informer acted from *morally bad motives: indifference* and *greed.* He did not care what happened to the Jews or his neighbors; what he cared about was getting the apartment for himself and his own family.

Once all of these relevant features have been spelled out, we can see that the informer's act makes him *morally blameworthy;* his act brings moral discredit on himself and makes him reprehensible. Why? Because he intentionally committed a terrible act, and he was motivated by greed and was completely callous and indifferent to the great harm he caused others. The degree of blameworthiness increases with the seriousness of the wrong act and the badness of the motives. Consequently, he deserves to be judged adversely by others; they are morally justified in regarding him as very reprehensible and holding him in great contempt. I call this *liability to judgmental blame.* Being morally blameworthy for wrongdoing in this sense is the most basic kind of responsibility that I address, since elements of it are presupposed in virtually all other aspects of our social practices and institutions—of holding people responsible for what they do. Being blameworthy for doing some particular wrong act is necessary for people to be properly held to account for the wrong they have done. This can be seen in the law, for example. The most important way of holding people accountable for their action is by imposing legal punishment. Some criminal penalties, such as imprisonment or death, are severe. Consequently, persons cannot be convicted of first-degree murder unless they have killed another human being intentionally; in legal terms, they must act with *mens rea* (a guilty mind). Thus an element of moral blameworthiness is a necessary condition for one important kind of legal responsibility: *liability to criminal punishment* for murder.

A second aspect of the theory of moral responsibility that I am previewing here falls in the area of moral philosophy called *virtue ethics,* which deals with standards of good and bad moral character. Good traits of moral character such as benevolence are called virtues, whereas bad traits such as cowardice are called *vices.* Some standard of character is presupposed in any judgment of moral blameworthiness, since in the most usual kind of case, persons act as they are predisposed to act, that is, they act "in character." The man who informed on the Jewish family betrayed his bad traits of character: the vice of greed and a moral defect, a lack of benevolence. Correspondingly, the behavior of the members of the German family that was hiding the Jews demonstrated such virtues as benevolence and conscientiousness. Traits of character are comparatively stable features of a person's psychological makeup; they are not ephemeral or episodic. The possession of virtues and vices determines whether a person is morally good or bad and how that person ought to be regarded morally, especially when questions of responsibility (blameworthiness) arise.

Of course, people sometimes act "out of character," and this complicates the issue of blameworthiness. For example, persons who do something wrong that is out of character for them may be judged less blameworthy than they might otherwise be, in effect, getting credit for the good moral character shown in their past conduct. Of course, people who have less than sterling characters may also act out of character by doing the morally right thing on occasion; yet, they are not deemed more praiseworthy on that account alone unless their right act is especially heroic or generous. For example, Oskar Schindler was a German businessman and war profiteer who seemed to many people to be utterly incapable of having any moral care or concern for others. Yet he splendidly rescued over a thousand Jews from death, and he is admired for it. Perhaps Schindler was (as Lawrence Blum has argued) a "responder" whose true moral character had never before been brought out until he was confronted with the brutality of his fellow Germans.[2]

A third aspect of the theory of moral responsibility that I am previewing involves *justified moral excuses*. Another way of indicating that the German informer was unquestionably blameworthy for his act is to state that he had no excuse. This does not mean that as a matter of psychological fact he would not have tried to make excuses if he had been accused of wrongdoing; rather, it makes the ethical claim that, given the relevant facts, he had no justifiable, valid excuse that would have exonerated him objectively for his action. If he had had a valid moral excuse in the strict ethical sense that I have described, he would have been completely blameless for his act of informing on his neighbors who were hiding the Jewish mother and her child. A valid excuse would block blameworthiness and would give him moral immunity from any kind of sanction or punishment; a blameless person does not deserve to be punished.

What kinds of circumstances would constitute a valid moral excuse? One condition that is generally recognized as a morally valid excuse is *ignorance,* that is, lack of relevant knowledge. For example, if the informer had not known that the mother and child were Jews who would be sent to Auschwitz, he might have had a valid moral excuse. His having been ignorant in this specific way would have blocked the otherwise justified inference that he had intentionally informed the Gestapo so that the Jews would be arrested; this in turn would have blocked questions about his motives and moral character, in short, questions about his moral blameworthiness. That is what makes ignorance a valid excuse. Another recognized valid excuse is *mistake*. For example, the informer might have sincerely believed that the Jewish mother was really a dangerous enemy agent working for the Allies. A complication that can be left for later is the question of whether the informer's ignorance and mistake were his fault; only nonculpable ignorance and mistakes can serve as valid excuses. A final example of an excuse that arises frequently in connection with the Holocaust is *coercion*. For instance, a soldier who acted under threat of dire punishment (e.g., execution) would have a justified excuse for complying with an order to kill an unarmed Jew.

A review of all the relevant circumstances and conditions of the informer's act fails to uncover anything that can serve the function of a valid moral excuse that blocks blameworthiness in the way that ignorance and mistake do; on the contrary, all of the facts point in the opposite direction. Indeed, the example of the informer's action serves as a paradigm to teach what it means to be fully blameworthy. Each of the conditions (e.g., ignorance and mistake, and others I will consider later) that are generally recognized as valid moral excuses serve to contradict or undermine one or more of the elements in my paradigmatic example of blameworthiness: a person (1) performs a wrong act, (2) knows it is wrong, (3) does it intentionally and (4) voluntarily, and (5) from a morally bad motive. Moreover, everything else being equal, the more seriously wrong the act, the greater the degree of blameworthiness of the agent.

One central implication of full moral blameworthiness is *deserving* the negative moral judgment of others and also deserving whatever additional adverse consequences are properly and justifiably incurred as a result. These *just deserts* can include informal moral sanctions like overt blame, withdrawal of love and friendship, and social ostracism, as well as formal legal sanctions like criminal punishment. In short, virtually any aspect of human relationships, social practices, or institutions can become involved when people who are blameworthy are made to "answer" for their wrongdoing.

The last topic in my preview of the theory of moral responsibility is *self-deception*. We deceive ourselves about many different things, some of which have nothing to do with morality and may be perfectly harmless. However, we often engage in self-deception about our own wrongdoing, and most of us have a strong propensity to avoid acknowledging flaws in our moral character. The explanation for this tendency lies in our desire to think well of ourselves; after all, self-respect and self-esteem are among the most important goods in life. The problem is that we all have shortcomings, moral defects, and vices, and we do things that are wrong or unfair, at least occasionally. Since it is not desirable for us to become complaisant about our moral character, we should take steps to improve it; but a necessary condition for being able to correct our shortcomings is to face them honestly. This is why *self-knowledge* is a principal moral virtue; the ancient precept "know thyself" was as much as anything else an admonition to face personal faults and vices honestly. Moreover, when we do something wrong, we should feel responsible for doing it—we should blame ourselves. Contrary to Freud, a feeling of guilt is not just neurotic anxiety; it is often the appropriate emotional response to the conscious and accurate recognition of wrongdoing that lacks any excuse or justification. Moreover, more serious wrongdoing should evoke deeper feelings of guilt.[3]

The feeling of guilt is painful and distressing, as are other moral feelings such as shame and remorse, but most of us find it very difficult to do the things that alleviate or remove conscious feelings of guilt and shame: taking responsibility for our actions, admitting our wrongs to others whom we have hurt, asking for forgiveness, making amends, and accepting blame and punishment as our just deserts. This helps to explain why self-deception is so attractive psychologically, but it also provides the ethical justification for calling it a principal moral vice.

One main tactic of self-deception is to "make excuses," which is parasitical on the ethically justified practices of giving and accepting valid moral excuses. A concocted excuse serves its self-deceptive function by misusing the ethical reasoning that underlies valid excuses. The all-important difference is that in a concocted excuse, the alleged facts that constitute the excusing condition either are false or are not justified by the available evidence. For example, the German informer who betrayed his neighbors for hiding Jews might avoid feeling guilty about his terrible act by convincing himself that he did not know for certain what was going to happen to the Jews once they were arrested by the Gestapo and thus convince himself that he did not intentionally help bring about their deaths. Other psychological tactics of self-deception include selective memory, willful ignorance, and avoidance of contrary evidence.

Part 1 of this book presents and defends the theory of moral responsibility that I have just previewed. In the remainder of this chapter I consider the variety of concepts and practices of responsibility. I discuss moral character, virtues and vices in chapter 2, valid moral excuses in chapter 3, and self-deception in chapter 4.

Concepts and Practices of Responsibility

It needs to be stressed from the beginning that moral responsibility is above all a social concept. That is why I consider each concept within its social setting—whether the setting is personal relationships between individual persons, informal social practices involving many people, or formal institutions like law and government. Setting is an essential feature of any close study of a complicated social phenomenon like the practices (note the plural) of responsibility.

Some Preliminary Issues

First, questions of responsibility may be raised not only by persons' positive acts—what they do (e.g., the German informing the Gestapo about the Jews in hiding)—but also by their omissions—what they do not do (e.g., the same German might refuse a request to hide a Jew). Second, most of the time questions of responsibility arise because of someone's morally wrong or bad act or omission; however, morally right or good acts and omissions are equally subject to assessments of responsibility such as being praiseworthy and deserving honor and admiration. Third, in addition, some acts and omissions are required while others are prohibited; in short, they are matters of duty. But there is also a category of acts and omissions that are neither required nor prohibited. Some of these are morally neutral, that is, they are neither right nor wrong, good nor bad. This leaves a very interesting class of supererogatory acts and omissions that go "outside" or "beyond" duty, for example, the positive act of volunteering one's time to work at a hospital once a week. It is a good thing to do, but because it is not required (i.e., it is not a duty), it is not wrong not to do it. Likewise, an act that one omits to do might have been a good thing to do but was not wrong not to do. For example, voluntarily not using one's fair share of water during a drought is a good thing to do (i.e., what one is "doing" is intentionally refraining from using water, and that is good because it helps lessen the severity of the drought), but it is not wrong not to refrain. After all, there is a fair share of water to which one is entitled. Fourth, there is an important subclass of supererogatory acts that involve great personal risk, danger, substantial sacrifice, or loss. These acts require a person to have extraordinary courage and self-control. People who can repeatedly engage in such activity over a period of time, like many of those who rescued Jews during the Holocaust, go far beyond ordinary moral duty and seem to be properly regarded as moral exemplars, some of whom were heroes or saints.

Causality versus Responsibility

In ordinary language it is possible to say that an electrical short circuit "was responsible" for a house fire, but obviously this does not mean that the short circuit is blameworthy and answerable for its physical effects. It only means that the short circuit caused the fire; there is no implication of moral blame or responsibility. Likewise, a hurricane can be "blamed" for a certain number of deaths, but that is only to say that the hurricane caused those deaths. Moral responsibility and just deserts are irrelevant when purely physical events and processes such as electrical short circuits and hurricanes are under consideration, since such events are devoid of human consciousness and intention, virtue and vice. There is no appropriate human subject to be held responsible. Thus I stipulate that moral terminology which is properly used to denote responsibility ("responsible," "blame," "deserve," etc.) should not be used to refer to causality involving purely physical events and processes. In other words, the terminology of moral responsibility should be used to characterize a situation only if it involves some action performed by a conscious human being.[4]

However, this restriction by itself is not sufficient to avoid all confusion about the distinction between responsibility and causality. Sometimes an event involving a conscious human being is relevant to an inquiry only because of its causal role in a situation. For example, suppose a man at a party is engaged in an animated conversation. Suddenly he is bumped by a running dog, loses his balance, and falls backward into an expensive vase, breaking it. His body falling on the vase causes it to break, but he is hardly blameworthy for the damage, even though he was conscious and performing an action (carrying on a conversation). This is because his carrying on the conversation did not cause his falling backward; the dog bumping into him was the cause. Although it is true that the man broke the vase by falling onto it, his falling was itself not an action at all. He was completely passive and was at the mercy of the physical forces causing his body to fall backward; what happened was not in his control.

Now suppose that the man engaged in the conversation is telling a joke that requires him to illustrate the comical events he is relating, and in the course of this he wildly swings his arm around, breaking the vase. In this scenario, his action directly causes the damage. Unlike the situation in which he was bumped by the dog, he is in full control of his body and is actively and intentionally moving his arm in order to tell his joke effectively. At the very least, some question about the man's blameworthiness can properly be raised, since it is his intentional action (telling the story with body movements) that has caused the harm. It seems doubtful that he is fully blameworthy, since he did not intentionally break the vase; it was an accident. Perhaps he is properly deemed negligent and thus is less blameworthy than he might otherwise have been. Still, it is reasonable to conclude that persons are often to some degree blameworthy for the unintended harm that is the causal consequences of their acts. Of course, there is no puzzle about why people are blameworthy when they intentionally cause harm.

Causing harm may seem to be a necessary condition for blameworthiness, but this is not so. There are many kinds of actions that cause no harm, at least no direct or immediate harm, for which the actor may still be blameworthy. For example, driving at high speed through a school crossing zone may not in fact injure or kill anyone, but it is still blameworthy because it shows recklessness and disregard for life. Likewise, attempted murder, by definition, does not result in death, but it is nonetheless morally blameworthy because of the perpetrator's intention and what it shows about his or her character.

To summarize, first, moral terminology ("responsible," "blame," etc.) that is properly used to hold human beings responsible for their actions should not be used in situations that only involve purely physical events and processes; the situation should involve some action performed by a conscious human being; second, in order for persons to be blameworthy for harm that occurs in a situation, the harm must have been caused by their consciously controlled action, not merely by bodily movements beyond their control; and third, causing harm by one's action is not a necessary condition for blameworthiness; some actions that cause no direct or immediate harm, like breaking a rule (speeding) and attempted murder, may still be blameworthy.

Moral Responsibility: Blameworthiness

Thus being fully blameworthy for one's action is being justifiably (deservedly) liable to judgmental blame because one has (1) performed a wrong act, (2) knowing it is wrong, (3) performing it intentionally, (4) voluntarily, and (5) from a bad motive; and so one has no excuse. Other things being equal, the degree of blameworthiness increases with the seriousness of the wrong act.

Judgmental blame is more complex than it might seem. First, there are two aspects to it: the judgment and the blame. The judgment is a putatively cognitive mental act, that is, it is supposed to be an unbiased and objective evaluation of the person's wrongful performance in the light of justified standards of good and bad moral character. It is not just a feeling or an emotion. It seeks to identify and assess the motives, as well as the virtues and vices, displayed in the person's behavior in order to be able to assess both the person's overall performance and his or her character as revealed in that performance. As a result, the person is judged to be of bad, poor, or not very good character. Thus this judgment also purports to embody the moral opinion that anyone ought to have, that is, what one (anyone) should think of the person, as a person, given what he or she has done, specifically, where one should place the person on a scale of moral worth (from evil and bad on the one extreme to very good and excellent on the other).

The noncognitive element in judgmental blame is, of course, the blame, that most basic element of just deserts, namely, to be regarded as reprehensible and/or to be held in moral contempt for one's action. Thus the blame in judgmental blame constitutes the affective, emotional component; one is justified in feeling a certain way, in having certain attitudes, toward the wrongdoer who has been found "worthy" of blame on the basis of the cognitive component of the judgment. We have a rich moral vocabulary to refer to the relevant emotions that can be involved in blame: indignation, wrath, contempt, anger, resentment, disapproval, and so on.

It bears repeating that persons who are blameworthy can recognize their own blameworthiness, feel responsible, and judgmentally blame themselves; when this occurs, we will most likely use an alternative moral vocabulary and describe them (or ourselves) as feeling guilty, ashamed, or remorseful, but the meaning is the same. The capacity to have a (justified) bad conscience is a litmus test for being a person with moral character.

The feelings and emotions involved in judgmental blame are not just subjective states of mind; they also involve dispositions to act in ways that overtly express the cognitive judgment and the feeling or emotion. A distinguishing feature of action dispositions involved with the feelings and emotions of blame is, of course, the tendency to engage in *overt blaming;* people often want to tell those they judgmentally blame what they think of them, and they are often equally inclined to tell others as well. Even though judgmental blame very frequently gets expressed in overt blaming behavior, it can also remain unexpressed. Indeed, a person could judgmentally blame someone else for years and never say or do anything about it. Moreover, it is morally important that the two kinds of blame be kept conceptually distinct, since even when judgmental blame is completely justified, overt blame might not be. For example, a person who has committed some seriously wrong act might feel so profoundly guilty and depressed that he or she becomes suicidal; in such a situation, an expression of severe condemnation could be very dangerous and would be morally unjustified. Thus a general caution is in order: We need to be careful about expressing our feelings of blame; even when the judgment that grounds the blame is well justified, the act of expressing the judgment is still distinct from it and may require its own justification.

In addition to the tendency to engage in overt blame, the feelings and emotions of blame usually involve dispositions to impose informal moral sanctions and/or to demand an account of himself or herself from the wrongdoer, both of which are involved in the social practices of holding one another accountable morally.

Moral Responsibility: Liability to Moral Sanctions

People take explicit steps and engage in a variety of activities that go beyond both judgmental blame and overt blame in order to hold people morally responsible for their wrongdoing. These include the myriad ways in which people show their moral disapproval of someone by informal sanctions such as withdrawing their love, affection, or friendship; being unwilling to participate with the wrongdoer in social activities that require cooperation and reciprocity; or by engaging with others in general shunning and ostracism. In addition to expressing disapproval, such sanctions can also be seen as just deserts that punish wrongdoers. Of course, there are moral limits both to the kinds and to the severity of harms that may be inflicted in these informal ways, and in a civilized society only the state can inflict such severe punishments as loss of freedom and property (leaving aside the still controversial death penalty). Moreover, the state can only punish someone who has been found legally guilty of a crime in a court of law. Still, the effect of informal moral sanctions can be very severe. It can be a devastating experience for someone to be held blameworthy by an entire community and shunned as a pariah. This is one of the main reasons for exercising care in judging others morally, particularly in regard to extremely serious immorality like genocide. It is, of course, of the greatest importance that people be held to account for their wrongdoing *if they are blameworthy for having done it*. However, there is a strong obligation to be quite sure that they are indeed to blame.

There are some guidelines and precautions that we should keep in mind in order to avoid judging someone unfairly. First, we should always maintain a certain level of moral modesty about our own powers of judgment; not many of us excel in the virtue of practical wisdom, so we are liable to make mistakes on occasion. Since we might be mistaken in our judgment that someone is blameworthy, we should make it a rule either to forego moral sanctions altogether or, if that is not acceptable, to use the least severe sanction consistent with our desire to treat the wrongdoer in some way to show our disapproval. Second, we should not cause any more harm to the wrongdoer than he or she has caused. And, finally, we should not take any steps that would irreparably damage or completely sever morally valuable relationships in which we stand with the wrongdoer that have the potential to lead to forgiveness, making amends, and other reparative actions. This last warning is especially relevant when the wrongdoers feel guilty and ashamed, have accepted responsibility, and ask for forgiveness.

Moral Responsibility: Liability to Being Made to Give an Account of Oneself (Moral Answerability)

Another concept of responsibility involves the familiar social practice of demanding that persons who are blameworthy for doing something wrong "answer" to those who have been harmed or, if there is no identifiable aggrieved party, that they give an account to someone in a position to ask for it. In effect, the person making the demand is asking the wrongdoer, "What have you got to say for yourself?" Social psychologists have studied the dynamics of this pervasive human activity and its role in allowing people to find some resolution to the troubling situations posed by the transgressions of wrongdoers. However, they tend to focus on the fact that many people use such situations as an opportunity to evade responsibility by making excuses.[5] Although such research has its value, it ignores other ways in which people can use the process of giving an account that can lead to outcomes that are morally preferable to the evasion and self-deception involved in making excuses. For example, wrongdoers can take the opportunity to admit their culpability, express remorse, ask for forgiveness, promise to make amends, and in other ways get started on the often arduous process of healing an injured relationship, which is one of the main goals that people have in mind when they demand an accounting in the first place. This is not to deny that often people demand an accounting, in part, because they are looking for an opportunity to engage in overt blaming. Because wrongdoers often sense that this is the aim, they are tempted to make excuses. But it is needlessly cynical to see this misuse of the process as the only (or the most important) example of it.

The dimensions of moral responsibility that I have surveyed in some ways resemble legal responsibility and punishment, but because they are very informal and unstructured, they are ill suited to provide the kind of consistency, predictability, and fairness needed to achieve justice as viewed from a general social perspective. Only a fully codified and institutionalized legal system can do that. Moreover, as I have already noted, use of the most severe punishments (e.g., loss of property or liberty) cannot be left in the hands of individual citizens. They must be reserved for the political state to administer under the constraints of the constitution and the rule of law.

Legal Responsibility: Liability to Criminal Punishment

Being liable to criminal punishment is possible only within the context of an existing legal system, since it is logically impossible to be legally liable to criminal punishment if there is no legal system, in the same way that it is logically impossible for a person to be a "batter" who is "out" unless the game of baseball exists. In our legal system a person becomes justifiably liable to criminal punishment only as the result of a complex procedure: One must have been found legally guilty of violating a valid law in a trial conducted by a duly constituted court of law, and one must have either waived one's rights to appeal or exercised those rights and lost. Once all of these conditions have been met with respect to some particular defendant, D, in a particular legal system, S, the statement "D is legally liable to criminal punishment in S" becomes a true description of a new social fact, namely, D's changed legal status in S. The salient feature of D's new legal status is that now the judge has the legal power to determine a specific criminal penalty for D and to order that it be imposed (by force, if necessary).

Liability to criminal punishment must be kept distinct from moral blameworthiness for wrongdoing. In law there is a decision procedure that (ideally) settles the question of whether someone is liable to criminal punishment; when that procedure has been followed to the end, the question is settled, at least as far as anyone can tell. (There is always the theoretical possibility that new evidence might be discovered that would warrant a new trial, for example.) However, being legally liable to criminal punishment for committing a crime is not sufficient to guarantee being morally blameworthy for wrongdoing because the complicated process by which someone becomes liable to criminal punishment is an example of imperfect procedural justice.[6] It is possible for the entire process to be fairly and scrupulously carried out and yet result in a mistaken verdict: A morally innocent person (i.e., someone who did not commit the crime) may be found legally guilty or a morally guilty person (i.e., someone who in fact committed the crime) may be found legally innocent. This means that even when a person is convicted of a crime such as first-degree murder, which has a legal definition that includes most of the elements required for moral blameworthiness (killing a human being with knowledge, intention, and bad motive), the person is not necessarily also morally blameworthy. Although there is always room for improvement in the way that criminal justice is carried out, there is probably no way that mistakes can be entirely avoided; it is a cliché, but true nonetheless, that humans are fallible.

Another reason legal liability does not guarantee moral blameworthiness is that many crimes are not morally wrong in the first place (e.g., miscegenation). Reforming the law to eliminate injustices like this is obviously possible, since miscegenation is no longer illegal anywhere in the United States; but historically such reform usually occurs slowly and incrementally. A third reason legal liability does not guarantee moral blameworthiness is that the legal definitions of some crimes ignore *mens rea* (a guilty mind) altogether; for example, in many jurisdictions possessing narcotics and having sexual intercourse with someone who is underage do not require knowledge or intention on the part of the perpetrator. These so-called strict liability offenses ignore the mental elements that are essential for moral blameworthiness. Using strict liability in criminal justice is a bad idea, for two main reasons. First, it poses a serious threat to individual liberty, since even conscientious, law-abiding citizens can incur criminal liability through no fault of their own, and it seems unreasonable to require everyone to curtail their freedom in order to avoid strict liability to punishment. Second, using strict liability subverts one of the main principles of criminal law, namely, *retribution* or *just deserts:* punishing people who commit crimes in proportion to what they deserve. One clear requirement of that principle is that a person who is morally blameless should not receive any punishment at all. Granted, there may be circumstances in which the principle of retribution is justifiably overridden by a utilitarian need to avoid very serious social consequences and criminal punishment is justified solely by deterrence. Yet even in such circumstances, severe penalties should not be employed. In actual practice, however, people who are convicted of strict liability offenses such as possession of narcotics need not be (and often are not) morally blameworthy, yet they can receive very severe penalties such as lengthy prison terms. Moreover, appealing to the goal of deterrence as an alternative justification for such severe penalties is not very convincing, since it is not clear how citizens can use rational deliberation to avoid strict liability. There are no precautions to take that would serve as reliable means of avoiding it; one is vulnerable no matter what precautions one might take.

In summary, there are conceptual reasons for differentiating between liability to criminal punishment and moral blameworthiness; there are ethical reasons for making distinctions between them; and for empirical reasons they do not always coincide with each other in the way that the principle of retribution would seem to require. In general, our legal system is designed to honor the principle of retribution (just deserts), and there are good reasons for making it live up to that principle. Citizens who are punished when they are blameless or receive harsh punishment out of proportion to their degree of blameworthiness are not likely to respect law or government. Victims who see the perpetrators of crimes get off with impunity or see them get the proverbial "slap on the wrist" are not likely to trust the law or government either. The rule of law is most effective if it is based on mutual trust among citizens and between the citizens and the officials who administer the criminal justice system. Conscientious adherence to the principle of retribution is a powerful means of building and maintaining that trust.

Role Responsibility

The concepts of moral and legal responsibility that I have considered so far involve *retrospective* responsibility for a *past* act or omission. By contrast, the concept of role responsibility, at least in its main uses, involves *prospective* responsibility for *future* acts and omissions.[7] This concept is expressed in the term "duties of office," which refers to those future actions for which someone who holds an office or position will be held accountable or answerable.[8] Thus a captain is responsible for the safety of his ship and passengers, and an officer in the military is responsible for the lives of the people who serve under him or her. Each general formula only indicates an area of responsibility; specific duties are identified through regulations, training, and similar institutional arrangements. In most cases, persons who are assuming a public office must take an oath to discharge the duties of the office; or the duties may be spelled out in a job description. The concept of role responsibility applies to more than offices and positions in formally defined institutions; it also applies to a wide variety of social roles involving "duties" that are at best only generally understood. For example, most people learn informally through socialization what parents are expected to do for their children.

The main idea contained in the concept of role responsibility is that a person assumes certain duties by virtue of occupying a social role or position, whether or not the duties are formally defined. Assuming that the social practice in which the role occurs is itself not morally bad or unjust, the fact that a particular person assumes or occupies a given position creates legitimate expectations (social, moral, or legal, as the case might be) about how that person ought to behave; and if that person fails to fulfill these expectations, he or she may be blameworthy and may be liable to appropriate moral and/or legal sanctions.

The great diversity of roles to which the concept of role responsibility applies makes it virtually impossible to generalize about the relationship between role responsibility and moral blameworthiness. Clearly, role responsibility is conceptually distinct from moral obligatoriness, so a failure to fulfill a role responsibility does not necessarily involve any blameworthiness. However, there is significant overlap between these two kinds of responsibility, since many of the role responsibilities attached to public offices, to professional occupations, and to basic social roles (e.g., mother and father) constitute prima facie moral duties; thus a failure to fulfill them is often blameworthy. On the other hand, examples of role responsibility that are morally questionable or categorically immoral also come readily to mind, especially in the study of the Holocaust. For example, SS guards at killing centers were supposed to deceive newly arrived Jews about the purpose of the "showers" to which they were being led, German judges were duty bound to enforce the racial laws that required the death penalty for a Jewish man convicted of having sexual intercourse with a non-Jewish woman, and members of the police battalions were supposed to kill their Jewish victims efficiently by delivering one shot at close range to the base of the neck. Conscientiously discharging the duties of these offices would almost always make a person to some extent blameworthy.

The safest course is to keep in mind that role responsibility by itself is never sufficient to establish actual moral duty, all things considered. It is especially important to remember this in regard to the ubiquitous excuse "I was only following orders," used by so many perpetrators as if it were a self-evidently valid moral excuse and legal defense. This is not to deny the validity of the moral excuse of coercion discussed earlier; persons acting under a threat of death for a failure to obey an order are generally not blameworthy for the wrongs they do. However, that valid excuse must not be confused with the bogus claim that the duties of one's office alone are sufficient to morally excuse murder.

Responsibility as Basic Capacity (the Possession of Powers of Agency)

All of the examples considered so far have involved persons who were assumed to be appropriate subjects for being held morally or legally responsible, that is, they were assumed to have the basic capacities that constitute being a competent human agent. We have not considered examples involving the behavior of very young children or persons who are mentally ill, and it is not difficult to understand why. For example, very young children often do not realize what they are doing or they do not appreciate the likely consequences, or both. The reason for their ignorance is that they do not have the capacity to acquire the knowledge or appreciation in the first place, not that they act in haste and do not take the time to study the situation. It would do no good to attempt to teach them how to make careful observations or how to draw logically valid inferences, since at their stage of psychological development they do not have the basic cognitive capacities to engage in these mental activities at all, much less learn to do them well. The implication of such a lack of capacity is not just that young children are not blameworthy for particular acts but that they are not yet competent persons and so cannot be held accountable in general. Suppose that a young child does something wrong, for example, starts a house fire. The correct explanation for this behavior is that the child lacks the cognitive ability to understand how matches work or to appreciate the likely consequences of playing with them. It would be very misleading (though true) to say only that on that account the child is not blameworthy for starting the fire, since the same could be said about a fully competent adult who started a fire unintentionally. The correct assessment of the child's status is that it is nonresponsible and so cannot be held accountable for starting the fire or for any other actions that would require the same level of cognitive capacity. Very young children lack what is called the powers of agency.

Similarly, persons may suffer from any one of a variety of mental illnesses that undermine or destroy their powers of agency — the capacities they need to act as competent moral agents pursuing their goals, making rational choices, and taking responsibility for their actions. What are these powers of agency? Three of them may be defined as follows:[9]

1. Sufficient *cognitive powers* to understand the nature of one's acts — what one is doing, that it is right or wrong, and what the consequences of doing it are likely to be. Very young children lack these cognitive powers; in addition, both children and adults can suffer from one of several kinds of psychosis that involve these kinds of cognitive deficits;

still other illnesses may involve active hallucinations and delusions that interfere with the ability to exercise the cognitive capacities that are possessed.

2. Sufficient *powers of deliberation* to make informed choices and decisions in the light of (1) one's aims and goals, (2) the priority attached to them, and (3) available evidence about which of the alternative means of reaching these goals is most likely to achieve them. These powers of deliberation are needed in all areas in which practical reason is used, whether it be in the pursuit of (rational) self-interest or in making moral decisions. Again, the most obvious example of those who lack sufficient powers of deliberation are young children, but some adults also lack powers of deliberation, for example, persons suffering from schizophrenia.

3. Sufficient *powers of volition* to enable one to carry out decisions and choices in action; in ordinary language these powers are often referred to as "self-control." In addition to young children, examples of people who lack the general capacity for self-control include severely neurotic persons whose personality style is dominated by impulsiveness, persons addicted to alcohol and other drugs, and psychopaths subject to "irresistible impulses."

Before concluding this discussion of the powers of agency, I want to make a few qualifications to avoid giving the impression that a person is either fully responsible (accountable, answerable) or not at all responsible. First, possession of each of these powers is a matter of degree; this is obvious with respect to basic cognitive capacity, since it is a familiar fact that individuals can differ significantly from each other in this respect. It is equally true, however, of powers of deliberation and powers of volition, even though the differences among individuals in these respects are not always as noticeable. Second, although these powers are to some extent interrelated, they can vary independently of each other. Third, a necessary condition for deeming a person fully responsible in this sense is that he or she have a sufficient degree of each of these three powers. This last point is true by definition; persons deemed to have insufficient cognitive capacities, for example, would be so little able to tell what they are doing or so at a loss to anticipate the consequences of their actions that they could not properly be held responsible or accountable for their acts at all. It follows that persons can be deemed to be nonresponsible persons for different reasons, and some persons deemed nonresponsible for the lack of one kind of power of agency may nevertheless have sufficient powers of agency of one or more of the other kinds. And, finally, some persons may have a combination of the three powers such that they are deemed to be neither fully nonresponsible nor fully responsible but are judged to have "diminished" responsibility.

The underlying moral justification for recognizing that people who lack relevant powers of agency should be deemed nonresponsible is that it is unfair to hold such people accountable for their actions. People who possess adequate powers of agency and choose to do wrong have failed to use their powers properly; people who lack those powers in the first place cannot be guilty of failing to use them. The same justification can by given for the legal insanity defense, which blocks liability to both moral and legal punishment.[10]

In chapter 5 I critically evaluate an argument sometimes advanced in discussions of the Holocaust, which holds that people who are socialized in a bad political culture like the one that existed in Germany in the 1920s and 1930s are not blameworthy (or at least are less blameworthy) for participating in the Holocaust because they lack the cognitive ability to realize the wrongness of genocide.

Summary

In this chapter I have provided a preview of the theory of moral responsibility that is used in this book. The theory includes four elements-concepts of responsibility (discussed in this chapter), moral character, justified moral excuses, and self-deception (each of which is discussed in the next three chapters). I introduced the basic concept of responsibility, moral blameworthiness, through a simple example of a German who informed the Gestapo that Jews were being hidden by his neighbor in the apartment next door. The German informer, I argued, was fully blameworthy because (1) he performed a wrong act, (2) he knew that the act was wrong, (3) he performed the act intentionally, (4) he performed it voluntarily and (5) from a morally bad motive. The conjunction of these conditions leaves the perpetrator with no valid moral excuse; there is no fact about the circumstances that can serve to block or mitigate blame.

Then I discussed the main kinds of *moral responsibility* and how they are related to each other: judgmental blame, overt blame, moral answerability, and liability to moral sanctions. The principal kind of *legal responsibility* is liability to criminal punishment. It is important to keep in mind that the relationship between moral and legal responsibility is not straightforward or simple; in particular, legal responsibility is not sufficient for moral responsibility. The concept of *role responsibility,* which cuts across both moral and legal responsibility, is a very useful and ubiquitous concept, but caution must be exercised in drawing inferences from it to either moral or legal responsibility. *Capacity responsibility* involves the possession of three broadly defined *powers of agency*—cognitive, deliberative, and volitional, each of which can be present in varying degrees. A person who has each of these capacities to a sufficient degree is a *responsible person* eligible for praise or blame, reward or punishment, in regard to his or her exercise of these capacities.

In the next chapter I consider ethical standards of good and bad moral character—the principal virtues and vices—which play a central role in judgments of moral blameworthiness and liability to criminal punishment. I provide an overview of virtue ethics and show how it is related to moral responsibility.

Notes

1. The justification for this and other moral judgments about the wrongness of actions performed during the Holocaust is discussed in chapter 2.

2. Lawrence A. Blum, "Moral Exemplars," in *Midwest Studies in Philosophy,* vol. 13, *Ethical Theory: Character and Virtue,* ed. Peter A. French, Theodore E. Uehling Jr., and Howard K. Wettstein (Notre Dame, Ind.: University of Notre Dame Press, 1988), 196–221.

3. David H. Jones, "Freud's Theory of Moral Conscience," *Philosophy* 41, no. 155 (January 1966): 34–57.

4. H. L. A. Hart, *Punishment and Responsibility* (Oxford: Clarendon, 1968), 214–215.

5. Bernard Weiner, *Judgments of Responsibility: A Foundation for a Theory of Social Conduct* (New York: Guilford, 1995), 217.

6. John Rawls, *A Theory of Justice* (Cambridge: Harvard University Press, 1971), 85–86.

7. Michael J. Zimmerman, "Responsibility," in *Encyclopedia of Ethics,* ed. Lawrence C. Becker (New York: Garland, 1992), 2:1089–1095.

8. Hart, *Punishment and Responsibility,* 212–214.

9. Hart, *Punishment and Responsibility,* 218, 227–230.

10. Hyman Gross, *A Theory of Criminal Justice* (New York: Oxford University Press, 1979), 292–313.

Suggestions for Further Reading

Aristotle. *Nicomachean Ethics.* Books 2–3. Many editions available.

Becker, Lawrence C., ed. *Encyclopedia of Ethics.* New York: Garland, 1992. See the articles on responsibility, coercion, excuses, and self-deception, among others.

Brandt, Richard. *Ethical Theory.* Englewood Cliffs, N. J.: Prentice-Hall, 1959. See the chapter entitled "Assessment of Persons and Character."

Feinberg, Joel. *Doing and Deserving.* Princeton, N.J.: Princeton University Press, 1970. Advanced discussion of many aspects of blame and blameworthiness.

Glover, Jonathan. *Responsibility.* London: Routledge & Kegan Paul, 1970. Good discussion of some basic issues, especially acting freely and voluntarily.

Gross, Hyman. *A Theory of Criminal Justice.* New York: Oxford University Press, 1979. Advanced discussion of virtually all aspects of responsibility in the law.

Hart, H. L. A. *Punishment and Responsibility.* Oxford: Clarendon, 1968. See the discussion of the various concepts of responsibility.

Kruschwitz, Robert, and Robert Roberts, eds. *The Virtues.* Belmont, Calif.: Wadsworth, 1986. An excellent collection of contemporary articles on the ethics of character, as well as on the nature of virtues and vices.

Lang, Berel. *Act and Idea in the Nazi Genocide.* Chicago: University of Chicago Press, 1990. Chapter 2, "The Knowledge of Evil and Good," covers some of the principal issues surrounding the relation of knowledge to blameworthiness. Lang defends the view that the perpetrators of the Final Solution knew that killing the Jews was immoral.

Chapter 2

Moral Character: Virtues and Vices

Virtue Ethics: An Introduction

Virtue ethics is concerned with identifying and justifying standards of good moral character; its main purpose is to answer questions such as, What kind of a person should I be? It seeks to identify the characteristics that answer the question, What makes a good person good? The traditional answer is, Possessing virtues that are complex psychological traits or dispositions to think, have emotions, and act in distinctive ways that constitute human excellences. Virtue ethics is also concerned with closely related issues of responsibility, such as justifying a judgment that a person is morally praiseworthy for having done something good or excellent. What makes a bad person bad? Virtue ethics tries to identify vices—psychological traits that make a person morally bad and reprehensible—and to provide reasoning that justifies a judgment that a person is blameworthy for having done something wrong or bad.

In contrast with virtue ethics, the ethics of right action is primarily concerned with answering questions such as, What makes a right action right? Although virtue ethics is distinct from the ethics of action, these two areas of ethics are interrelated in important ways, one of the most important of which is that a great deal of people's virtuous motivation depends on their cognition, especially their beliefs about right and wrong. For example, one principal virtue is conscientiousness, the character trait that consists in part in having a strong and effective desire to do one's duty and to fulfill one's obligations. However, this desire is not activated unless the person sincerely believes that some particular action is a duty or an obligation; thus, the person's conscientious motivation to do the act depends in part on his or her antecedent belief that doing the act is a duty. However, the virtue of conscientiousness by itself is not sufficient to guarantee that the person's belief is correct, all things considered. This is especially true when the person has been socialized in an authoritarian culture, for example, Germany during the 1930s. Most Germans were socialized to respect legitimate authority, both public and private. Thus most Germans had a strong sense of duty to obey parents, teachers, and public officials. As long as the political system was accepted as legitimate, they were very law abiding. Because most Germans came to accept the Nazi regime as legitimate, they consequently believed that they had a serious duty to obey anti-Semitic laws that discriminated against the Jews and stripped them of citizenship. Thus they complied conscientiously. In this way, the virtue of conscientiousness was subverted by authoritarian beliefs instilled through socialization. (It is worth noting that most Germans did not accept the Weimar Republic as legitimate, so there was a great deal of illegal violence between 1919 and 1932.)

Other virtues, such as self-control and practical wisdom, also depend on beliefs about right and wrong for their operation. In short, virtue ethics is not self-sufficient; it must be supplemented by the ethics of action. Before beginning this study of some principal virtues and vices, I want to identify and justify some basic moral principles and rules of action that provide the core content of morality—to sketch out how people ought to arrive at their beliefs about the right and wrong way to act, all things considered. These basic principles serve as standards by which to judge the beliefs of the people who participated in the Holocaust, particularly the perpetrators. They also serve as reminders of the social purposes served by morality and explain why it is desirable for people to have the particular virtues being discussed as well as why people should not have the vices that I identify, an awareness that is especially needed for a consideration of the conduct and character of individuals involved in the perpetration of the Holocaust.

The core content of morality captured in the basic principles and rules of action presented here falls well short of being a comprehensive ethical theory of the kind that philosophers often attempt to provide. Such a comprehensive theory would include (ideally) not only a theory of right action for individuals but also principles of justice for institutions, an account of nonmoral intrinsic value, and a complete virtue ethics. However, my position is that a comprehensive ethical theory is not needed in order to appreciate the wrongness of the unprovoked mass killing of defenseless men, women, and children that constitutes the Holocaust. The core content of morality is sufficient. What this core content lacks in the way of comprehensiveness it makes up for in the degree to which it is noncontroversial in contemporary moral philosophy. Or so I shall argue.

The Core Content of Morality I: Basic Moral Rules Not to Harm Others

Every society has to prohibit positive acts that harm others (whether directly or indirectly); if persons were free to kill, steal, injure, rape, lie, and make false promises, society would be very unstable and could hardly survive. Thus basic rules that prohibit individuals from harming each other by positive acts have one very clear and straightforward justification: They are necessary for the survival and stability of society. These basic rules, especially those that prohibit direct killing, maiming, causing pain, and the like, are also necessary for the sense of security (if not the survival) of the individuals who make up the society. People would hardly have a reason to be cooperative and trusting unless these rules were sanctioned and generally obeyed. Every member of society is able to see and appreciate that these rules are meant for the good of everyone alike; it is taken for granted that the main point of human association is mutual survival. As philosopher of law H. L. A. Hart has noted, society is not a suicide club.[1]

Clearly, general compliance with the basic rule prohibiting harm to others is a necessary condition for the survival and stability of society, but it only identifies one reason (albeit an important one) for the wrongful nature of harming others in one's own society. It says nothing about harming others outside one's society, and thus it leaves out one principal kind of killing at the heart of the Holocaust. Another reason appeals to the overall utility of general compliance with the prohibition against harming others. Everything else being equal, a society that abides by a complex set of rules that prohibit both harming others directly (e.g., killing and causing pain) and harming others indirectly (e.g., lying and breaking promises) creates a greater amount of net utility (the total amount of happiness over unhappiness in society) in the long run than a society that abides by none or few of these rules; therefore, moral rules that prohibit harming others also have a strong utilitarian justification.[2]

Nevertheless, rules that prohibit harm to others seem to ignore the most significant characteristic of doing harm, namely, that it affects an individual human being whose particular interests and aims are at stake. In the worst kind of harm, killing someone, the person's basic interest in staying alive is ignored and nullified. It is this kind of extreme harm that is at the center of the Holocaust. Showing that it is immoral requires identifying and articulating a reason that is distinct from the general social effects cited above. I propose to justify the conclusion that there is a prima facie duty not to harm others by positive acts by appealing to a principle of equal consideration for all persons. This principle calls our attention to the claims we humans have on each other just because we are individual persons, not because we are members of some particular society or group and not because refraining from harm will maximize utility in the long run. Before using this principle to justify the duty not to harm others, I shall outline the justification for equal consideration itself. The justification consists of the following four-point argument.

First, an empirical premise in the justification for equal consideration is the fact that all (normal) human beings share a characteristic: the potential to lead a life as a person. Every (normal) human being is either actually leading a life as a person already or is in the process of developing the capacity to lead such a life. What does it mean to lead a life as a person? It means being conscious and being capable of experiencing pleasure and pain, feelings and emotions, happiness and unhappiness; having a sense of personal identity constructed out of one's own beliefs and values, plans and goals; making choices in the light of those plans and goals; and carrying out those choices. In the most fundamental sense, to *respect* another individual as a person is to acknowledge and appreciate this (complex) fact about him or her. To respect every person equally is to be prepared to acknowledge and appreciate this fact about each person equally. But this is precisely what traditional anti-Semites and Nazi ideologues were not prepared to do.

To be capable of leading a life as a person does not guarantee anyone the opportunity to do so; a galley slave who spends years in agonizing drudgery may be capable of leading a life as a person even if he gets no chance to exercise that capability. Moreover, leading a life as a person does not guarantee any particular kind of outcome, since people who in fact lead lives as persons are not necessarily free, happy, or successful. The weight of evidence from the behavioral and social sciences (biology, psychology, anthropology, and sociology) is that all (normal) humans are genetically endowed with the potential to lead a life as a person. Whether this potential is realized depends on a wide variety of contingent circumstances, such as adequate medical care and nutrition (especially during childhood), together with psychological nurturance and development in a supportive social environment. It is, of course, an empirical truth that no human being can be born, survive, and develop completely outside society; consequently, all human beings live in some society or other (however poor or meager it may be), at least during childhood.

Second, something is an interest of an individual if its realization is either intrinsically or instrumentally good for that individual, or both. Being able to realize one's potential for leading a life as a person is a basic interest of human beings. It is a basic instrumental good because it is necessary in order to obtain any other good in the course of leading a life as a person; it also constitutes a basic intrinsically good component in the lives of people who manage to lead their lives as excellent and virtuous persons.

Third, a thesis in social theory states that since one essential purpose of any society is to further (i.e., protect and enhance) the interests of its members as far as it is possible to do so, the culture of any society should recognize the fundamental interest that all humans beings have in being able to realize their potential to lead a life as a person. The culture of a society consists in the way it is structured and organized, including the shared communal understanding of what members are required to do or required not to do in their dealings with each other. In short, a relevant consideration for arriving at the content of basic rules of conduct for society is the fact that all human beings have an interest in realizing their potential for leading a life as a person.

Fourth, there is a reasonable presumption that no individual human being's interest outweighs any other's interest. Unless there is a sound justification to the contrary, every person's interest is to be given equal weight in arriving at the content of basic rules of conduct. This presumption is especially important with regard to each person's interest in staying alive, a necessary condition for having the chance to lead his or her life as a person.

If this justification of the principle of equal respect for persons is sound, then it provides additional and powerful support for including a duty not to harm others by positive acts among the basic rules of conduct. The fourth point deserves some further comment to avoid possible misunderstanding. Notice that it does not discuss specific rules for particular social practices that may permit individuals to be treated differently from each other. For example, most people who break the law are justifiably punished for their misbehavior; they bring the punishment on themselves, so to speak. This particular exception to equality of treatment is justified by reasons having to do with a particular person's own past actions. Likewise, individual people are often rewarded differently according to their past services and efforts. Unlike a basic principle of human inequality (e.g., one that purported to justify slavery), these practices are not grounded on alleged basic differences among human beings that are supposed to justify overriding the presumption of equality. The poor record posted by past attempts to justify inequality seems to justify the conclusion that no sound justification for basic inequality exists; at the very least, none has yet been found. History and anthropology furnish countless examples of cultures that purport to provide a justification for the basic inequality of human beings in terms of caste, race, sex, aristocracy, religion, and nation, to mention only the most obvious examples from among many more. None of these alleged justifications (particularly German anti-Semitic ideology with its fantastic and paranoid views of the nature of Jews and the alleged justification it provided for genocide) for inequality has been able to withstand rational scrutiny. This does not rule out some possible justification (heretofore undiscovered) for inequality; after all, the presumption of equality is deemed rebuttable in large part because it is not true a priori.[3] Therefore, the following proviso should be added to the four-part justification: Fifth, the burden of proof is on the inegalitarian to provide a reasoned and rationally persuasive justification for dropping the presumption of equality of respect for all persons.

The rules that prohibit doing harm to others have to be understood as rules of prima facie duty, that is, there is a strong presumption in favor of obeying each of these rules as they would ordinarily apply; considering only that one fact: People ought to obey the rule. Indeed, the rules are binding in the vast majority of cases. However, I have been assuming a general conception of morality according to which moral judgments are judgments about what rational agents ought to do and be, *all things considered*.[4] Thus, when making a particular choice, given all the circumstances, one can sometimes be morally justified in overriding a rule of prima facie duty if it would be morally worse, all things considered, to abide by it. For example, one may kill justifiably if it is necessary to stop a terrorist about to explode a bomb, or a doctor may cause a patient severe pain without anesthetic in an emergency. Of course, an alleged justification for overriding a rule of prima facie duty in a particular situation must be compelling; there must be clear, relevant, and convincing reasons why it is permissible to break the rule, all things considered.

There is one especially important feature of duties not to perform positive acts that harm others that makes them *impartially binding* in a way that no other duties are. Unlike a duty to do good for someone else, which requires a positive act that necessarily involves the expenditure of some time and effort, and, perhaps, actually giving up one's own possessions, a negative duty not to harm others requires only that one refrain from doing harm and nothing else. Assuming that the agent has neither a justification nor a valid excuse for inflicting the harm, the only issue is whether one chooses to refrain or not. In such situations, it is always physically and morally possible for a competent person to fulfill a negative duty not to harm someone else. Put another way, there is no valid excuse not to refrain from doing harm. One has a choice, regardless of who the beneficiary is. One cannot pick and choose someone to be harmed; one's duty is not to harm anyone. In addition, the prima facie duty not to harm is owed to all persons, whether they belong to one's own society or group or not. For example, the fact that another person is a stranger is morally irrelevant to the question of having a prima facie duty not to harm him or her. This feature of the duty not to harm others, that it is *universally owed to everyone,* is what differentiates it so sharply from any duty one might have to perform positive acts of doing good for others.

It is fairly common to find people believing that their moral obligations to outsiders are different from their obligations to people in their own society. This is partly true, since (obviously) it is not possible to do good for all others equally. Thus, much of the time it is permissible to treat outsiders differently from insiders. However, this is not so where doing harm is concerned; it is basically *arbitrary* and thus unjustifiable to inflict harm on outsiders that one would not inflict on people in one's own society. Even Nazi ideology implicitly recognizes this basic moral point; the pseudo-scientific biological and anthropological theories about the "value" of "Aryan blood" and the "criminal blood" of Jews are supposed to provide a justification for genocide where, in fact, no justification exists.

The Core Content of Morality II: Doing Good for Others

Of course, morality is as much about doing good for others as it is about not harming them. Every society has to have some way to ensure that all of its members at least have their basic needs met; these good things include water, food, shelter, mutual aid in emergencies, and defense against enemies. A moment's reflection reveals that there is a fundamental asymmetry between not harming and doing good; the model of an impartially binding duty owed to all persons that is applicable to the former is impossible with the latter.[5] For example, how could anyone even try to comply with the following rule: It is the duty of every person to provide the basic needs to everyone else. Obviously, it would be impossible to put such a rule into practice; furthermore, it would do no good to try to make the duty less onerous by selecting one basic need instead of all of them. It would be equally impossible for everyone to have a duty to provide, say, food for everyone else.

The asymmetry between a negative duty not to harm others and a positive duty to do good for others stems from the fact that the former can be impartially binding and owed to others in all instances but the latter cannot. When it comes to doing good, we must necessarily be "partial," if only because it is always impossible to help everyone in exactly the same way. Doing good necessarily takes time, energy, and (perhaps) possessions, and individuals have only limited amounts of each.

These rather abstract considerations help both to explain and (to a certain extent) to justify a familiar feature of conventional morality everywhere, namely, its pervasive "partiality." Where doing good for others is concerned, people do not believe it is wrong to be partial to persons who belong to their own family, community, church, or nation. Indeed, most societies recognize a positive duty to help members of one's own family and community that routinely take precedence over giving help to strangers and outsiders, especially when these come into direct conflict. Such preferences may on occasion be taken to extremes that are unjustified, but all things considered, most of the time they are both necessary and desirable as a means of addressing the general problem of meeting the basic needs of all members of society. Indeed, most societies provide some basic needs, such as water and protection from enemies, as a matter of communal provision, that is, goods that are deemed to be the responsibility of the community as a whole to provide to all.[6]

Societies differ greatly from each other, both in the kinds of goods that they make available through communal provision and in the kinds of social practices and institutions that do the providing. They also differ greatly in the mix of public (communal provision) and private practices and institutions that are involved in making these basic needs available to their members. One obvious reason for these variations is a difference in size and complexity. A very simple society with a small population might not need the variety of practices and institutions found in a complex society with millions of members. However, all societies need some version of the family to provide for the care and rearing of children, and even the simplest society needs some form of communal government.

The relevance of these social practices and institutions for my sketch of the core of morality lies in their capacity to provide a structure within which individuals can do good for others that is practical and logistically feasible; the fundamental social strategy is one of division of labor. Individual members of a particular society ordinarily participate in several different social practices and institutions at any given time, and some of these are involved in providing basic needs to members of society. To a large extent, participation in any one of these practices or institutions can be defined by the role or position that an individual occupies; the roles or positions, in turn, can be defined by the responsibilities (i.e., the duties of office) that they involve. (This is another application of the concept of role responsibility mentioned in chap. 1.) If, as I am assuming, the practice or institution itself is morally justified (i.e., it has among its aims the provision of some basic need for members of society, its other purposes are morally permissible, and its procedures are fair), then the role responsibilities of a person participating in it are also prima facie moral duties. For example, a married man with children occupies both the role of spouse and the role of father in the social institution of the family. Assuming that the institution is in other respects fair, the role responsibilities he has to provide the basic needs of his children are also prima facie moral duties. Likewise, the role responsibilities of a hospital nurse to care for his or her patients are also prima facie moral obligations. Other examples include participation in schools, churches, civic service organizations, emergency rescue, police, the military, and government itself.

Thus individuals in a particular society ordinarily have at least two complementary sets of moral duties: (1) the prima facie negative duties not to inflict harm on others, duties that are universally and impartially binding on all competent persons in any society and owed to all persons, whether inside or outside of one's society, and (2) the prima facie positive duties to do good for others that are generated by their participation in some of the particular social practices and institutions that exist in their particular society. To these role responsibilities should be added (3) occasional duties of *mutual aid* to do good for others that arise in emergency situations not covered by any practice or institution. In these so-called Good Samaritan situations a person needs emergency help (because of serious illness, injury, or imminent death) and there is no one with a role responsibility to render aid; any person present who is able to render aid without great risk or loss has a prima facie duty to do so. Clearly, the duty of mutual aid in emergencies is owed to all persons, regardless of whether they belong to one's own society or group or not. For example, it would be wrong to ignore pleas for help from a Mexican family injured in an automobile accident solely on the ground that one is merely a foreign tourist on vacation in Mexico. (In chapter 9 I discuss the implications of this duty for helping and rescuing fugitive Jews during the Holocaust.) Note, however, that a particular duty of mutual aid can involve some risk, cost, or loss, as long as it is not unreasonable. These three sets of duties constitute the core content of morality.

The Core Content of Morality and the Immorality of the Holocaust

Clearly, the core content of morality is sufficient to justify the judgments that the contemporary consensus makes about the immorality of the Holocaust.

First, the mass killing of defenseless men, women, and children was a flagrant violation of the prima facie duty not to harm others. Second, the widespread complicity in the implementation of the Holocaust on the part of lawyers, doctors, churchmen, public officials, the military, and the police, not to mention the millions of ordinary citizens, represents a wholesale failure to do good for others in accordance with their justified role responsibilities. Third, the great majority of people who were bystanders in the Holocaust failed to fulfill the prima facie duty to give aid in an emergency by not helping or rescuing Jews and other victims of the Nazi regime. It is obvious that had people lived up to the prima facie duties at the core of morality, there either would not have been a Holocaust or its extent would have been drastically reduced.

The Nonegoistic Character of the Virtues

Benevolence and Conscientiousness: Two Nonegoistic Virtues

The duties that constitute the core content of morality require people to refrain from harming others and to do good for others in accordance with their role responsibilities or the principle of mutual aid. In short, in order to live up to the basic demands of morality, people must be motivated to act in ways that take into account the interests of other people; sometimes this involves overriding their own self-interest. Thus it seems quite plausible to conclude that morality requires people to have considerable nonegoistic and unselfish psychological capacities of motivation and action, an opinion shared by both common sense and the mainstream of traditional virtue ethics (secular as well as religious). This view is further confirmed in virtue ethics, which identifies the two principal virtues of motivation as benevolence and conscientiousness. Both virtues are demonstrably nonegoistic in nature.

The virtue of *benevolence* can be defined as the character trait whose salient feature is a direct care or concern for the well-being of other persons for their own sake. For example, rescuers who stop to give a ride to a stranded motorist in a snowstorm can be motivated by sympathy aroused by the sight of the stranded motorist who is suffering from the severely cold weather or by fear that he or she might in fact freeze to death if left alone in the storm, or both. Rescuers with these motives care about the well-being of the stranded motorists for the sake of the motorists; they are reacting to what they perceive to be the plight of another person, and they are concerned to do something to alleviate it; that is the purpose of their action. Moreover, rescuers are likely to be worried and concerned as long as the stranded motorist's plight continues, and they are happy and relieved when aid is rendered (either by themselves or others). Furthermore, if benevolent persons should fail to give help to someone who needs it, and they have no justification or valid excuse for the failure, they will feel guilty and ashamed of themselves. Finally, if their failure to help resulted in the death of a stranded person, benevolent people would also feel remorseful. In all of these ways benevolent people show that they are not purely egoistic; on the contrary, they have genuine concern for the well-being of others for their sake.

The virtue of *conscientiousness* can be defined as a character trait whose salient feature is a strong and effective sense of duty or obligation. Conscientiousness is most clearly exhibited in situations that require a person to act purely on principle, and benevolence plays no role. For example, people often turn in lost wallets that they find, even when the wallets contain large sums of money or credit cards and no one observed them finding the wallet. No doubt, some people return a lost wallet out of benevolence; they may feel sympathy for the (unknown) owners because they can imagine how worried they probably are. However, some people return lost wallets simply because they think its the right thing to do; they would feel guilty and ashamed of themselves if they kept a wallet that did not belong to them. They do not need to know anything about the owners (e.g., their wealth or poverty) in order to have a good reason to return the wallet. It is the principle involved: One should not keep something that belongs to someone else. People do conscientious acts like this all the time for the same kind of reason based on principle: One should not lie, a promise should be kept, and so on.

People can also perform acts like rescuing a stranded motorist out of conscientiousness. But in contrast with a person acting from benevolent motives such as sympathy and fear for the victim (which are triggered by the perception of, and sympathy with, the plight of the stranded person), a person acting from conscientiousness perceives the situation as one covered by a relevant moral principle or rule, and this perception causes the feeling of duty. The person may view the situation as one covered by a role responsibility (e.g., as an officer in the highway patrol) or, perhaps, as covered by the principle of mutual aid. We should not assume that conscientious persons lack benevolence or vice versa, since the traits of benevolence and conscientiousness are not mutually exclusive, either conceptually or empirically. Whether a person is acting out of benevolence or out of conscientiousness in a particular situation depends on the correct psychological explanation of the action.

Even though persons acting out of conscientiousness need not have (and in practice often do not have) any altruistic feelings such as sympathy for the persons they help, nonetheless, their motives are nonegoistic. They have a sense of duty to the people they help and are likely to view the help they give as something owed to others as a matter of right. This means that they take the interests of others seriously into account; they have a strong and effective desire to protect those interests as an end. Thus the object of their action is something distinct from, and often (though not necessarily) in conflict with their own self-interest. If conscientious persons fail to fulfill what they sincerely believe is their duty to others, and they have no justification or valid excuse for the failure, they feel guilty and ashamed of themselves. Furthermore, if conscientious persons cause serious harm to others through a failure to do their duty, they feel remorseful. Clearly, conscientiousness, like benevolence, is nonegoistic in its aims.

The Challenge of Psychological Egoism

The precept "ought implies can" encapsulates the moral intuition that one cannot have a duty to do something that is impossible to do. If doing X is one's duty, then one must be able to do X. We have seen that the core content of morality requires that people be able to perform acts and omissions for the sake of other people and that these acts and omissions sometimes conflict with their own self-interest. So the question that most requires an answer is, Are human beings in fact psychologically capable of having nonegoistic motives to act in the unselfish way that morality requires?

Psychological egoism (hereafter PE) is the claim that human beings are not capable of having nonegoistic motives; on the contrary, they are capable of having only egoistic motives. Expressed more precisely, PE is the view that people are capable of desiring or pursuing only their own self-interest for its own sake, as an end. Defenders of PE do not deny the obvious fact that people sometimes desire the happiness of others or that they act in ways that in fact make others happy. However, they deny that the motives for such acts are truly unselfish—that they express a concern for the well-being of other people for their sake—as an end. Rather, people help others only because they believe that it is a means to their own happiness, which is their ultimate end.[7]

One obvious objection to PE is that there seem to be plenty of examples of people helping others in ways that in fact involve a genuine cost or sacrifice, for example, returning a lost wallet full of cash to its owner. Defenders of PE typically reply that despite the loss of the money returned with the wallet, people are still made happier than if they had kept it because they have avoided such bad feelings as guilt and shame and gained the good feeling of a clear conscience. However, this reply does not show that people's motives are egoistic or selfish; on the contrary, it presupposes that people have some nonegoistic concern for the interests of the owners of lost wallets—that they think it would be wrong to keep the money, that they would feel guilty and ashamed if they kept it, and that they feel happy when they in fact return lost wallets and the money. Defenders of PE who use this kind of argument take the feeling of guilt for granted instead of recognizing that they need to explain why people feel guilty when they act selfishly. The commonsense explanation seems correct: The feeling of guilt would be caused by the person's sincere belief that keeping the wallet is wrong.

This last example displays one pervasive flaw in arguments used to defend

PE, namely, conceptual confusion over what exactly makes a motive nonegoistic rather than egoistic. A motive is nonegoistic if it has as its *objective* something other than one's own interest *as an end*. Thus wanting to help the owner *as an end* is sufficient to make the person's desire to return the lost wallet nonegoistic; it would have been an egoistic motive if the objective of the desire to return the wallet to the owner had been to enhance the finder's reputation, with the return of the wallet *as a means* to that end. But how can it be determined that helping the owner is being sought *as an end?* By using the very same set of criteria I used to critically analyze the argument for PE: by the good feelings (a clear conscience, self-respect, satisfaction) that would result if the end is achieved and by the bad feelings (guilt and shame) that would result if the end were not achieved.

A defender of PE might reply that the analysis in the last paragraph is inconsistent because (1) it assumes that wanting to return the wallet as a means to the end of enhancing one's reputation makes the desire egoistic, but (2) it assumes that wanting to return the wallet as a means to the end of keeping one's conscience clear, though it is a perfectly parallel example, does not make the desire egoistic. This reply is mistaken, however, because despite a superficial similarity in their descriptions the two examples are quite different. The end of enhancing one's reputation may or may not be achieved by returning the wallet; it is a causally contingent effect that depends on what other people happen to think. By contrast, the end of keeping one's conscience clear depends only on what one thinks of oneself, specifically on how one morally assesses one's own motives, intentions, and actions. If, by hypothesis, people do what they sincerely believe is the right thing to do (in this example, returning the wallet and money for the sake of the owner), then they ipso facto have a clear conscience, that is, they keep their self-respect and they avoid feelings of guilt and shame. Defenders of PE assert that it is a matter of "wanting to return the wallet as a means to the end of keeping one's conscience clear" in order to obscure this fundamental difference. Moreover, their description of the alleged motive is internally inconsistent; this can be seen when its implications are fully spelled out: "wanting to return the wallet solely for the egoistic end of keeping one's conscience clear, that is, avoiding bad feelings of guilt and shame due to the belief that it is wrong to disregard the interests of another person."

It seems safe to conclude that the challenge of PE dissipates once the conceptual confusions on which it is based have been identified and guarded against. There are other arguments for PE, but I will not try to refute them because they are not directly relevant to virtue ethics and because they are generally considered fallacious or inconclusive.

Even if PE, strictly interpreted, is false, it is still a fact that people do have rational, self-interested motives. Moreover, these self-interested motives have great importance for ethics as a whole, if not for virtue ethics in particular. Rational, self-interested motives constitute a "second-best" model for human action and motivation after the moral virtues themselves. For example, in the last chapter I pointed out that legal sanctions are often needed to supplement moral sanctions for the retributive purpose of expressing moral disapproval of blameworthy wrongdoers. Of equal importance is the role that legal sanctions have in morally justified *deterrence* of crime. The fear of punishment and the desire to avoid public disgrace are rational self-interested motives that can deter people from committing crimes; in this way they supplement the moral motives that most people also have to be law-abiding. Rational self-interested motives can also play a significant role in maintaining cooperation and reciprocity among competitors who are participating in a mutually beneficial activity but have only limited benevolence or a weak sense of duty toward each other. Especially important in the study of the Holocaust is the way in which the political culture in a society can mobilize the rational self-interested motives of citizens in support of crucial institutions such as the rule of law and social practices such as racial, religious, and ethnic tolerance. In all of these examples, however, the background social institutions and practices are necessary in order to generate the kinds of self-interested motives in individuals that supplement rather than conflict with moral motives.

The Virtues and Vices

Some Definitions of Key Terms

Good moral character is constituted by the possession of a set of virtues; each virtue, in turn, is a complex trait with distinctive features. Paying attention to these distinctive features is helpful both in appreciating the nature of each particular virtue and in distinguishing it from others. Consequently, I define *character trait* as a complex psychological disposition that can be expressed or realized (1) in thought, (2) in feeling and emotion, and (3) in action. For example, the virtue of benevolence, which I have defined simply as being a direct care or concern for the well-being of other persons for their sake, can be defined as a complex psychological disposition (i.e., a set of tendencies) consisting of, first, *thought*—a tendency to think of others, to notice that they need something, to remember that they are ill, and the like, as well as to engage in mental activities such as taking time to deliberate about the best means to help someone; second, *feeling* and *emotion*—a tendency to worry anxiously when someone is in danger, to be relieved or joyful when someone is put out of danger; and, third, *action*—a tendency to do favors, to give help, and to make sacrifices for others.

For a psychological disposition to be a virtue or a vice it must be a trait of one's character, that is, it must be a relatively permanent feature of one's psychological makeup, not temporary or fleeting. It need not be immutable, however; people can both acquire and lose virtues and vices. A *moral virtue* like benevolence is a trait of character that makes the one who possesses it to some extent morally good or excellent and worthy of respect and admiration; it also justifies some degree of self-respect. A *moral fault* or *character defect* is the lack of a moral virtue or the possession of a virtue in a weak or truncated form, which makes a person to some extent morally bad or unworthy; it also justifies some diminished self-respect. For example, the lack of benevolence is the moral fault of callousness or indifference. A *moral vice* is a trait of character that makes a person to some extent morally bad or unworthy and deserving of moral disapproval; it also justifies some diminished self-respect. Most vices involve dispositions that are in direct conflict with one or more of the virtues. For example, the vice of cruelty, which is a disposition to place intrinsic value on directly harming others by inflicting humiliation, pain, and death and to receive satisfaction and enjoyment from it, conflicts with the virtue of benevolence.

Several principal virtues are needed for people to be able to act in accordance with the prima facie duties that make up the core content of morality: benevolence, conscientiousness, courage and self-control, self-knowledge, practical wisdom, and autonomy. The basic moral rules were flagrantly violated in the Holocaust, and it comes as no surprise to discover that it was to a large extent the lack of these virtues (together with the presence of vices such as cruelty) that explains the failure of *individuals* to refrain from participation in the genocide. I will not attempt to present or defend a comprehensive theory of all the virtues and vices; the choice of the virtues and vices I include in this survey is dictated by the subject of this study: moral responsibility in the Holocaust.

The Virtue of Benevolence

The virtues of motivation can vary both in strength and in scope. In the case of benevolence, *strength* refers to the degree to which each of the three tendencies—thought, feeling and emotion, and action—is present in an individual; whereas *scope* refers to variation in the degree of inclusiveness of the class of persons who are potential objects of a given individual's benevolence.

Thought

A tendency to have certain kinds of thoughts and to engage in certain kinds of mental activities amounts to a benevolent *cognitive style*. People who are benevolent exercise their cognitive capacities such as perception, attention, awareness, memory, and reasoning in ways that exhibit their underlying care and concern for the well-being of others. To say that they are thoughtful of others captures the general tendency of their cognitive style, since they are inclined to engage in a variety of cognitive activities that enable them to discover opportunities for doing a favor, being of help, or preventing harm. They tend to notice someone who needs help, to think of ways to give it, or to remember (for example) that today is the day when a friend needs a ride to get to a doctor's appointment. Clearly, people differ from each other in the degree to which they have a benevolent cognitive style, both in the size of their personal repertoire of these activities and in the frequency with which they engage in them. Since both the complementary tendencies to have benevolent feelings and emotions and to engage in benevolent actions are in large part causally dependent on the person's cognitive style, it is perhaps the most important variable for explaining differences in the strength of benevolence among individuals.

Most variations in the scope of benevolence are explained, at least in part, by a particular kind of cognitive variation, namely, the different ways that individuals conceive of other people that determine whether they are regarded as suitable recipients of benevolence in the first place. Such cognitive factors are especially important for explaining prejudice and hostility toward people who fall entirely outside one's immediate family or social group, for example. These different ways of conceiving other people are highly correlated with (and often caused by) the kinds of social relationship in which individuals find themselves. These fall into three main categories: close personal attachments, communal and cooperative relationships, and relations of universal and equal consideration.

Examples of benevolence that develop in *close personal attachments* include maternal bonding with newborn infants, parental love in general, family affection, and friendship. Benevolence is an essential feature of such close attachments to particular individuals. Moreover, the benevolence involved is highly personal because, in an especially crucial way, it depends on the unique identity of the individuals who are the objects of benevolence. Even in the simplest cases there is a crucial cognitive factor. The mother bonds with "her" baby (even if, as sometimes happens, she has been given someone else's baby by mistake). Family members conceive of each other *as* belonging to the same family, as well as occupying a specific role in it (my sister or my father). And friends usually like each other because of the unique set of valued characteristics they perceive in each other, together with the experiences and memories they share that constitute the history of their friendship.

Although the forms of benevolence found in these personal attachments are likely to be very strong, they are necessarily of *limited scope*. First, no matter what the culture, there is a limit to the number of opportunities for personal attachments that an individual can have and, second, even when there are many opportunities, most people are psychologically incapable of becoming personally attached to more than a few dozen individuals. Consequently, although the from of benevolence that emerges in personal attachments is both of fundamental importance to the individuals involved in them and morally desirable, it cannot be relied on it to provide the motivation required to fulfill the duties that constitute the core content of morality.

Examples of *communal and cooperative relationships* include being neighbors, being fellow workers, and being members of organizations such as a church, union, club, athletic team, and the like. These are "local," face-to-face relationships, usually in a particular place or community. They are not as inclusive as, say, the relationship of being a fellow citizen is within a modern political community. People who participate in such activities, especially when doing so is mutually beneficial, are likely to develop benevolent feelings of mutual trust, liking, and solidarity for each other that they do not have for people who do not participate or "belong." Although these forms of benevolence are usually not as strong as those found in personal attachments, they have greater scope, since they tend to include anybody regarded as a fellow participant or member in good standing. Consequently, the benevolence generated by the pervasive communal and cooperative relationships found in nearly every society has much greater potential to supply the motivation needed to fulfill the duties at the core of morality.

However, in practice, many such social activities fail to realize that potential fully; for example, members of a neighborhood may feel isolated from each other, fellow workers may be too competitive, and a church may be split by a theological dispute. Much more worrisome, though, is the fact that all too often people involved in local communal and cooperative relationships use the criteria of membership (whatever they happen to be) not merely as ways to encourage benevolence within the group (a process that necessarily excludes some people) but also as a way to denigrate people who are excluded and to see them as unworthy of care or concern, or (in the worst case) deem them so evil that they need to be exterminated.[8] This is the dark side of community and fellowship. Because it was so successfully exploited by the Nazis, it looms large in the study of the Holocaust. On balance, then, despite the great value of the forms of benevolence associated with these kinds of social relationships and their pervasiveness, they cannot be relied on alone to provide the motivation required to fulfill the duties that constitute the core content of morality. This has been confirmed by some empirical studies of the psychology of rescuers of Jews during the Holocaust. For example, although there was at least a prima facie duty to help Jews whose lives were in jeopardy, relatively few people actually came to their aid. One in-depth study of the motivation of people who rescued Jews found that a characteristic of "extensivity" (what I call unlimited scope benevolence and/or conscientiousness) was a 70 percent reliable predictor that a person would be a rescuer. In other words, people who saw Jews as fellow human beings who deserved equal consideration and concern were much more likely to come to their rescue than controls who did not share this conception.[9]

The principal example of *relations of universal and equal consideration* is being fellow citizens in a political community, especially as citizenship is generally understood in modern states, namely, as being universal and equal. People who participate together as citizens in a political community, especially if its basic structure is just and fair, tend to develop benevolent feelings of mutual recognition, trust, equal consideration, and national solidarity.[10] Citizens think of each other *as* fellow citizens, as compatriots. In contrast with the two forms of benevolence already considered, this form of benevolence is relatively impersonal; the mutual consideration that citizens have for each other is independent of family ties, personal love, friendship, and local communal memberships; consequently, this impersonal benevolence is potentially of *unlimited scope*. Although in routine situations this kind of benevolence is likely to be somewhat weaker than that associated with personal attachments and local communal activities, in emergencies it has the potential to provide very strong motivation for fulfilling the duties at the core of morality. Moreover, if a favorable political culture exists to complement individual benevolence, citizens may well be more than merely adequately motivated to meet that purpose even in routine situations.

It is a very short step, conceptually and emotionally, from the virtually universal benevolence involved in the mutual and equal consideration among citizens to actual universal equality of care and consideration for all persons. This is the ideal form of the virtue of benevolence, since it is of truly *unlimited scope*. All merely local and political criteria for being a fit object of care and concern fall by the way, and what remains is just the fact that a person is a fellow human being who needs help. I call this *universal benevolence;* it is the only form of benevolence that is likely to provide individuals with the kind of reliable motivation that is required to meet the demands of the core content of morality. Universal benevolence is especially needed when the well-being of people outside one's own society or political community is at stake, for example, in natural disasters, famine, and war. For our purposes, however, the most striking example of the need for universal benevolence is the threat of genocide. There is no doubt that many people have this ideal form of the virtue (as attested to by the findings of studies of rescuers already noted), in addition to the two forms with more restricted scope. It is this ideal form that I have in view as I discuss the other two tendencies that constitute the virtue of benevolence.

Feeling and Emotion

Benevolent people have a tendency to worry when others are in danger, to feel compassion when they are injured or ill, to be unhappy when they die, and to miss them when they are gone. They are free of the moral defect of callousness (or indifference). They are likely to derive satisfaction from doing favors for others or helping them when they are in need, to be happy or relieved when someone they are concerned about escapes from danger or recovers from illness. These emotions can be aroused by the weal and woe of others who are anonymous strangers, regardless of whether or not they can do anything to help;

indeed, they may only learn of someone else's good or bad fortune from viewing television or reading the newspaper. Since the vice of cruelty is in conflict with benevolence, people who are benevolent tend not to have unjustified feelings of hatred or anger, of vengeance and retribution, and do not enjoy inflicting pain, humiliation, and death on others. If they are ever intentionally cruel, they feel guilty and ashamed, and if they inflict serious injury or harm on someone, they feel remorse. Finally, they tend to have affection and friendly feelings toward others who are benevolent and tend to dislike, disapprove of, and feel anger toward others who are callous or cruel. These characteristic feelings and emotions help to provide benevolent people with the reliable motivation to abide by the basic duties not to harm others, to live up to one's role responsibilities to do good, and to provide mutual aid in emergencies.

Action

Leaving aside desert island counterexamples, a person who had a tendency to have benevolent thoughts and a tendency to have benevolent feelings and emotions but never actually did anything benevolent would be suspected of not really having the virtue. "By their actions you will know them" is almost an axiom in virtue ethics because a trait of character would have very little, if any, instrumental social value if it did not include a strong tendency to act in accordance with its defining cognitive and emotional features. This is why so much attention had been paid to the psychology of rescuers—they put their benevolent care into action to save lives. (This is not to say that the value of moral virtues is only instrumental. As I shall argue shortly, they also have intrinsic value, both for those who possess them and for others.)

The action tendencies of benevolent people are easily described. They have a strong and effective desire to fulfill whatever role responsibilities they may have to do good for others because they have care or concern for their well-being as an end, distinct from any sense of duty they may have; for the same reason, they are strongly inclined not to harm, injure, or show cruelty to others and to give aid in emergencies when they are able to do so. Moreover, they are strongly disposed to do morally optional acts that lie outside the realm of duty, such as kindnesses and favors, as well as to give generously, above and beyond duty. Thus benevolent people are motivated both to act in accordance with the demands of the core content of morality and to act beyond the call of duty.

The Virtue of Conscientiousness

Conscientiousness (along with benevolence) is a principal virtue of motivation, the salient feature of which is a sense of duty or obligation. Like benevolence, conscientiousness can vary in strength (because of individual differences in the degree to which the tendencies that constitute it are present) and in scope (because of individual differences in cognitive style). From the perspective of virtue ethics, the ideal is for everyone to have the virtue of conscientiousness with the widest possible scope so that they will be motivated to live up to the duties that constitute the core content of morality. This ideal is taken for granted in the discussion of the three main tendencies (in thought, feeling and emotion, and action). As with benevolence, the most important factors that determine the scope of conscientiousness are cognitive ones.

Thought

Conscientiousness is defined as the disposition to do acts that one sincerely believes are one's duty or obligation. People who are conscientious also have a tendency to think of (notice, pay attention to, remember) the features of a situation that evoke a relevant general moral principle or rule. The basic moral rules that forbid killing, robbing, raping, and stealing are assumed (correctly) to be virtually exceptionless. Recall the example of the person who returns a lost wallet just because it is the right thing to do; it is the person's belief that it is a matter of principle that causes the sense of duty. Conscientious people tend not to emphasize either prudential self-interested reasons or utilitarian consequentialist reasons when they deliberate about what they ought to do. They are, of course, especially keen to fulfill whatever role responsibilities they have, simply because they are expected to do so. As noted earlier, if they help someone in accordance with the principle of mutual aid, they tend to see it as something that is owed to the person helped rather than as a good that meets some need. Conscientiousness primarily involves treating people with respect, according them their rights, and not disappointing what are regarded as their legitimate expectations.

One feature of the cognitive style of conscientious people has become somewhat notorious, perhaps because of the way it was viewed in Freudian theory. Conscientious people tend to be somewhat compulsive. They are not just concerned to do their duty; they want to do it properly—carefully, thoroughly, accurately, and in a timely fashion (as the case warrants). They tend to pay attention to the details of what they are doing, notice when things are not going as they should, and the like. Similarly, they try to avoid harming others by not taking risks that would endanger others; they do not want to be negligent or careless.

Although conscientiousness has an important role in most personal relationships, it is especially needed in areas of public life that are impersonal, structured by rules, and institutional, such as the workplace, the marketplace, business, and government. In these areas there is often little room for personal feelings of love, affection, and friendship, and yet it is essential that people tell the truth, keep their word, respect property, and obey the law. That is why conscientiousness has to be very wide in scope; society cannot function if people cannot trust each other's word. So it is extremely important that there be a publicly shared conception of people as individuals with a capacity to lead a life as persons who are all equally deserving of respect and consideration.

One very conspicuous lack of this aspect of conscientiousness among Germans emerged eight years prior to the Holocaust when their fellow citizens were being persecuted just for being Jewish. The ever more stringent anti-Semitic laws and policies pursued by the Nazi regime explicitly targeted Jews as undeserving of equal respect under the law long before the Holocaust was implemented. The fact that very few Germans objected to these laws and policies shows that they had at best a severely truncated form of the virtue of conscientiousness.

Feeling and Emotion

Conscientiousness is ordinarily defined (as it is earlier in this study) primarily in terms of a cognitive psychological tendency to do what one sincerely believes is one's duty or obligation. However, this cognitive feature typically triggers corresponding feelings and emotions, for example, a belief that doing something that is one's duty can be experienced subjectively as an anxious sense of duty or a worrying feeling of obligation. People who do their duty from conscientiousness will have a sense of self-respect, a "clear conscience." But when they fail to do their duty, without a valid excuse or justification, they feel guilty and ashamed. Correspondingly, they tend to feel respect for those who fulfill their duties and obligations but indignation and resentment toward those who are unreliable or untrustworthy.

Actions

People who have the virtue of conscientiousness are strongly inclined to do what they believe is their duty and to fulfill what they see as an obligation. Moreover, since they also have conscientious cognitive habits, their beliefs about what their duties and obligations are tends to be well justified. Thus they are very likely to recognize a situation that is covered by a basic principle or rule belonging to the core content of morality. This, together with the fact that they are motivated by a strong sense of duty, makes it highly likely that they will in fact act in accordance with the core content: they will refrain from harming others, they will fulfill their role responsibilities to do good, and they will give aid in emergency situations when they are able to do so.

Before proceeding any further in this study of the Holocaust, I should note that we will encounter many examples of pathological forms of conscientiousness, especially among perpetrators who believed that their role responsibilities in genocidal institutions were moral duties that they had an obligation to fulfill. It bears repeating that an agent's beliefs about which actions are duties must be correct and justified; otherwise, the virtue of conscientiousness can be pernicious or evil in its effect. Understanding how the problem of misguided conscientiousness might be avoided is just one of the reasons for considering the role of practical wisdom in relation to other virtues.

The Virtue of Practical Wisdom

A morally good person has to have considerably greater capacity for practical reasoning than the discussion of the virtues up to this point may have suggested. This can be illustrated through a problem that has been alluded to briefly, namely, the fact that the basic moral rules are rules of prima facie duty. This means that there is always a strong presumption in favor of obeying them and that, in fact, they are binding in nearly all situations; nevertheless, it is sometimes morally permissible to override them. Of course, breaking a basic rule requires a compelling moral justification—one supported by clear, relevant, and convincing reasons. There are some cases in which the decision to break a rule seems so obviously correct, for example, when one has to kill in self-defense, that there is a temptation to say that it is not really an exception, since the rule should be understood to include it. But in many situations there may well be a justified exception to a basic rule, but the reasons that provide the justification are not at all obvious or noncontroversial, and finding them may require powers of analysis, reflection, and deliberation of a fairly high order. In short, the virtue of practical wisdom is often needed.

A closely related problem that calls for practical wisdom is the notorious fact that moral rules of prima facie duty often conflict with each other. For example, I cannot both keep a promise to meet a friend at a specified time and stop to help persons injured in a car accident. Of course, many times conflicts like this are easily resolved (I can telephone my friend to explain why I shall be late), but sometimes they are not. So-called hard cases are pervasive in ethics textbooks for a good reason; they present a serious challenge to our moral understanding. Unfortunately, the study of the Holocaust provides far too many examples of such hard cases. For example, some of the Jewish councils appointed by the Germans to run the ghettos decided that it was permissible for them to sacrifice some Jews in order to meet weekly quotas for transports to killing centers (perhaps a thousand or more each time), in the hope that the rest would be saved to perform valuable work for the Germans.[11]

A moral judgment, recall, is a judgment about what people should do or be, all things considered. Consequently, in order to deliberate effectively, one needs to be aware of basic moral principles and rules and to have relevant factual information. Ideally one should try to arrive at beliefs that are empirically well founded, but often one has to be content with estimates based on what little evidence happens to be available. For example, the life-and-death choices that faced the Jewish councils would have been tragic no matter how much more they had known, but they might have chosen differently if they had had better information about the Germans' true intentions and how long the war was going to last.

The virtue of practical wisdom can be defined as the possession of (1) knowledge of basic moral principles, rules of prima facie duty, and standards of goodness for actions and persons; (2) an inclination to become well informed about relevant facts in any situation in which a moral judgment is to be made; and (3) a capacity to deliberate, that is, to weigh different moral considerations such as conflicting duties in a particular situation, in the light of relevant facts with objectivity and fairness in order to make a justified decision about what ought to be done, all things considered.

Practical wisdom is a master virtue in the sense that it mediates all the other virtues.[12] This function can be appreciated by considering the way in which practical wisdom can prevent some of the pathologies to which individual virtues are subject. Benevolence in practice sometimes degenerates into unjustified favoritism, for example, when an unqualified family member is appointed to an important public office with heavy responsibilities. This is one reason why Kant gave a low ranking to the moral worth of "inclinations" like kindness.[13] It is not necessary to agree with Kant entirely to see that benevolence unchecked by practical wisdom can be morally pernicious.

In a study of the Holocaust, pathologies of conscientiousness take center stage. Conscientiousness can all too easily become mindless rule worship or blind obedience to authority, as it did with Adolf Eichmann and many other perpetrators of the genocide. However, it is a mistake to think that it was only blind obedience at work. There were also some radical cognitive failures and they were pervasive, not only in the minds of fanatical Nazis but also in the minds of many ordinary Germans. For example, it was widely (but mistakenly) believed that Jewish treachery was responsible for Germany's defeat in World War I and that the Jews were also behind an international conspiracy that was responsible for the presumed evils of both capitalism and communism (including the Russian revolution of 1917). These and a number of other paranoid fantasies played an essential role in justifying the persecution of Jews and in motivating the genocide. These cognitive mistakes made it possible for Germans to believe that it was permissible to violate the basic moral rules that forbid doing harm, and many of them came to believe that it was actually their duty to kill Jews.

In addition, Germans were socialized into an authoritarian political culture in which the state and its officials were deemed to be virtually beyond criticism and accountability, and obeying the law was considered to be a nearly absolute duty. The core content of morality includes a rule of prima facie duty to obey valid laws, but a person with practical wisdom would never accept it as an absolute duty to obey any law regardless of what it required. If a law is clearly in conflict with the core content of morality (e.g., the German law that required the death penalty for a Jewish man convicted for having sex with a non-Jewish woman), the prima facie duty to obey it may be overridden. The same reasoning applies all the more to wartime military orders that conflict with basic rules not to harm, since the potential for causing harm to defenseless civilians is so great. One of the major changes in U.S. military ethics is a direct result of the catastrophic breakdown of restraint by the German military during World War II.[14] There are now significant restrictions on the concept of legitimate orders and new definitions of what constitutes a war crime.[15]

The Virtue of Autonomy

Autonomy is the trait of being self-directed and intellectually independent in moral matters, with a strong sense of responsibility for making up one's own mind in particular situations and for leading one's own life as a whole. It might seem that any person who had the virtue of practical wisdom would also have the virtue of autonomy. This may well be correct, and perhaps autonomy would be best viewed as a feature of practical wisdom. Still, it seems advisable to treat autonomy separately in order to emphasize its moral significance, especially in the study of the Holocaust. A person who lacks (or is seriously deficient in) autonomy has a serious *moral defect,* a tendency (among other things) to defer to presumed authority or to the conventional morality of the community, even on the most basic issues of life and death. One especially pertinent example of the importance of autonomy is the fact that thousands of Jews were actually saved by relatively few individual rescuers. Several studies have found that the people who rescued Jews were a very small minority among a large majority of perpetrators and bystanders; moreover, there is some evidence that most rescuers were not only courageous (as one would naturally expect) but were also autonomous individuals, being very little influenced by social pressure or conventional moral attitudes.[16] Particularly interesting is the fact that few of them were anti-Semitic, even when they lived in very anti-Semitic cultures.[17] (I consider rescuers in greater detail in chap. 9).

Virtues of Self-Control

Traditionally these virtues were referred to as "willpower" because they involve the capacity to manage and overcome one's desires, aversions, and fears in the light of one's moral principles and ideals. Although the virtues of self-control require some cognitive knowledge ("knowing that"), they are primarily a kind of practical skill ("knowing how").[18]

Temperance

This is the classical virtue of self-control. It consists of the capacity to counter or block desires, especially for pleasure, that threaten to interfere with doing what is morally right or good. It is important to see that temperance is not necessarily "puritanical" in the popular sense; its function is not to repress desire or thwart pleasure as an end but rather to check the pursuit of pleasure when indulgence will lead, or is likely to lead, to wrongdoing. For example, temperate persons do not drink alcohol when they are driving a car or have unprotected sex if they are HIV positive. A *moral defect* in relation to temperance is the trait of impulsiveness. *Vices* that interfere with or subvert the virtue of temperance often involve an inordinate or uncontrollable desire for some good. Examples include greed, which is a voracious need for possessions, especially money or wealth, though sometimes greed displays itself in a willingness to take advantage of people in dire straits. This happened on a large scale when many Germans took over valuable Jewish properties and businesses at ridiculously low prices under the provisions of Nazi Aryanization laws in the 1930s.[19] Other vices include gluttony, addiction to alcohol or drugs, sloth, and predatory sexual promiscuity.

Courage

Courage is the capacity to overcome fear and aversion in order to do what is morally right. Although people can exhibit courage in the pursuit of nonmoral goals (e.g., athletes) and earn people's admiration for it, I am interested only in the moral form because it alone has moral worth. In any case, the sphere of action in which moral courage is a relevant virtue is virtually unlimited, so it is a mistake to think of it only in connection with overcoming fear of physical danger. Courage is needed to face all kinds of moral challenges, for example, overcoming the social pressure to conform to conventional anti-Semitism that faced rescuers of Jews during the Holocaust. The salient vice related to courage is cowardice.

It is sometimes thought that a person with truly good character would be literally fearless, that is, not subject to fear in the first place. Such an ideal person would not have the need for courage as I have defined it. However, there are empirical reasons for thinking that this ideal is quite unrealistic. According to evolutionary psychology, possessing the capacity for realistic, cognitively based fear has great survival value, and this explains why we are genetically programmed to feel fear. Since almost all human beings do in fact have the capacity to feel fear, and we know that fear often interferes with meeting the demands of the core content of morality, virtue ethics recognizes the need for the virtue of courage.

Patience

Patience is the capacity to manage irritation, provocation, or distraction that threatens to interfere with doing one's duty or achieving some morally worthy goal. Patience is required in many different kinds of situations, but it seems to be especially valuable for people who occupy stressful social roles such as law enforcement officer or parent. The people who rescued Jews during the Holocaust again serve as good examples, since they often hid the Jews in their homes, living with them in cramped quarters, sharing their scarce, rationed food, all the while taking precautions not to be discovered. A related *moral fault* is irritability, or, simply, impatience.

The Virtue of Justified Moral Self-Respect

The strongest desire in nearly all humans is that for self-preservation, but the desire for self-respect comes in a close second. Indeed, it is a commonplace in psychology that people who suffer an abrupt or catastrophic loss of self-respect often become suicidal. Before analyzing this virtue, I need to explain the use of the qualifiers "justified" and "moral" in the subheading for this section. In virtue ethics, self-respect is justified self-assessment of one's own character, all things considered. This needs to be kept distinct from a wide variety of nonmoral self-assessments that are called self-esteem. Examples of people who base their self-esteem on nonmoral or immoral traits abound. For example, a frontier gunslinger who took pride in having killed dozens of men in gunfights based his self-esteem, at least in part, on the moral vice of callousness toward the lives of others. Likewise, people who specialize in swindling others through confidence games often derive a profound sense of self-satisfaction and pride in their ability to "con" others. Clearly, such nonmoral (or immoral) self-esteem must be distinguished from the virtue of self-respect based on the possession of good moral character. Hence, the need for the seemingly redundant use of the term "moral."

The term "justified" is also needed because self-respect should involve an assessment of oneself, all things considered. Even if we confine our attention to people whose self-respect is (ostensibly) based on the possession of good character traits, we often find that their feelings of pride and self-respect are unjustified because they are mistaken or self-deceived about the morality of their actions and/or the goodness of their characters. Indeed, some forms of self-deception are vices and constitute one of the most pervasive problems encountered in the study of the Holocaust. (See chap. 4 for a fuller discussion of self-deception.)

The psychological explanation for the pervasiveness of self-deception is that most people find it easier (and in most cases it is easier, at least in the short run) to engage in self-deception than to take responsibility for their wrongdoing and acknowledge the defects and vices in their character. Taking responsibility for wrongdoing involves blaming oneself and feeling guilty, while acknowledging character shortcomings causes feelings of shame. These can be very distressing and anxiety-ridden emotions. Moreover, taking responsibility for wrongdoing often requires acknowledging it to others and having to accept their disapproval and any appropriate moral and legal sanctions. There is no getting around it; honestly and openly taking responsibility can be an exceedingly difficult thing to do, and for most people self-deception is a constant and powerful temptation.

When self-deception is used systematically to evade moral responsibility, it is a principal moral vice; it not only keeps people from taking the morally desirable steps that would bring a resolution to the problems caused by their own wrongdoing as far as others are concerned, but it also blocks whatever motivation for reform they might otherwise have. It is for these reasons that justified moral self-respect, based on an honest self-assessment of one's true moral worth, is a moral virtue. False pride bought at the cost of self-deception has no moral worth; self-satisfaction based on false or unfounded beliefs is a delusion.

Thus, *justified moral self-respect* consists of (1) an inclination to engage in cognitive activities such as paying attention to, noticing, remembering, and morally evaluating one's actions in order to attain knowledge of one's conduct and character that is as accurate and complete as possible, (2) being relatively free of the vice of self-deception with respect to one's character and conduct, which together result in (3) having explicit beliefs about one's conduct and character that are, overall, reasonably accurate and complete, and (4) having a sense of proper pride that is justified by these beliefs about one's conduct and character.

Summary and Justification of the Virtues

I began the chapter by noting that virtue ethics, which is concerned with identifying and justifying standards of good character, is not self-sufficient; it must be supplemented by principles and rules of action that constitute the core content of morality: a set of rules of prima facie duty not to do harm, to do good in accordance with role responsibilities, and to give aid in emergencies in accordance with the principle of mutual aid. Then I surveyed the reasons for the nonegoistic character of the virtues, especially benevolence and conscientiousness, and critically evaluated the challenge of psychological egoism. I reached the conclusion that the principal arguments for psychological egoism are based on conceptual confusions about what constitutes a nonegoistic motive. However, even if psychological egoism is false, there is still an important role for rational self-interested motives in ethics.

The individual virtues discussed in the chapter are *benevolence, conscientiousness, practical wisdom, autonomy, self-control,* and *justified moral self-respect.* Each of these virtues is a complex psychological trait, with several of them involving distinctive cognitive styles. The virtues of benevolence and conscientiousness are virtues of motivation, whereas those of self-control involve both motivation and practical skills, a kind of "knowing how." Moreover, benevolence and conscientiousness should be universal in scope. I also identified several principal vices: *cruelty, untrustworthiness, negligence, greed, cowardice,* and *self-deception.*

Once some principal virtues have been identified, it is necessary to justify the moral judgment that they are indeed good traits that make people who possess them worthy of respect and admiration; providing this justification can also serve to show that the corresponding moral defects and vices are morally bad and make people who have them reprehensible.

There are three main kinds of reasons that justify the judgment that these traits are indeed virtues: (1) they have *instrumental value* because they provide people with the motivation to meet the demands of the core content of morality, (2) they have *instrumental value* because they enable people to participate in communal and cooperative social relationships that foster *intrinsically valuable* feelings of belonging, friendship, and solidarity, and (3) they have *intrinsic value* for the individuals who possess them because they constitute the bases for moral self-respect. Each of these deserves further discussion.

The *instrumental value* of providing people with the motivation to meet the demands of the core content of morality should be obvious. If people have these traits, they will do less harm and more good overall than they would if they did not have them. Moreover, the greater the strength and the scope of traits like benevolence and conscientiousness, the greater will be the harm not done and the amount of good brought about. The degree to which people have the additional traits of practical wisdom, autonomy, self-control, and justified self-respect can only make it even more likely that they will be able to meet the basic demands of morality. By contrast, the greater extent to which people are callous, cruel, negligent, deferential to authority, or self-deceived, the more they will fail. The study of the Holocaust provides horrible confirmation of this last point.

The *instrumental value* of enabling people to participate in communal and cooperative social relationships that foster *intrinsically valuable* feelings of belonging, friendship, and solidarity may not be so obvious. People who have the traits that I have identified as virtues are much more likely to participate in communal and cooperative social relationships, both because they have a greater ability to participate effectively and because they are more likely than people who lack these traits to derive intrinsic satisfaction from it. Some of this intrinsic satisfaction will often be ordinary nonmoral (not "immoral") pleasure that is the natural consequence of achieving the goals of the cooperative activity; but there are also deeper satisfactions that depend on a sustained sense of the meaningfulness of the social relationship itself, quite distinct from the activities engaged in. People value belonging, friendship, and solidarity for their own sake, distinct from the value they place on what is achieved by means of the cooperative activity in which they are engaged.

The *intrinsic value* of the virtues for the individuals who possess them has long been recognized. For example, it is implicit in the old saying that virtue is its own reward, which is used to drive home the point that one should not be motivated to do something morally right in order to be praised or rewarded (a self-interested goal), but only because it is morally right. The implicit assumption is that there is indeed a reward for acting in this principled way and that it has intrinsic value. Conscientious people who do what they think is their duty as a matter of principle will have a "clear conscience," referring to the fact that they have maintained their self-respect. This observation applies equally to all of the other virtues as well, since each time people intentionally exercise their capacity for, say, self-control or practical wisdom, they create an opportunity to reflect on the fact that they are leading a principled life and take satisfaction in it. It is very important to see that justified moral self-respect always has this distinct intrinsic value for the people who have and appreciate it, independent of any other value that good character might have for them.

People with the strongest moral character will have developed a sense of personal identity and integrity based to a large extent on their moral commitments and values. Consequently, such moral exemplars find it psychologically impossible to act against their principles even if doing the right thing means risking death. In chapter 9 I describe some individuals with moral character of this excellent kind who rescued Jews under extremely dangerous conditions.

Notes

1. H. L. A. Hart, *The Concept of Law* (Oxford: Clarendon, 1961), 188.

2. See J. S. Mill, *Utilitarianism,* chapter 5; many editions available. For brief introductory discussions of the place of rules in morality, see Bernard Gert, "Moral Rules," in *Encyclopedia of Ethics,* ed. Lawrence C. Becker (New York: Garland, 1992), 2:859–862.

3. Lawrence C. Becker, *Reciprocity* (London: Routledge & Kegan Paul, 1986), 60–61.

4. Becker, *Reciprocity,* chap. 2.

5. Gert, "Moral Rules," 2:859–862.

6. Michael Walzer, *Spheres of Justice* (New York: Basic, 1983), chap. 3.

7. Joel Feinberg, "Psychological Egoism," in *Reason and Responsibility,* ed. Joel Feinberg (Belmont, Calif.: Wadsworth, 1993), 461.

8. Pierre L. van den Berghe, "The Biology of Nepotism," in *Bigotry, Prejudice, and Hatred: Definitions, Causes, and Solutions,* ed. Robert L. Baird and Stuart E. Rosenbaum (Buffalo, N.Y.: Prometheus, 1992).

9. Samuel P. Oliner, *The Altruistic Personality: Rescuers of Jews in Nazi Germany* (New York: Free Press, 1988), 253.

10. Robert D. Putnam, *Making Democracy Work: Civic Traditions in Modern Italy* (Princeton, N.J.: Princeton University Press, 1993), chap. 6.

11. Raul Hilberg, *The Destruction of the European Jews* (New York: Holmes & Meier, 1985), 3:1034–1039.

12. Becker, *Reciprocity,* chap. 3.

13. Immanuel Kant, *Groundwork of the Metaphysics of Morals* (Indianapolis: Hackett, 1964).

14. Hilberg, *Destruction of the European Jews,* 1:299–304.

15. Paul Christopher, *The Ethics of War and Peace: An Introduction to Legal and Moral Issues* (Englewood Cliffs, N.J.: Prentice-Hall, 1999), chap. 9, "Responsibility for War Crimes"; Telford Taylor, *Nuremberg and Vietnam: An American Tragedy* (Chicago: Quandrangle, 1970), 56–57.

16. Nechama Tec, *When Light Pierced the Darkness: Christian Rescue of Jews in Nazi-Occupied Poland* (New York: Oxford University Press, 1986), 188–193.

17. Eva Fogelman, *Conscience and Courage: Rescuers of Jews during the Holocaust* (New York: Doubleday-Anchor, 1994), 176–177; Tec, *When Light Pierced the Darkness,* 99–112.

18. Robert C. Roberts, "Will Power and the Virtues," *Philosophical Review* 93 (April 1984): 227–247.

19. John Weiss, *Ideology of Death: Why the Holocaust Happened in Germany* (Chicago: Ivan R. Dee, 1996), 310.

Suggestions for Further Reading

Becker, Lawrence C., ed. *Encyclopedia of Ethics.* New York: Garland, 1992. See the articles on altruism, benevolence, character, duties and obligations, and moral rules, among others.

Blum, Lawrence A. *Friendship, Altruism and Morality.* London: Routledge & Kegan Paul, 1980. A defense of the moral value of friendship and benevolence and a rejection of narrow Kantian views that focus exclusively on feelings of duty.

Kruschwitz, Robert, and Robert C. Roberts, eds. *The Virtues: Contemporary Essays on Moral Character.* Belmont, Calif.: Wadsworth, 1987. See articles by Robert C. Roberts, Susan Wolf, Robert M. Adams, and Lawrence Blum.

Wallace, James D. *Virtues and Vices.* Ithaca, N.Y.: Cornell University Press, 1978. Advanced study of several virtues, including benevolence and conscientiousness.

Chapter 3

Excuses

The topic of excuses is another major element of the theory of moral responsibility. Ordinarily, when people have done something wrong, we are justified in making an inference that they are blameworthy, at least to some degree, for having done it. However, if the wrongdoer has a justified excuse, the usual inference that he or she is blameworthy is blocked. Moreover, someone who is blameless for wrongdoing does not deserve overt blame, moral sanctions, or legal punishment. Thus, it is easy to appreciate why excuses are a central feature of our social and legal practices of responsibility. This discussion of excuses is not primarily interested in the role they play as a means of coping with awkward social situations or of evading responsibility by "making excuses," that is, offering plausible (but bogus) excuses. Our topic is *morally justified excuses,* a topic that belongs to ethics. The purpose of this chapter is to achieve a better understanding of the (often implicit) reasoning involved in offering an excuse and to see what features all valid excuses have in common that block blameworthiness. I also discuss the difference between the philosophical inquiry into the reasoning that underlies justified excuses that belongs to ethics, on the one hand, and the experimental investigation of activities such as "making excuses" that belongs to social psychology, on the other. I begin with ethics.

In chapter 2, as part of an initial overview of theory, I offered several examples that show how excuses are related to moral blameworthiness. The first example described a German who informed the Gestapo that his neighbors were hiding Jewish persons (1) knowing that the act of informing was wrong, (2) doing it intentionally, (3) doing it voluntarily (i.e., he could have done otherwise), and (4) from a bad motive of greed. Taken together, these features make the man unquestionably blameworthy for his act; another way to state this judgment is to say that "he had no excuse." This does not mean that as a matter of psychological fact he would not have tried to make excuses for himself were he to have been accused of wrongdoing; rather, it is an ethical judgment that (given the features 1–4) there is no justifiable excuse that would objectively exonerate him from responsibility for his wrongdoing, all things considered.

Absent any of these features, however, or if they were altered in certain relevant ways, the man's blameworthiness either would not exist or would be diminished. Suppose, for example, that the man did not know that the people who were being hidden were Jews, and, furthermore, that his only purpose in informing was to stop what he believed to be a violation of safety regulations designed to prevent overcrowding in housing. Given this new set of facts, features 1–4 no longer apply; consequently, there is very little, if any, reason to blame the man. Objectively the act is still wrong, since it led to the arrest and deportation of the mother and her child, but the informer did not know it was wrong. Furthermore, if his ignorance about the victims being Jews was not his own fault (i.e., his ignorance was nonculpable), then he was not at all to blame for their terrible fate, even though it was his action that brought it about. (Causing harm to others, by itself, is ordinarily not sufficient for moral or legal responsibility.) Moreover, there is also the mitigating factor that his motives are not morally reprehensible in the way that the greed present in the earlier example is. This example thus helps us appreciate how a morally justified excuse serves to block the usual inference from the fact that someone has done something wrong to the conclusion that the person is therefore blameworthy.

In this chapter I am mainly concerned with ethics, identifying some principal excuses and mitigating factors that are commonly accepted as morally justified and providing a theory to show why the common view is correct. Before beginning this investigation into the ethics of excuses, I shall consider the closely related but distinct investigation of excuses pursued in social psychology.

The Psychology of "Making Excuses" versus the Ethics of Justified Excuses

Social psychologists have a great interest in learning as much as they can about the pervasive and important human activity of "making excuses," since it plays such a central role in how people manage threats to their self-respect and avoid overt blame and punishment from others.[1] Whereas ethicists are concerned with what makes an excuse morally justified, psychologists tend to focus almost exclusively on how, and under what conditions, people make up bogus excuses, false alibis, and merely plausible stories in order to avoid some "aversive outcome" such as a loss of self-respect, disapproval from others, or punishment. Although there are exceptions,[2] most psychological studies pay scant attention to the moral reasoning that even a fake excuse must follow if it is to have any chance of succeeding. It is important to recognize that "making excuses" is necessarily a parasitic activity dependent on a background moral activity of giving and accepting justified excuses. Making bogus excuses is like using counterfeit currency, which has value only if it succeeds in imitating a genuine currency that people generally trust and accept. Thus the ethical inquiry into justified excuses has a logical priority over the psychological study of making excuses, independent of whatever may be said about the overall importance or value of each inquiry considered independently.

It is not clear why most psychologists pay attention to "making excuses" while generally neglecting the pervasive activity of making and accepting honest excuses. One reason may be that psychologists often insist on drawing a sharp distinction between scientific and empirical inquiry into how humans in fact behave, on the one hand, and ethical inquiry into how humans ought to behave. This distinction (which is useful and valuable for many purposes) might be seen as justifying psychologists' relative neglect of the genuine activities. However, this distinction does not constitute a plausible justification, if only because the genuine activities are just as pervasive, just as much a fact of life, as activities of feigned excuses that are parasitic on them. In order to study genuine moral activities, social psychologists would need a greater understanding of both ordinary moral reasoning and ethical theory than is extant in much current work. However, the benefits from such a research orientation would be enormous, especially if it led to a more balanced view of how genuine and feigned excusing activities are related to each other in everyday life. This is not to say that the study of the parasitic activities is unimportant; far from it. In the very next chapter I take a closer look at both the ethics and the psychology of self-deception in which excuses play a prominent role.

Some Basic Distinctions: "No Act" Explanation, Justification, and Excuse

A person can block responsibility for an act by means of either a *"no act"* explanation or a *justification,* both of which differ from an *excuse.* All three of these ways of blocking responsibility appeal to relevant facts, and in order to be rationally acceptable in their primary social functions, these alleged facts must be true in actuality. False explanations, bogus justifications, and made-up excuses are often mistakenly accepted at face value by others, but when this happens the primary social purposes of holding people responsible for their actions are subverted.

"No Act" Explanations

A person who gives an explanation for an alleged act says, in effect, "I did not do the act." Such an explanation is described in chapter 2: A running dog causes a man to lose his balance, fall backward, and break a vase. Although the motion of the man's body causes the damage, he is not acting at all; the movement of his body is determined by the forces acting on it, forces over which he has no control. Thus the true and correct explanation of how the vase was broken is complete without having to make any mention of the man's intentions, motives, beliefs, or any other fact about his psychology or moral character. In this particular example, the gist of the explanation is, in effect, that there was no act at all.

Whenever bodily movements can be completely and correctly explained by causes over which the person has no control, there is an explanation for the behavior that blocks any moral or legal responsibility. The same holds true even if the causes are internal. For example, in an epileptic seizure, neurons firing in the brain directly cause behavior, completely bypassing the person's powers of cognition and control. This is the crucial feature of any explanation purporting to show that strictly speaking no act was performed. It is important, of course, that the explanation be in fact true. Some explanations of this kind (e.g., acting under posthypnotic suggestion and sleepwalking) are controversial, in part because it is often difficult to tell whether the alleged explanation is true; but the principle is still the same.

In some cases a person may be blameworthy for the fact that his or her powers of agency are bypassed in the way alleged by a "no act" explanation. For example, someone who drives a car might negligently fail to take medication that prevents epileptic seizures and, as a result, suffer a seizure that causes an accident.

Justification

A person who gives a justification for an act says, in effect, "I did the act, but the act is not wrong." For example, a police officer on duty shoots an armed fugitive who threatens to use a gun; the officer acts in a morally permissible way, nothing else considered. As with "no act" explanations, the alleged facts appealed to in a justification must be true. Of course, police have been known to lie about their use of deadly force, and even when they believe they are justified, they can still be mistaken. The invocation of an alleged justification is especially important in the study of the Holocaust, since many German perpetrators were convinced that killing the Jews was not only not wrong but was actually necessary and right. In short, they felt justified in committing genocide. However, the alleged facts that were used to justify genocide against the Jews were not based on personal empirical observation, historical evidence, or scientifically confirmed theories. Instead, they consisted of pseudo-biological racial doctrines, historical myths, paranoid fantasies, and politically motivated lies.[3]

Excuse

A person who offers an excuse for an act says, in effect, "I did the act, the act is wrong, but I am not to blame for doing it because. . . ." In order for an excuse to be morally justified, the facts or conditions used to complete it must be true. The fact that the person offering the excuse sincerely believes it is not sufficient to make it a justified excuse, if only because making excuses is one of the main psychological tactics employed in self-deception. In short, an excuse is not justified just because the person offering it finds it convincing. Just as with explanations and justifications, there is a requirement that the relevant facts appealed to in offering an excuse be objectively correct.

What Makes an Excuse Morally Justified?

Valid versus Being Justified

In addition to the requirement that the alleged facts appealed to in offering an excuse be true, the ethical principles and standards used must also be relevant and justified. Often these principles and standards are not stated explicitly because they are taken for granted as obvious truths that everyone recognizes. In virtue ethics, however, all assumptions must be made explicit in order to clarify the reasoning by which an excuse can be justified. Presumably, reasoning that justifies a particular excuse for an act of wrongdoing can always be formulated in a deductive argument; the premises state the relevant facts, ethical principles, and standards that, when taken together, justify the conclusion; the conclusion (which follows deductively from the premises) is that the person is not blameworthy.

The distinction between the validity of an excuse and its being justified is modeled on the distinction in logic between the validity and the soundness of arguments. An argument is deductively *valid* if its conclusion follows necessarily from its premises. For example, the following argument is deductively valid:

1. All illegal immigrants must register with the police.
2. John is an illegal immigrant.
3. Therefore, John must register with the police.

If both premises are true, then the conclusion must also be true. This particular argument would also be *sound* if both of its premises were indeed true. Soundness allows us to infer that the conclusion is in fact true; validity alone does not.

When an argument is used to support an excuse, the concept of *being justified* replaces the concept of soundness; otherwise, the distinctions are the same. An excuse is morally *valid* if its conclusion (i.e., that the person is not blameworthy) follows deductively from premises that state the relevant facts adduced as the excusing condition or conditions, together with relevant ethical principles and standards. For example, the following argument represents a morally valid excuse:

1. Intentionally causing Jews to be deported to Auschwitz and killed is wrong (ethical principle).
2. The German who informed on the people hiding next door did not know that they were Jews who would be deported to Auschwitz and killed (empirical fact).
3. Therefore, the German who informed on the people hiding next door did not know that his action was wrong. (Validly inferred from 1 and 2.)
4. People are blameworthy for doing a particular wrong act, A, only if they know that A is wrong (ethical principle).
5. Therefore, the German who informed on the people hiding next door was not blameworthy for his action. (Validly inferred from 3 and 4.)

This particular excuse would also be *morally justified* if the premises 1 and 4 were each morally justified and premise 2 were in fact true. Assessing the premises in an argument that is meant to justify an excuse is the main focus of this discussion. The remainder of this chapter is devoted to identifying and explaining the principles that cover the most important of the excusing conditions and to showing how they justify a judgment that a person is not blameworthy for doing something wrong. The empirical investigation into the truth of alleged facts stated in the premises is distinct from the ethical investigation into the relevant principles and standards, but it is equally essential to the overall task of establishing that the excuse is justified.

I have offered several examples of excuses that are commonly regarded as having moral validity, such as coercion, ignorance, and mistake. Do these excuses have something in common that makes them all valid? The widely accepted Hume-Brandt theory holds that there is indeed something common, namely, that persons have a valid excuse for wrongdoing whenever their act or omission was *not* produced by a defective character, that is, by a lack of virtue or the presence of a vice.[4] To illustrate, I return to an earlier example: the German soldier who kills an unarmed Jew under coercion of a threat of death for disobeying an order. The soldier has a morally valid excuse because he is motivated to kill the Jew solely by a justified fear of death, a motive that is neither bad in itself nor indicative of a vicious character trait. There is nothing in the soldier's character or motive that brings moral discredit on him; he is blameless (assuming that the soldier would not kill the Jew if he were not being coerced; obviously, this assumption does not hold for many actual German soldiers who killed Jews). Thus the study of excuses has brought us back full circle to moral blameworthiness (discussed in chap. 2). I shall now survey some of the principal excuses commonly regarded as morally valid to see whether the Hume-Brandt theory can be confirmed.

Some Principal Valid Excuses

This survey of valid excuses is organized around three of the four features of an unquestionably blameworthy act that were noted earlier: a person who performs a wrong act or omission (1) knowing that it is wrong, (2) doing it intentionally, and (3) doing it freely or voluntarily. Assuming that each of these features is necessary for being blameworthy, the absence of any one (or more) of them constitutes an excuse that renders the person not blameworthy. Thus a list of familiar excuses can be inferred: *ignorance* (the absence of relevant knowledge); *accident, mistake,* or *negligence* (the absence of intention); and *coercion, lack of ability,* and *lack of opportunity* (the absence of freedom; lacking the ability or opportunity to do otherwise). I discuss an additional feature, (4) acting with a morally bad motive, in a section on mitigating circumstances.

Nonculpable Ignorance (Lack of Relevant Knowledge)

People who do not realize the nature of what they are doing and are not to blame for their ignorance are not to blame for the wrong they do. This is the valid excuse of *nonculpable ignorance.* For example, a garbage collector throws an abandoned baby into a trash compactor, not realizing that the baby has been concealed in the trash barrel.[5] He does not kill the baby knowingly, but by *mistake* and thus wholly unintentionally. The fact that the baby is in the trash barrel is unforeseeable and thus entirely unexpected. Moreover, since it would be impractical to require that garbage collectors search each barrel of trash, this is not his role responsibility; therefore, he is *not negligent.* Clearly, the garbage collector's act, although it is morally wrong, is not the product of any moral defect in his character, and so his act brings no discredit on him. He is blameless. Thus this excuse clearly satisfies the Hume-Brandt test for moral validity.

By contrast, people are blameworthy for doing something wrong out of ignorance when they themselves are at fault for being ignorant. For example, suppose that a pharmacist mistakenly fills a prescription with the wrong medication, causing someone's death. Unlike the garbage collector, the pharmacist does have a clear role responsibility, namely, to make certain that the correct medications are used to fill all prescriptions. Because of the high risk of causing serious injury, illness, or death, it is reasonable to require all pharmacists to take every precaution against filling a prescription incorrectly. Therefore, the pharmacist's act is produced by his *negligence,* a moral defect. This example illustrates how *culpable ignorance* fails the Hume-Brandt test for moral validity; thus it does not belong on our list of valid excuses.

A related problem that is encountered frequently in the study of the Holocaust is how to justify a judgment that a particular example represents culpable ignorance. Not all cases are as clear as the example of the negligent pharmacist. For example, most Germans did nothing to help the Jews during the years of persecution and genocide, so they seem to be blameworthy for what they failed to do. However, after the genocide was over, many German accomplices and bystanders claimed that they had not known at the time that deported Jews were actually being killed; in effect, they claimed an excuse of ignorance. This raises two questions: Was this a justified excuse? Were the Germans in fact ignorant? Although it is surely unwise to make sweeping judgments about what all Germans "must" have known, the historical evidence indicates that it is highly probable that by the end of 1942 a majority of them either knew or strongly suspected that the Jews were being systematically killed or left to die.[6] So it appears that most Germans did not have a justified excuse of ignorance. The second question concerns those Germans who genuinely did not know that the Jews were being killed: Was their ignorance nonculpable? Again, it would be unwise to make any generalization. Some Germans lived in remote rural areas far removed from both the war and the camp system. Very few Jews had ever lived in those regions, and thus many of the Germans probably had no inkling of the genocide. However, most Germans lived in cities that saw conspicuous deportations of Jews, the sudden availability of blocks of vacant apartments, and the Aryanization of Jewish businesses. Remaining ignorant or unsuspecting in this case would have required people to engage in extensive tactics of self-deception for which they would most likely be to some extent blameworthy. (I discuss the morality of self-deception in more detail in chap. 4.)

It seems safe to conclude that many Germans were afflicted with *culpable ignorance* of the fate of the Jews, and so they did not have a valid moral excuse for their failure to aid the Jews. Individuals who were not to blame for their ignorance might justifiably claim an *excuse* (if it was impossible for them to get the information), or perhaps a *mitigating circumstance* (if it was merely difficult), that makes their failure to help less blameworthy than it would have been had it been done with full awareness.

Unintentional Action (Accident, Mistake, and Negligence)

People who do something wrong intentionally not only know what they are doing (intent presupposes knowledge, though the reverse is not true), but they also mean to be doing the wrong. Doing wrong with both awareness and intent clearly puts the agent's character in question and, barring some other excuse, makes him or her blameworthy. We may not know the specific vice or defect of character that accounts for the motivation to do wrong intentionally, but we can infer that something must be lacking in the person's character. People who do something wrong *unintentionally* are not fully blameworthy for doing it. Acting unintentionally usually constitutes a valid excuse, but it may be only a mitigating circumstance, depending on the nature of the specific factor that explains why the act is unintentional. I have already discussed how the valid excuse of nonculpable ignorance can explain unintentional wrongdoing, but the validity of that excuse depends on a specific kind of cognitive failure, the absence of knowledge that is necessary in order to have the relevant intention. Now I shall proceed with a consideration of some other factors that can make a wrong act unintentional and thereby serve as either a valid excuse or a mitigating circumstance.

Sometimes people do something wrong purely by *accident*. For example, a batter hits a high fly ball that lands on a spectator's head, causing a brain concussion. This act is wrong (because it causes pain and injury) but unintentional. It is *not negligent* because (unlike the example of the pharmacist) the batter did not violate clear role responsibility; there are no precautions or safeguards that all batters are expected to take that he failed to take. Indeed, the harm is not produced by any defect in the batter's character. This example illustrates why the excuse of pure accident clearly passes the Hume-Brandt test for moral validity.

Doing something wrong through *negligence* does not constitute a valid excuse, despite the act's being unintentional, because negligence itself is a moral defect. There is no way it can pass the Hume-Brandt test for moral validity. The pharmacist who filled a prescription incorrectly was negligent; in that case the negligence consisted primarily of a cognitive failure. However, there are many other kinds of negligence besides the purely cognitive one. For example, people can be careless, thoughtless, or forgetful in ways that endanger or hurt others, not because they have made a cognitive mistake but because they are indifferent and do not care enough to give the matter any thought to begin with. They are not motivated to be careful in behavior that might affect others. It is a small thing to tighten the cap on a gasoline can, but some people fail to do it. People can also fail to perform a manual job (e.g., building a piece of furniture) as thoroughly or carefully as they promised and thus unintentionally fail to keep their promise. There is always a cognitive element in regard to intentional action because the person must at least be aware that he or she is doing it, but there is room for great variation in the performance of it. Although negligence is not a valid excuse, it can, nevertheless, serve as a *mitigating circumstance* relative to a possible accusation of intentional wrongdoing; doing something wrong through negligence is not as reprehensible as doing it on purpose.[7]

There is also a form of acting negligently in which persons are aware that their wrong actions entail possible harm to others. They knowingly risk that harm, even though they do not intend to cause harm to others. In law this is known as *recklessness*. For example, firing a high-powered rifle outdoors in a residential neighborhood is very dangerous and shows wanton disregard for the lives of others. A person who recklessly kills someone in this way is even more blameworthy than someone who kills through inadvertent negligence. In general, doing wrong recklessly is more blameworthy than doing it negligently, precisely because it reflects a conscious willingness to risk harm to others. Like ordinary, inadvertent negligence, recklessness is not a valid excuse, and if it

serves as a mitigating factor at all, say, in comparison with intentionally causing harm, it ordinarily does not lessen a wrongdoer's blameworthiness to any
great extent.[8]

Coercion and Lack of Freedom ("Could Not Do Otherwise")

The general precept "ought implies can" is a maxim of practical reason. It
means that one can have a duty to do some act, X, only if it possible for one to
do X. This maxim is directly relevant to the validity of any excuse involving a
claim that it is impossible to do some act, X, which is prima facie the morally
right act in a particular situation. One can hardly be at fault for a wrong act, failing to do X, if doing X is impossible. This can be rephrased in the language of
responsibility: People who do something wrong are blameworthy only if they
"could have done otherwise," that is, they had the personal ability and the opportunity to act differently than they did in fact. When people who do wrong
lack either the ability or the opportunity to do otherwise, and their lack is not
their own fault, they are not to blame for the wrongdoing. We say of them that
"they could not help doing it," "it was beyond their control," or "it wasn't up
to them." By contrast, when people do wrong even though they have both the
ability and the opportunity to do otherwise, we say of them "it was their
choice," "no one made them do it," or "they have no one to blame but themselves." At work here is the assumption (discussed in chap. 2) that everyone except small children and the mentally ill are competent persons with basic powers of agency who are morally answerable for their conduct. People who do
wrong when they have both the ability and opportunity not to do wrong have
failed to exercise their powers of agency properly.

But competent persons are not omnipotent, and sometimes there are conditions that make it impossible for them to do otherwise than they in fact do, even
when they do something wrong. When these conditions themselves are not the
fault of the wrongdoer, they constitute a valid excuse by the Hume-Brandt criterion. There are basically two kinds of excuses that are related to being free to
do otherwise: those that involve a *lack of personal ability* and those that involve
a *lack of opportunity*. Each category is further subdivided into excuses that are
factual/descriptive and excuses that are *moral/normative*. In ordinary language
the expression "I could not do otherwise" is used to refer to any situation in
which one of these four different excuses applies. Consequently, "could not do
otherwise" is often quite ambiguous because it is not made clear which of these
four kinds of excuse is at issue.

Lack of Personal Ability

An excuse of lack of ability appeals to some condition of the person (hence it
is "internal"), whereas an excuse of lack of opportunity (discussed in the next

section) appeals to some external condition in the person's situation or environment.

The Factual/Descriptive Sense of Lack of Personal Ability to Do Otherwise. Sometimes it is impossible, in a very strict and uncomplicated sense, for people to do other than what they in fact do because they lack the ability to do an alternative and morally preferable act. The lack of a physical ability (e.g., being able to lift a heavy object) is perhaps the kind of example that is easiest to understand. Trying one's utmost to lift a heavy beam that is crushing someone trapped underneath it but failing to do so is not blameworthy if, in fact, one does not have the physical strength to do it. Lacking a specific cognitive skill can also make it impossible to do an alternative act. For example, not knowing how to speak French can make it impossible to use the telephone to report an accident in an isolated area of the French countryside. The lack of emotional control that is present in phobias of various kinds can make it impossible to do certain kinds of acts in particular situations, for example, a fear of public speaking.

People who do something wrong but lack the requisite ability to do otherwise have a valid moral excuse. It is important, however, that they themselves are not to blame for their lack of ability; for example, someone who is unable to render aid in an emergency because of self-induced intoxication would be blameworthy. An excuse of *nonculpable* lack of ability, however, would pass the Hume-Brandt test for validity. Most abilities and skills can be present in varying degrees; consequently, people often find it merely difficult, not impossible, to act otherwise. In many cases, a limited ability or skill, even if it is nonculpable, serves only as a mitigating condition, not a full-fledged excuse, because the agent could have tried harder to exercise whatever level of ability or skill he or she possessed. Thus someone who did not even try to report an accident merely because of limited proficiency in French would be to some extent blameworthy but not as blameworthy as someone fluent in French.

The Moral/Normative Sense of Lack of Personal Ability to Do Otherwise. Although sometimes wrongdoers could have done otherwise in the factual/descriptive sense, it may still be justified to conclude that they are *not* able to do otherwise but in a different, moral/normative sense, namely, they had no reasonable or fair alternative way of exercising their ability. For example, a person with a newly fractured leg could say, "I could not get up to answer the telephone because my leg was broken," meaning not that she lacks the physical ability to get up and walk but that she cannot reasonably be required to walk on her broken leg because the costs to her would be too high. (Let us suppose that it would have caused her severe pain and additional injury to her leg.) Whether a particular excuse like this is justified depends on the relevant details in the specific situation. If the failure to answer the telephone involved, say, a matter of life and death for someone else, then the woman might be blameworthy, but if the failure to answer caused only some minor inconvenience, it would not be fair to hold her responsible. Finally, we should add that the person herself should not be to blame for being in the debilitating condition; it should be a *nonculpable debility.*

Lack of Opportunity

An excuse of lack of opportunity appeals to some *external* condition in the person's situation or environment that prevents acting in a specific way.

The Factual/Descriptive Sense of Lack of Opportunity to Do Otherwise. People who have the personal ability to do a specific kind of act often find themselves in circumstances that prevent them from exercising their ability. For example, a doctor may find it physically impossible to visit a seriously ill patient because his or her car is caught in a flash flood. Assuming (as usual) that the doctor is not to blame for getting caught in the flood, he or she has a valid excuse for not visiting the patient. The external conditions that prevent action need not be a natural event beyond human control like a flood; they can also be conditions intentionally brought about by the actions of other humans. Indeed, excuses that appeal to such human interference are so transparently valid that they are stock features of melodrama. The hero is taken by surprise, bound, gagged, and blindfolded so that there can be no question of moral blame for his failure to come to the heroine's rescue.

The Moral/Normative Sense of Lack of Opportunity to Do Otherwise. This kind of excuse, like the moral/normative sense of lack of personal ability, involves a moral judgment: Although there are no preventing conditions that make it literally physically impossible for the person to do otherwise, it would, nevertheless, be unreasonable or unfair to require that he or she do so. The German soldier who shoots an unarmed Jew under a threat of death for disobeying an order is acting under *coercion;* his act is not free in the sense that it is *not voluntary.* Of course, he has the physical ability and the opportunity to refrain from killing the Jewish victim; after all, this is one of the underlying reasons for a basic moral duty prohibiting acts of commission like killing: It is so easy to comply. However, in this coercive situation, refusing to kill is not a reasonable alternative and it would be morally unfair to require him to disobey and risk being shot himself. We would characterize the soldier's situation as one in which "he has no choice"; what he does is "not up to him." He is motivated by a reasonable fear of death and not by hatred for the victim. Such an excuse of coercion easily meets the Hume-Brandt test of moral validity.

Unfortunately for many Germans who attempted to use coercion as an excuse for their participation in genocide, the historical evidence is more complex and mixed. For example, membership in the SS (Schutzstaffel, the principal organization charged with carrying out the genocide) was voluntary throughout the years of Nazi rule until 1944 and 1945.[9] Moreover, there is extensive evidence that soldiers in both the SS and ordinary police battalions could avoid participating in the killing without any serious punishment.[10] Finally, there is extensive evidence that a great many German perpetrators believed that killing the Jews was morally justified and participated willingly.[11] I discuss these issues in detail in chapter 7.

Some Additional Mitigating Circumstances

Negligence and recklessness constitute two examples of mitigating circumstances that lessen the degree of blameworthiness of wrongdoers who cause harm unintentionally but fall short of excusing them. There are some additional examples that are noteworthy because they function primarily to undermine feature 4 of a fully blameworthy act, namely, that it was the product of a bad motive. People who intentionally do something wrong sometimes act from motives that do not reflect badly on their character, or if they do, they bring only slight discredit on them because their motives and relative lack of control are understandable in the situation. For example, people who intentionally steal food because they are both poor and starving probably do not have a valid exculpatory excuse, but they are not as blameworthy as they would be if they had enough money to buy food and/or were not suffering from hunger. This is especially true if, like so many people who live in underdeveloped countries, they are not to blame for their poverty. When people are faced with adverse circumstances largely beyond their control, it is often unfair and unreasonable to expect them to have the degree of self-control and conscientiousness appropriate to people in affluent societies. The more dire the circumstances, the closer the case comes to being one in which the person has an excuse because there is no reasonable or fair opportunity to do otherwise. Another example is someone breaking into a cabin to seek shelter during a blizzard, which would be recognized in law as a case of *necessity*. Of course, stealing food and breaking into locked homes are both prima facie morally wrong and illegal, but when the motives that prompt these acts are elemental ones, like the desire to avoid starving or the fear of freezing to death from exposure, the perpetrators are not as blameworthy as they would be otherwise. In the first place, it is perfectly natural for people to have such desires and fears in these circumstances; second, it is generally recognized that any person, no matter how good his or her character, would find it very difficult to exercise self-control and refrain from acting on such fears and desires. Finally, diminished capacity responsibility that makes it difficult (though not impossible) to realize that one's acts are wrong can lessen the degree of blame one might otherwise deserve.

The Moral Importance of Justified Excuses

What is the moral significance of recognizing justified excuses and mitigating circumstances in our various social practices of holding each other responsible? The practices of overt blaming, imposing informal sanctions, and carrying out legal punishments are themselves morally justified only to the extent that the persons being held responsible in these various ways deserve what they get. Just desserts is an elemental moral notion that requires us to treat each other fairly, and this means that we may blame and punish people only if they are blameworthy and/or legally culpable for their wrongdoing. It is no exaggeration to state that recognizing and honoring justified excuses keeps our practices of holding each other responsible from degenerating into groundless faultfinding and despotic abuse of legal power. That is the main reason why so-called strict liability offenses in the law are dangerous and undermine respect for law. Being harshly punished for something like possession of narcotics when one had no knowledge and did nothing wrong intentionally is a paradigm of injustice.

The importance of justified excuses is demonstrated by the fact that all too often people think of excuses only in connection with the pervasive, but parasitic, practice of making bogus excuses in order to avoid blame and punishment that are in fact deserved. Many psychologists contribute to this popular view by ignoring the underlying moral reasons for recognizing and honoring morally justified excuses. Of course, psychologists did not create the widespread practice of making bogus excuses; most of us find it easier (at least on occasion) to avoid taking responsibility for our wrongdoing by making excuses, and it is understandable why psychologists are drawn to study the endlessly fascinating ways that we devise to do so.

However, the ever present subversion of the social practices of giving and accepting justified excuses should not tempt us into thinking that it would be a good thing to do away with excuses altogether. Recognizing justified excuses is the only way we can have truly humane and fair relationships to each other, whether these are personal attachments or bonds of common citizenship under law.

Summary

Clarifying the reasoning that underlies justified moral excuses belongs to ethics. The social practice of offering and accepting justified excuses must be kept distinct from the parasitic practice of "making excuses" studied by social psychologists, since the latter depends on the former in the same way that using counterfeit money depends on the existence of genuine currency that is trusted. The main function of justified excuses is to block inferences from wrongdoing to blameworthiness, but they should not be confused with two other ways to block blame: "no act" explanations and justifications. The principal excuses are nonculpable ignorance, acting unintentionally, and lack of ability and/or opportunity, both of which can take either a factual/descriptive sense or an ethical/normative one. The principal mitigating circumstances are negligence, recklessness, and necessity.

Notes

1. C. Snyder, R. Higgins, and R. Stucky, *Excuses: Masquerades in Search of Grace* (New York: Wiley, 1983); Bernard Weiner, *Judgments of Responsibility: A Foundation for a Theory of Social Conduct* (New York: Guilford, 1995).

2. Snyder, Higgins, and Stucky, *Excuses;* Kelly Shaver, *The Attribution of Blame: Causality, Responsibility, and Blameworthiness* (New York: Springer-Verlag, 1985).

3. Raul Hilberg, *The Destruction of the European Jews* (New York: Holmes & Meier, 1985), 3:1007–1029.

4. Holly M. Smith, "Excuses," in *Encyclopedia of Ethics,* ed. Lawrence C. Becker (New York: Garland, 1992), 1:344–346.

5. Smith, "Excuses," 344.

6. David Bankier, *The Germans and the Final Solution* (Oxford: Blackwell, 1992), chap. 6.

7. Hyman Gross, *A Theory of Criminal Justice* (New York: Oxford University Press, 1979), 82–88.

8. Gross, *Criminal Justice,* 85–86.

9. John Weiss, *Ideology of Death: Why the Holocaust Happened in Germany* (Chicago: Ivan R. Dee, 1996), 260.

10. Christopher Browning, *Ordinary Men: Reserve Police Battalion 101 and the Final Solution in Poland* (New York: HarperCollins, 1992), 170.

11. Daniel Jonah Goldhagen, *Hitler's Willing Executioners: Ordinary Germans and the Holocaust* (New York: Knopf, 1996).

Suggestions for Further Reading

Baker, Brenda. "The Excuse of Accident." *Ethics* 93 (1983): 695–708.

Beardsley, Elizabeth. "Blaming." *Philosophia* 8 (1979): 573–583.

Becker, Lawrence C., ed. *Encyclopedia of Ethics.* New York: Garland, 1992. See the articles on coercion, double effect, excuses, negligence, and responsibility, among others.

Brandt, Richard B. "A Utilitarian Theory of Excuses." *Philosophical Review* 78 (1969): 337–361.

Snyder, C., R. Higgins, and R. Stucky. *Excuses: Masquerades in Search of Grace.* New York: Wiley, 1983. Recent work in social psychology on the construction of the self-concept, making excuses, self-deception, rationalization, and denial.

Williams, Granville. "The Theory of Excuses." *Criminal Law Review* (November 1982): 732–742.

Chapter 4

Self-Deception

Self-Deception and Moral Responsibility

Self-deception is related to moral responsibility in several important ways. One of the ways in which people use their skills to make bogus excuses is mainly in the service of self-deception to evade feeling responsible for their wrong acts and omissions. Self-deception interferes with the ability to publicly accept responsibility for one's own wrongdoing, ask for forgiveness, and make amends; it also destroys any motivation to engage in self-criticism or strive to become a better person. A good example of self-deception is the way in which a great many Germans evaded acknowledging the fact that the Jews were being deported to their death while the Final Solution was being carried out. I use this example to help define self-deception and investigate its relationship to moral responsibility.

Because nonculpable ignorance is a justified excuse for a wrong act or an omission, it is not surprising that after the Holocaust many Germans claimed that they had not known about the extermination of the Jews, maintaining instead that they had been led to believe that the Jews were being "resettled in the East" where they would be put to work. It would appear that Germans who truly believed this cover story provided by the Propaganda Ministry were not blameworthy (or at least not as blameworthy as they might otherwise have been) for failing to help the Jews, since they were nonculpably ignorant of what was actually happening to them.

There is a great deal of historical evidence, however, that many Germans either knew or had very good reason to suspect that the Jews were being exterminated. For one thing, it has been estimated that at least 100,000 Germans were perpetrators in the Final Solution who knowingly participated in the killing institutions (Einsatzgruppen, police battalions, work camps, or death marches).[1] Moreover, even the vast majority of Germans who were merely bystanders had available a great deal of evidence that the Jews were being exterminated, even if they did not know the exact methods and all the details. In his public speeches and broadcasts, Hitler had proclaimed again and again that the Jews would be killed. Furthermore, Jews were rounded up and deported in full public view in cities like Berlin, Frankfurt, and Vienna. There was already widespread public knowledge of the so-called euthanasia program begun in 1939, two years before the deportation of Jews, in which thousands of German Christians were killed for reasons of "racial purification." It seems highly improbable that people could believe that the Jews were going to be treated differently. In 1942, there were 6 million Nazi party members, 200,000 SS, and 52,000 Gestapo and other security forces. Even if many members of these organizations did not participate directly in the killing, they most likely would still have known about the extermination by word of mouth through their comrades. In addition, the open-air killings in the areas conquered during the invasion of the Soviet Union in 1941 were witnessed by thousands of soldiers, photographs were taken and sent home, and men went home on leave and related what they had seen. Killing centers such as Auschwitz in occupied Poland were supposed to be secret, but many Poles and Germans knew of them and knew what was happening to the Jews there. For one thing, the stench from the crematoria and bodies that were burned outdoors carried for miles. Gradually, knowledge of the extermination spread throughout Germany.[2]

It seems fair to conclude that many Germans, both perpetrators and bystanders, did in fact know, or strongly suspected, that Jews were being exterminated and that these Germans were lying when they claimed to have been totally ignorant. Thus making a judgment of the blameworthiness of Germans who fall into this category is not complicated by the presence of self-deception. For example, many of the people who knew or strongly suspected the truth had opportunities to help Jews avoid deportation without great risk to themselves,[3] and so they had a prima facie duty to give aid. But relatively few did so. The great majority of Germans who failed to live up to the basic duty of mutual aid are blameworthy for that failure; they are even more blameworthy if they lied about knowing or suspecting that the Jews were being killed.

Some Germans fall into a second category: those who remained genuinely ignorant of the extermination through no fault of their own, despite the wealth of evidence available to Germans generally. For example, some Germans lived in isolated rural areas with very few Jewish residents and were nonculpably ignorant of what was happening to them in the rest of Germany and the occupied territories in the "East." Here again, making judgments of blameworthiness is not complicated by the presence of self-deception. Germans in this second category have a justified moral excuse and so are not blameworthy for their failure to help the Jews.

I am primarily interested in a third category of German bystanders, probably quite large, who engaged in various tactics of self-deception in order to avoid the conclusion that the Jews were being exterminated. These people successfully engaged in self-deception and thus kept themselves ignorant of the fate of the Jews and could truthfully say that they did not know. Can they, therefore, also claim that they were not blameworthy for failing to help the Jews? In short, does ignorance induced through self-deception constitute a justified excuse for failing to help? Answering this question requires a consideration of the nature of self-deception in some detail, both as a set of psychological activities engaged in as tactics to achieve a state of self-deception and as the resulting state itself. A state of ignorance resulting from self-deception is almost always something for which the person is to some degree blameworthy and cannot serve as a completely exculpating excuse for wrong acts and omissions. This conclusion is all the more important in light of the nearly universal temptation to engage in self-deception as a means of avoiding feelings of guilt, shame, and responsibility.

The Nature of Self-Deception

Self-Deception: A Generic Characterization

There is a wide variety of psychological processes that can be called self-deception, ranging all the way from short-lived and innocuous episodes of wishful thinking to full-fledged psychotic delusions over which the person has no control. I am focusing on a kind of self-deception that is quite pervasive in everyday human life but hardly ever involves any kind of clinically defined psychopathology. This kind of self-deception is something that persons consciously engage in and have some control over, at least initially. Consequently, it is something for which they are potentially blameworthy, especially when it contributes to immorality.

The kind of evasive self-deception most directly relevant to moral responsibility has been characterized very well by Michael W. Martin:

> Deceiving oneself is the evasion of full self-acknowledgment of some truth or of what one would view as truth if one were to confront an issue squarely. The truth or apparent truths may concern oneself, others, one's immediate situation, or the world at large. The evasion may have any number of motives, although what is evaded will be perceived as unpleasant or onerous in some way.[4]

Let us imagine that we are living in Germany in 1942 and apply this characterization to the example of someone engaged in self-deception about the belief that the Jews are being exterminated. It is best to begin by considering the positive case, that is, someone who does in fact fully acknowledge the truth that the Jews are being exterminated, and see what that involves before attempting to explain what is involved in evasion of such self-acknowledgment.

People who fully acknowledge to themselves the truth that the Jews are being exterminated keep that belief (or knowledge) active by integrating it into their conscious thoughts, reasoning, emotions, and actions. This means that they

(1) are willing to have explicit thoughts in consciousness of the Jews facing death, being killed, their bodies being disposed of, and so on; (2) believe the proposition that the Jews are being exterminated (let us call this proposition J); (3) have a disposition to use J in reasoning when it is relevant (e.g., noticing that J is confirmed to some degree by the fact that trainloads of used clothing are returning to Germany from the "East"); (4) have appropriate emotional responses such as horror, sorrow, and indignation; and (5) have a disposition to express J in appropriate actions, given their desires, other beliefs, and basic commitments.

By contrast, people whose goal is to *evade the full self-acknowledgment* of proposition J, the belief that the Jews are being exterminated, engage in one or more of a variety of tactics of self-deception. They may (1) avoid thinking explicitly about Jews facing death or being killed; (2) distract themselves with rationalizations, such as thoughts that the Jews are safe and working somewhere in the "East"; (3) evade belief in J by systematically failing to make any inquiries, distracting their attention from and ignoring available evidence (such as the trainloads of used clothing); (4) block appropriate emotional responses such as horror, sorrow, and indignation and assume an attitude of indifference; (5) evade and be disinclined to engage in any actions that would be appropriate for genuine belief in J, given their desires, other beliefs, and basic commitments. For example, they might have no inclination to help Jews still facing deportation.[5]

A sustained project of evasion of this kind results in a state of self-deception that is best characterized as *willful ignorance*. It is "willful" because the state of ignorance is not an accident but is a goal that is purposefully and intentionally sought; once it is achieved, it is assiduously maintained and protected. The person is motivated by a desire not to know or find out the truth of the matter. Moreover, some of the tactics used to achieve and sustain this state of ignorance, such as ignoring available evidence and refusing to look for possible additional evidence regarding the truth of J, clearly violate norms of rationality. It is prima facie irrational to deliberately remain ignorant regarding a matter that is of great moral importance; thus, willful ignorance is a kind of *motivated irrationality*.[6]

These considerations should not lead to the conclusion that self-deceptive evasion of self-acknowledgment is always something undesirable that should be avoided. As Martin makes clear, there is a great variety of possible subjects about which people deceive themselves, and, correspondingly, the motives for engaging in self-deception can also vary greatly from case to case. Only some of these motives open up the self-deceiver to possible reproach, not to mention moral blameworthiness.

The Variety of Motives for Engaging in Self-Deception about the Extermination of the Jews

It is possible to identify a number of different possible motives that people could have had for evading full self-acknowledgment of the truth of J, even when the discussion is restricted to the example of self-deception about proposition J, that the Jews were being exterminated. People who were bystanders at the time when the evidence became available to them should have begun to have some concern about the fate of the Jews. They were in a preliminary stage of awareness and possible reflection "before the fact," not yet having considered whether there was any problem that should concern them. Many people in that situation could have been motivated to evade full self-acknowledgment of J simply by a vague fear of being drawn into something that they regarded as being none of their business or by an aversion to doing anything that might possibly be inconvenient or slightly risky. It should not be assumed that everyone fully realized the great danger involved in making inquiries about the fate of the Jews or in actually helping them, or that it was the fear of official punishment that motivated self-deception about J. Of course, explicit fear of punishment and reprisal would motivate many people to deny the truth of J, if only because they might happen to know some Jews personally whom they might have been tempted to help if they had come to believe that they were in danger. Others might have engaged in self-deception because they anticipated that even if they knew that J was true, they would not have the courage to help. Since they had a strong desire to keep their self-respect and avoid feeling guilty and ashamed of themselves, they were likely to find it very easy to avoid reaching the conclusion that J was true.

In addition to enabling people to avoid psychological stress "before the fact," self-deception also serves to maintain self-respect "after the fact" when people have already failed to help the Jews and want to avoid feeling guilty and ashamed. It is a sad fact that many people had opportunities to help Jews facing deportation, often with relatively little risk, and yet they did not help them. Once the Jews had been deported and evidence of the extermination began to mount, the motivation to deny the truth of J naturally grew much stronger.[7] There was a continuing need to maintain self-respect in one's own mind and possibly a growing fear of blame and recrimination by others. One very potent psychological defense against such fear is to convince oneself that J is false so that one can in turn convince others that their recriminations are unjustified. Such a project of self-deception can be so successful that the person achieves a state of what Martin calls "inner hypocrisy," a conviction of being a person of strong moral character who is blameless.[8] It is very likely that many bystanders availed themselves of this kind of self-deception.

Not all self-deception is motivated by a desire to maintain self-respect. Some fanatical anti-Semitic bystanders who approved of exterminating Jews engaged in self-deception about the truth of J out of an irrational, ideologically based fear of deadly reprisals by the (allegedly) all-powerful world Jewish conspiracy or by a somewhat more rational fear of severe punishment by the victorious Allies.[9] In addition, a lot of self-deception is motivated by rational self-interest, unlike that driven by an irrational fear based on anti-Semitic ideology.

It is often both beneficial to the self-deceiver and harmless to others. Finally, as I demonstrate in the next section, some kinds of self-deception are not only morally permissible but positively good.

The crucial steps in such projects of purposeful evasion of self-acknowledgment are *intentional acts* (mental or physical) that are controlled by the people engaged in them. They choose to do them; they are not psychologically compelled to do them. Of course, there is often very little (if any) premeditation in, for example, the choice not to pay attention to some piece of evidence pointing to the ongoing extermination of a group of people. Nonetheless, one is aware at the moment of shifting attention from the disturbing facts to something else. However, one is not necessarily aware of the overall direction of the project and its goal, which is to maintain a state of ignorance about the fate of the Jews. To dwell on that would undermine the project of evasion, whereas one wants to stay "innocently" ignorant. That's the whole point of this kind of self-deception. A more difficult version of purposeful self-deception would involve selective attention to, and biased weighing of, available evidence in order to convince oneself positively that the Jews are not being killed. In any case, the intentional nature of the individual steps in a project of evasion of truth has important implications for the moral blameworthiness and praiseworthiness of people who engage in it.

Why Self-Deception Is Sometimes Desirable and Morally Good

It seems fairly clear that what can be called *ordinary coping self-deception* plays a pervasive and generally beneficial role in people's lives. It is almost a truism in psychology that some degree of self-deception is essential for minimal self-respect and mental health. Most people are not psychologically capable of being completely honest with themselves and systematically ignore or play down their shortcomings, including moral faults and vices.[10] In addition, most people use various tactics of self-deception on occasion to motivate themselves to overcome life's recurring difficulties, sometimes against objectively high odds, such as recovering from serious illness or injury or overcoming addiction or depression. Since very often ordinary coping self-deception is beneficial to the self-deceiver and innocuous to others, it cannot be condemned as inherently bad or undesirable. This is not to deny that all too often self-deception is unattractively narcissistic and even silly, even if it is not vicious or evil; in general, it is prudent to resist succumbing to its lure.

Sometimes self-deception can be not only personally beneficial but also morally good and praiseworthy. For example, people who rescued Jews during the Holocaust often engaged in self-deception about the objective risk and danger involved in their work. In occupied Poland, for example, people caught hiding Jews in their home were usually killed on the spot together with the Jews. Had rescuers dwelled on what would happen to them if they were caught, they might not have been able to maintain the self-control needed to continue taking the often enormous risks. Some rescuers are quite explicit about this: "And sometimes I think we were unconscious, not aware of the danger we were taking on."[11] Some of what the rescuers did to help the Jews (for example, give them a warm meal or hide them overnight until they could be taken to a safe place in the countryside) carried only a slight risk and could reasonably be required as an obligation of mutual aid. However, many things that rescuers did was clearly supererogatory and admirable. Many rescuers hid Jews for months and even years; others guided groups of Jews across heavily guarded borders into Switzerland and Spain. There are also many examples of Jews and other victims surviving the ghettos and slave labor in camps like Auschwitz by similar tactics of self-deception; they purposefully refused to acknowledge the seemingly insurmountable odds of living through the experience of those institutions of death.[12]

When Self-Deception Is Morally Bad and Blameworthy

But self-deception can contribute to moral wrongdoing and evil, thus serving as a justifiable basis for judgments of blameworthiness. I discuss the morality of individual episodes of self-deception first and then turn to a consideration of the morality of self-deception as a character trait or full-blown vice. This discussion focuses on intentional activities of purposeful evasion of self-acknowledgment and the resulting states of willful ignorance. Self-deceivers engaged in purposeful evasion have some degree of control and awareness of what they are doing; they choose to do it and thus are usually blameworthy for it to some degree.

Individual Episodes of Self-Deception

As used here, individual episodes of self-deception refer not only to particular acts of purposeful evasion (some of which may be momentary and fleeting) but also to projects of evasion (some of which may occupy long periods of time), as long as they are focused largely on the evasion of a single primary subject. For example, a bystander might engage in purposeful evasion of evidence that Jews were being exterminated for months or years. An individual episode includes both the activities of evasion and the resulting state of willful ignorance.

There is a variety of bad-making characteristics that an individual episode of self-deception can have that contribute to the blameworthiness of the self-deceiver:[13] first, *morally bad motives for engaging in self-deception.* For example, an episode of self-deception about the extermination of the Jews was bad to some degree if it was motivated by a desire to avoid any inconvenience that might result from discovering the truth. Such a desire is itself bad because it betrays a selfish concern for one's own comfort together with callousness, instead of benevolence, toward others. A person who truly cared about the well-being of someone else who might (for all one knows) be in danger of being killed, would not consider it an "inconvenience" to try to find out what was happening to the Jews and to help them if it is required, especially if the risk was not great (as was very often the case during the Holocaust). Second, *the instrumentally bad effects of a state of self-deception on the rest of the self-deceiver's character*. A state of willful ignorance is usually bad to some degree because it interferes with or undermines whatever degree of practical wisdom the self-deceiver person happens to have, especially the disposition to be fully informed about morally relevant facts. Moreover, willful ignorance tends to block or further weaken the self-deceiver's benevolent responses, as well as undermine inhibitory impulses of self-control. Third, *instrumental badness of wrongful acts of commission and omission that result from an episode of self-deception*. An episode of self-deception about the extermination of the Jews, for example, was instrumentally bad if it resulted in a wrongful act of omission, such as failing to help a Jew who could have been helped without great risk. This violation of the basic moral duty to give aid in emergencies was made worse if it resulted in Jews being deported and killed. Moreover, since the activities that bring about the state of ignorance are intentionally engaged in, such self-deceivers have no one but themselves to blame for being ignorant; they are willfully ignorant. Thus their ignorance is no excuse for failing to help the Jews, because it is culpable ignorance.

Fourth, *the badness of remaining in self-deception: secondary projects of evasion*. Persons whose state of self-deception causes them to be guilty of wrongful acts of omission like failing to give aid often engage in a secondary project of evasion, now with the wrongful omission itself as the target. People may embark on a secondary project of evasion either because their primary project of evasion (whose target was the extermination of the Jews) has in fact failed or because they may still be engaged in the primary project, although it is in continual danger of collapsing. In either case, their cognitive style, that is, the way in which they employ their cognitive faculties such as memory and interpretation of information, is likely to become distorted by the desire to avoid confronting their past failure and the feelings of guilt and shame that would be brought with it. They may have a strong tendency not to think about the fact that they did not help Jews, they may be unable to remember exactly what happened, or they may even misremember and come to believe that they did in fact give help. They may tell themselves and others elaborate stories about how and when they helped the Jews and come to believe the stories so strongly that they are in a state of "inner hypocrisy" of the kind already alluded to. However, most people are not psychologically capable of sustaining a project of pure denial of this kind; vivid memories are hard to repress and conflicting evidence keeps cropping up.

A much easier strategy for a secondary project of evasion is to make unjustified excuses to oneself. Recall that making an excuse involves admitting one's wrongful act or omission but arguing that because of certain conditions one is not blameworthy for it. For example, one might argue that one could not have helped Jews avoid deportation because it was impossible to do so (because, e.g., there was no room to hide them or because the Gestapo would have certainly discovered the hidden Jews). Adopting such a strategy is easier because it does not require convincing oneself of something that did not happen and hence would be continually undermined by conflicting evidence; instead, it rests largely on hypothetical claims about what it was possible to do or what was likely to happen if one had tried to help Jews, or on claims (like the one that there was no room to hide Jews) that are often matters of judgment and are, therefore, difficult to disprove. Moreover, a successful strategy of making unjustified excuses to oneself enables one to avoid feeling guilty and ashamed just as well as a strategy of denial of wrongdoing. Clearly, people are blameworthy for engaging in a purposeful strategy of making unjustified excuses motivated by a desire to avoid recognizing one's responsibility for wrongdoing, a strategy itself brought about by earlier self-deception. Successful secondary self-deception may be a derivative wrong, but it is a wrong nonetheless.[14]

A third strategy for a secondary project of purposeful evasion is self-justification. People might convince themselves that although they did not help Jews, it was morally permissible, even right, for them to refuse to help. For example, they could convince themselves that traditional anti-Semitic myths about the alleged criminality and dangerousness of Jews were actually correct and that the Nazi regime was justified in pursuing a policy of genocide. (Keep in mind that I am not discussing fanatical anti-Semites who both knew about and approved of the Final Solution from the beginning. Such people felt no need for self-deception.) Clearly, persons who pursue a self-deceptive strategy of justification based on irrational and empirically unfounded myths of anti-Semitism are seriously lacking in practical wisdom and are prima facie blameworthy on that account.

Self-Deception as a Vice (Character Trait)

The phenomena of self-deception raise an important question, namely, whether particular episodes are in character or out of character for the individual self-deceiver involved. For example, an individual bystander's self-deception about the fate of the Jews would be out of character if it were an isolated instance in a life that is otherwise virtually free of self-deception, especially about something as morally serious as genocide. Moreover, everything else being equal, a morally bad episode of self-deception that is clearly out of character ordinarily does not make a person as blameworthy as it would if it were one among many instances in a recurring pattern of morally bad self-deception about a wide variety of subjects, thus indicating that the person has a strong tendency to engage in self-deception. When such a tendency is entrenched enough to be a trait of character, self-deception becomes a full-blown vice.

It has already been noted that individual episodes of self-deception have a variety of bad-making characteristics: (1) being brought about by morally bad motives, (2) causing bad effects on one's character, (3) giving rise to wrong acts, and (4) involving secondary projects of evasion that maintain and prolong the state of self-deception. When self-deception becomes a full-blown vice (character trait), individual episodes exhibit bad-making characteristics 1–3. In addition, they are *in character* for the particular person, which tends to aggravate the person's blameworthiness. Furthermore, characteristic 4, *remaining in self-deception,* becomes salient, and this also makes the person's character more reprehensible.

The vice of self-deception needs to be closely examined in order to discern why episodes of self-deception that are in character are usually more blameworthy than those that are out of character. Recall that a character trait is a complex psychological disposition that is exhibited in the person's thoughts, feelings, emotions, and actions. The disposition that constitutes the vice of self-deception differs from person to person, depending on the individual's salient motive or motives for engaging in episodes and projects of self-deception. A fairly prevalent type of personality that virtually requires the vice of self-deception in order to function psychologically is made up of persons whose sense of self-respect depends on being able to maintain their own belief that they have a morally superior character when in fact they have a major moral fault such as a lack of one or more of the virtues of self-control (e.g., temperance, courage, or patience).[15] Such people can be called *akratic* (i. e., weak-willed) *self-deceivers* because they have a very conflicted personality; they are highly motivated to engage in self-deception by a persistent need to avoid feeling guilty and ashamed about their continual failure to live up to their own unrealistic standards of moral worth. It is important to gain an understanding of the way in which akratic self-deceivers function psychologically in order to assess their moral blameworthiness. Their psychological functioning is marked by four major features, including their sense of personal identity, a pervasively biased cognitive style, motivated excusing tactics, and self-deceptive tactics of self-presentation.

Akratic self-deceivers accept the exceedingly high standard that self-respect is justified only if one is a rigorously conscientious and wise person. But, at the same time, they are psychologically unable to endure the feelings of guilt and shame that would emerge if they were to fully acknowledge their own (predictable and frequent) failure to live up to this standard. Consequently, they are highly motivated to engage in a wide range of self-deceptive tactics in order to maintain their self-respect. Because their need for and belief in their own moral superiority constitutes an essential feature of their sense of personal identity, they are extremely threatened by any thought that they should modify or discard these elements of their personality. Thus they are caught on a psychological treadmill; the constant and strong motivation to engage in self-deception is supplied by the joint operation of the implacable need to be superior and the recurring need to deny the reality of their failure to meet that standard.

People engaged in a project of self-deception tend to have biased attention, memory, reasoning, judgment, and imagination with respect to the subject about which they are deceiving themselves. But there is no implication that these biases extend beyond that particular project. At least there is no need for this to happen. With the vice of self-deception, however, this is exactly what inevitably occurs. For example, akratic self-deceivers' attention and memory are highly selective; they not only fail to pay attention to or remember their own wrongdoing, but they are perpetually on the lookout for wrongdoing by others and are sure to remember it when it happens. By contrast, they have little interest in the actions of others that seem right or permissible and they are sure to forget it if, perchance, they cannot avoid noticing a good deed by someone else. The effect of this biased cognitive activity is to make the wrongdoing of others vivid and readily available in their memory (what psychologists call the availability heuristic), thus reinforcing their belief in their own superiority.

Making unjustified excuses is a favored tactic in ordinary episodic self-deception regarding a particular wrongful act or omission. Thus it comes as no surprise that akratic self-deceivers have a tendency to make unjustified excuses. Nevertheless, the strength of the tendency, the pervasive role it plays in their lives, and the virtually automatic and impulsive manner in which they employ unjustified excuses is striking. People with the vice of self-deception become very adroit at hitting on a plausible excuse for almost any situation without giving it any reflection or deliberation. Nevertheless, at the moment they are conscious of what they are doing; they are not passive victims of unconscious motives working behind the scenes, but active agents engaged in largely intentional and purposeful activities of self-deception. It is true, of course, that because their motivation for self-deception is so strong and insistent, they have relatively little control over the choice to engage in the excusing activities, which tend to become habitual and automatic.

Akratic self-deceivers may also employ what has been called the self-presentation feedback loop, a process in which such activities as self-pretense, roleplaying, and hypocrisy are used to complement biased cognition and unjustified excuses.[16] By definition, the goal of evasive self-deception is to enable oneself to avoid knowledge or belief about some subject; by contrast, the goal of self-presentation is to get others to accept beliefs about oneself. Such presentations can be sincere and honest or they can be manipulative and dishonest. The use that akratic self-deceivers make of the self-presentation feedback loop falls into the latter category. The implicit logic of this process is that self-deceivers present themselves to others in ways calculated to persuade them to accept the self-deceivers' own favorable view of themselves; if they succeed in persuading others, they, in turn, treat the self-deceivers in accordance with this favorable view. Having conveniently forgotten that they engaged in prior self-presentation tactics to elicit precisely this response, self-deceivers seize on this feedback from others as if it were independent evidence that confirms their own distorted beliefs.[17]

Clearly, the vice of self-deception, as found in akratic personalities, makes purposeful evasion of self-acknowledgment of one's own wrongdoing especially pernicious and the person who has the vice especially reprehensible. In addition to enabling the person to evade self-acknowledgment of particular acts and omissions of wrongdoing, the pervasive tactics of self-deception also have the cumulative effect of entrenching the tendency to self-deception, making it a stable trait of character that is virtually immune to change. Moreover, with some exceptions, isolated states of self-deception that are not brought about by the vice of self-deception tend to be relatively fragile, unstable, and short-lived. Projects of evasion that are manifestations of a deceptive character, however, are almost guaranteed to be stable and long lasting because the vice of self-deception undermines or destroys virtues such as practical wisdom and self-knowledge that a person needs in order to change and become more fully integrated and responsible. Akratic self-deceivers are ignorant of many of their particular wrongful acts and omissions, and they are also very likely to be ignorant of their own character flaws as well, although seriously lacking in the capacity to overcome that ignorance. Nonetheless, because their state of self-deception is initially the result of their own intentional and purposeful project of evasion, it constitutes culpable ignorance. For all of these reasons, akratic self-deceivers tend to be more blameworthy than self-deceivers who do not have the vice, all things considered.

Thus purposeful self-deceptive evasion of acknowledging one's own wrongdoing or defects of character, whether it is an isolated episode or one resulting from the vice of self-deception, is almost always something for which the person is to some degree blameworthy. It cannot serve as a completely exculpating excuse for wrongful acts or omissions.

The Difficulty of Knowing When Someone Really Is (or Was) in a State of Self-Deception: The Case of Albert Speer

A number of difficult practical questions face anyone trying to assess the blameworthiness of perpetrators and bystanders in the Holocaust. How can it be determined whether an individual knew about the extermination or was ignorant? If it is established somehow that a person was ignorant, how can it be determined whether the ignorance was nonculpable or was caused by culpable self-deception? What weight should be given to persons' claims not to have known? To these questions one must add another that may at first seem rather odd: What weight should be given to a person's claim (admission?) to have remained ignorant of the ultimate fate of the Jews by having engaged in a project of willful evasion? This claim (admission) was at the heart of Albert Speer's defense of his failure to do anything to stop the Holocaust or help the Jews, even though he had been one of the most powerful men in the Third Reich during the period in which most of the Jews were killed (1942–1945). Speer exemplifies some of the problems that are encountered in the course of trying to answer these questions.

The central practical difficulty is created by the fact that the great majority of Germans (aside from perpetrators who were known to have been directly involved in the killing) denied knowing that the Jews were being killed. Even though both common sense and the overwhelming historical evidence indicate that many Germans knew or strongly suspected the truth (as was pointed out at the beginning of the chapter), this does not solve the practical problems posed by the need to identify the individuals who knew and assess their blameworthiness on the basis of sufficient credible evidence. Furthermore, from an ethical point of view, properly assessing blameworthiness lays the foundation for other activities of holding someone responsible, such as overt blaming, demanding an account, or punishing.

Large numbers of people claiming not to have known about the extermination of the Jews creates a need for some reliable way to distinguish (1) those who are telling the simple truth because they were genuinely and nonculpably ignorant from (2) those who in fact knew or suspected the truth and are now lying and from (3) those who were really self-deceived. However, it is very doubtful that any reliable method actually exists; at any rate, in practice it is often impossible to identify the individuals who belong in each of these categories. It is impossible to get direct knowledge of people's subjective state of mind, what they really believed, remembered, or intended; this must be inferred from objective evidence. There are only two kinds of objective evidence relevant to making these distinctions: the person's overt behavior (including self-presentation) and factual evidence (including the testimony of others) arrived at independently of what the subjects do or say. Overt behavior is not a reliable guide for making these distinctions because both those who know the truth and those who are self-deceived about it are highly motivated to engage in similar deceptive tactics of self-presentation designed to convince others that they are nonculpably ignorant. If no independent evidence is available, a fairly common occurrence, then there is no objective way to make the distinctions. In short, it is often impossible to tell whether someone is really self-deceived or not.

The example of Albert Speer is especially revealing, not only with respect to the general problem of being able to tell when someone is really self-deceived but also because it alerts us to some exceedingly subtle interrelationships between strategies of self-deception and the presentation of the self to others. Albert Speer was one of the twenty-one principal leaders of Nazi Germany who were tried for war crimes and crimes against humanity by the

Allied International Military Tribunal in Nuremberg in 1945–1946. Although Speer formally pleaded not guilty, he was the only defendant to admit that he shared responsibility for Germany's aggression in World War II and the "catastrophe" that resulted, since he had served as a government minister (munitions and armaments) from 1942 to 1945.[18] However, in his court testimony and in his memoirs and other writings, Speer always insisted that his responsibility was "general" and consistently denied any responsibility for "particular" crimes committed during the Nazi regime. This carefully limited admission of responsibility seems to have been part of a general strategy of self-presentation that Speer engaged in to vindicate himself at Nuremberg and thus possibly save his life. When he described his responsibility as a government minister as being "general," he probably meant to refer only to his official and institutional role responsibility, not to any personal moral or legal responsibility. He hoped that this limited admission, taken together with his denial of any responsibility for "particular" crimes, would both give him credibility with the court and reduce the risk of criminal liability for any of the most serious German atrocities, especially the extermination of the Jews.[19]

This strategy might have been sufficient to minimize Speer's criminal liability in the face of accusations that he had personally performed seriously wrong acts of commission; although he sent people to concentration camps (not killing centers), there is little evidence that he actively participated in the Final Solution. However, acts of omission are another matter; and Speer must have realized from the beginning that there would be serious questions about his knowledge of atrocities and extermination and about his failure to intervene or to help victims. The problem he faced was fourfold. First, there was a reasonable presumption that Speer had known about the extermination of the Jews; he had been the head of the Ministry of Armaments and Production, which, among other things, used millions of slave workers (both Jewish and non-Jewish) and had powerful influence over the use of the government-run railroads, which operated the Jewish deportation trains in addition to transporting munitions and troops to the front. Second, he therefore could not plausibly claim to have been completely ignorant about the extermination of the Jews. Third, if he had admitted that he had known about the extermination and had done nothing to stop it or to help the Jewish victims, he would almost surely have been hanged. Fourth, he therefore had to claim that he had been ignorant but had to explain his ignorance in a way that would be credible but not too incriminating.

Speer's solution to his problem was to admit that he had engaged in a project of willful evasion in order to avoid finding out precisely what was happening to the Jews. At his trial Speer defended his evasion with the excuse that he was an apolitical technocrat who was uninterested in ideology and was only trying to do his job. In his memoirs, Speer goes further and describes his evasion explicitly in terms of the tactics of purposeful self-deception. A good example is the way he describes his response to a warning from a close friend to never visit a certain concentration camp in Lower Silesia (he was alluding to Auschwitz) because he had seen something there that was to be kept secret and was indescribable:

> I did not query him, I did not query Himmler, I did not query Hitler, I did not speak with personal friends. I did not investigate—for I did not want to know what was happening there. . . . From that moment on, I was inescapably contaminated morally; from fear of discovering something which might have made me turn from my course, I had closed my eyes. This deliberate blindness outweighs whatever good I may have done or tried to do in the last period of the war. [Here Speer is referring to his largely successful efforts in the very last months of the war to countermand and sabotage Hitler's orders to destroy the German infrastructure.] Those activities shrink to nothing in the face of it. Because I failed at that time, I still feel, to this day, responsible for Auschwitz in a wholly personal way.[20]

This admission of purposeful self-deception and the expression of a deep sense of responsibility for having failed to do anything to stop the extermination are the salient features of Speer's portrait of himself as a remorseful and tortured person that he presented to the public until his death in 1981.

However, this portrait was seriously challenged as new and very damaging evidence came to light. As early as 1971, Speer's claim not to have known about the Holocaust was challenged by an American history professor, Erich Goldhagen, who argued that Speer had been present at a 1944 speech in which Himmler informed Nazi leaders of the true nature of the Final Solution. According to Goldhagen, the transcript of the speech shows that Himmler directly addressed Speer. Although Goldhagen made some errors in the article, his central accusation remained unrefuted. Speer felt so threatened by it that he solicited letters from friends supposedly proving that he had left the meeting before Himmler's speech. However, Speer's account of how the friends spontaneously volunteered the information that he then asked them to put in writing is not very credible, so the question whether Speer heard Himmler's speech remains unresolved. Nevertheless, there are good reasons to think that Speer was fairly familiar with at least the general nature of the killing centers and the concentration camp system; there is a great deal of other circumstantial evidence that by May 1943 Speer knew about Auschwitz. We know that he visited Mauthausen, the notorious labor camp in Austria, and we have his correspondence with Himmler in which he complains about the "luxurious" construction standards he found there.[21]

More recently, however, evidence has surfaced that Speer had direct knowledge of and responsibility for a significant aspect of the Holocaust that he assiduously covered up for years; indeed, he went so far as to tamper with some of the historical evidence in order to keep it a secret. Since 1937 Speer had been the Inspector General of Construction for the Reich Capital (GBI) directly responsible to Hitler, who considered him his personal architect for carrying out his grandiose plans for redesigning Berlin as the capital of the Third Reich. In 1940 Speer ordered one of his architects, Rudolf Wolters, to begin keeping an unofficial diary of the activities of the GBI, which came to be known as the *Chronicle;* it was based on reports from the offices under Speer's direction. Later in 1942, when Speer took over as Minister of Armaments and Production, he retained his position and authority as GBI, and Wolters continued to keep the *Chronicle,* an uncensored inside record not intended for public use. Among the activities of GBI recorded in the *Chronicle* was the forceful eviction of 75,000 Jews from thousands of apartments in Berlin, some as part of a massive resettlement to make room for the huge building projects, and some to free up apartments for non-Jews made homeless by Allied bombing raids. The Jews who were displaced had been suffering already because they were not allowed in bomb shelters during raids; now most of them had no regular housing either. Eventually all of these evicted Jews were deported to the "East." None of these activities were mentioned in the Nuremberg indictment against Speer and, if they had been discovered later, could easily have been the basis for a new trial.[22]

It is now known that while he was serving his Nuremberg sentence in Spandau prison, Speer persuaded his still loyal friend Wolters to sanitize the original copy of the *Chronicle* by deleting the incriminating passages about the eviction of the Berlin Jews.[23] Later, after Speer's release from prison, he used a copy of the sanitized *Chronicle* to write his memoirs. When the memoirs were completed in 1969, Speer carelessly sent his copy of the sanitized *Chronicle* to the German Federal Archive so that it could be used for historical research. On receiving Speer's copy of the *Chronicle,* the director of the Federal Archive sent Speer a letter in which he thanked him and asked him to have Wolters send him the original of the *Chronicle,* at least temporarily, so that he could check the accuracy of the copy. Now the fat was in the fire and Speer had to take some drastic steps to maintain the cover-up. After he and Wolters had made several suggestions and countersuggestions about what to do with the original *Chronicle,* Wolters wrote Speer an ironic letter claiming that the original *Chronicle* no longer existed. Both Speer and he knew that this was not so. Speer then asked Wolters to write him a new letter stating that the *Chronicle* no longer existed, but in a form that he could send to the Federal Archive. Wolters duly complied. The cover-up worked until after Speer's death in 1981; however, in 1980 Wolters had already revealed the deception to Matthias Schmidt, whose expose was published in Germany in 1982.[24] Finally, when Wolters died, the original *Chronicle* was sent to the Federal Archive. Speer's deception was now public knowledge.[25]

Speer's elaborate and sustained project of self-deception over a span of nearly forty years illustrates how difficult it is to be sure that a person really was in a state of self-deception. There is no doubt that he had some genuine regrets about the years during which he was a loyal servant in Hitler's regime, but these doubts developed very late in the war primarily because he was horrified by Hitler's orders to destroy the German infrastructure and by his callous disregard for the suffering of the German people. In view of his cynical cover-up of his role in the eviction of thousands of Jews, a cover-up that continued right up to the time of his death, however, it is difficult to credit Speer's repeated claim that he felt deep remorse and guilt over his failure to help the Jews and other victims of the Nazi regime. A more accurate portrait would probably stress his inordinate ambition, his love of power, and his willingness to sacrifice individuals in order to achieve his goals as a technocrat in the service of an inhuman totalitarian dictatorship. This portrait supports the conclusion that Speer was never really self-deceived about the extermination of the Jews, as he continually claimed, just as he was not self-deceived about the eviction of thousands of Jews and his role in it (as proven by the documentary evidence). Instead, Speer's alleged self-deception was itself an elaborate sham, part of a project of self-presentation that began at Nuremberg, designed to avoid liability to harsher criminal punishment.

Notes

1. Daniel Jonah Goldhagen, *Hitler's Willing Executioners: Ordinary Germans and the Holocaust* (New York: Knopf, 1996), 164–168.

2. John Weiss, *Ideology of Death: Why the Holocaust Happened in Germany* (Chicago: Ivan R. Dee, 1996), 374–379.

3. Marion Kaplan, *Between Dignity and Despair: Jewish Life in Nazi Germany* (New York: Oxford University Press, 1998), chap. 8, "Life Underground."

4. Mike W. Martin, *Self-Deception and Morality* (Lawrence: University Press of Kansas, 1986), 13.

5. Martin, *Self-Deception,* 14–15.

6. R. Nisbet and L. Ross, *Human Inference: Strategies and Shortcomings of Social Judgment* (Englewood Cliffs, N.J.: Prentice-Hall, 1980), chap. 1.

7. Kaplan, *Between Dignity and Despair,* 194–200.

8. Martin, *Self-Deception,* chap. 3.

9. Raul Hilberg, *The Destruction of the European Jews* (New York: Holmes & Meier, 1985), 522–523.

10. Martin, *Self-Deception,* chap. 6; *Self-Deception: An Adaptive Mechanism?* ed. Joan S. Lockard and Delroy L. Paulus (Englewood Cliffs, N.J.: Prentice-Hall, 1988).

11. *Rescuers: Portraits of Moral Courage in the Holocaust,* ed. Gay Block and Malka Drucker (New York: Holmes & Meier, 1992), 122.

12. Primo Levi, *Survival in Auschwitz* (New York: Collier, 1993), 40–41.

13. Martin, *Self-Deception,* 104–108.

14. Martin, *Self-Deception,* 37–48.

15. David H. Jones, "Pervasive Self-Deception," *Southern Journal of Philosophy* 27, no. 2 (1989): 217–237.

16. D. Gilbert and J. Cooper, "Social Psychological Strategies of Self-Deception," in

Self-Deception and Understanding, ed. Mike W. Martin (Lawrence: University Press of Kansas, 1985).

17. Erving Goffman, *The Presentation of Self in Everyday Life* (Garden City, N.Y.: Doubleday-Anchor, 1959).

18. Telford Taylor, *The Anatomy of the Nuremberg Trials* (New York: Knopf, 1992), 448–454.

19. Taylor, *Anatomy of the Nuremberg Trials,* 448–454; Gitta Sereny, *Albert Speer: His Battle with the Truth* (New York: Knopf, 1995); Dan van der Vat, *The Good Nazi: The Life and Times of Albert Speer* (Boston: Houghton Mifflin, 1997).

20. Albert Speer, *Inside the Third Reich* (New York: Macmillan, 1970), 447.

21. van der Vat, *Good Nazi,* 134–135, 349–351.

22. Sereny, *Albert Speer,* 220–222, 228–230; van der Vat, *Good Nazi,* 96, 135–136.

23. van der Vat, *Good Nazi,* 320, 328.

24. Matthias Schmidt, *Albert Speer: The End of a Myth,* trans. J. Neugroschel (London: Harrap, 1985).

25. van der Vat, *Good Nazi,* 338–343.

Suggestions for Further Reading

Becker, Lawrence C., ed. *Encyclopedia of Ethics.* New York: Garland, 1992. Articles on authenticity, deceit, hypocrisy, self-deception, and weakness of will, among others.

Fingarette, Herbert. *Self-Deception.* London: Humanities, 1969. A brief and illuminating study.

Martin, Mike. *Self-Deception and Morality.* Lawrence: University Press of Kansas, 1986. A study of the evasion of self-acknowledgment along with authenticity, inner hypocrisy, and "vital lies" (beneficial self-deception).

Martin, Mike, ed. *Self-Deception and Self-Understanding: New Essays in Philosophy and Psychology.* Lawrence: University Press of Kansas, 1985. Advanced essays.

Taylor, Shelley E. *Positive Illusions.* New York: Basic, 1989. The psychological role of self-deception in mental health.

PART 2

APPLICATION OF THE ETHICS OF RESPONSIBILITY TO PROBLEMS RAISED BY THE HOLOCAUST

Chapter 5

Political Culture, Socialization, and Responsibility

The remaining chapters in this book assess the moral responsibility of individuals in the Holocaust. One very general thesis about the responsibility of individuals is that people who have been socialized in a bad political culture cannot justifiably be held responsible, or at least not fully responsible, for some of their immoral or evil conduct.[1] If true, this thesis presents a fundamental challenge to the validity of trying to assess individuals' moral responsibility. It can be stated in an overly simple way and applied to Germans who perpetrated the Holocaust: People who are socialized in a bad political culture like the one that existed in Germany before and during the Holocaust may lack the ability to see and appreciate the wrongness of killing Jews. Since they develop without some of the basic capacities to know right from wrong, they have diminished responsibility and therefore are not blameworthy (or at least are less blameworthy) for their participation in the Holocaust than they would otherwise be. I call this the bad political culture thesis (hereafter BPC). Contrary to the implication of BPC, diminished capacity most probably played a minor role in the perpetration of the Holocaust and therefore can have only a marginal effect, overall, in the assessment of the blameworthiness of individual Germans for their role in the Holocaust.

Here are two sample formulations of BPC from the recent literature:

Consider the ordinary citizen living in Germany in the 1930s, the white child brought up on a southern plantation in the 1850s, or anyone brought up forty years ago to become a "lady" or a "gentleman" and to accept conventional sex roles as deep features of human nature and civilized society. Although it would be difficult to establish, even in individual cases, that such people were unable to see and appreciate the injustice of some of the practices, attitudes, and institutions of their communities, insofar as we regard social pressure and norms as potential obstacles to sound moral judgments, we lessen the blame that we would otherwise

99

direct toward individuals who, surrounded by these obstacles, fail to reach these judgments.[2]

A man raised in the society of Mundurucu headhunters is socialized into behavior that might be judged immoral by outsiders. Many groups require males to kill designated enemies. To the extent a group completely socializes its members into such conduct, we cannot expect them to have a separate perspective or to question its conduct or their own.[3]

Proponents of BPC do not go so far as to claim that people socialized in a bad political culture lack the capacity to know right from wrong altogether (that would make anyone who was socialized nonresponsible), but they do claim that such people can have specific deficiencies in capacity that render them either not blameworthy or less blameworthy for some of their wrong acts.

My point here is simply *if* we believe that they are unable to recognize that their values are mistaken, we do not hold them responsible for the actions that flow from these values, and *if* we believe that their ability to recognize their normative errors is impaired, we hold them less than fully responsible for the relevant actions.[4]

I have already shown that blameworthiness is a central concept used in a wide range of social and legal practices. To say that a person is blameworthy for performing a particular wrong act is to claim that the person has brought discredit upon himself or herself and deserves disapproval and blame for having performed the wrong act without sound justification or excuse. To think that someone is "responsible" in this sense is just to believe that the person is discredited by performing the wrong act and deserves to be blamed. Such judgmental blame should not be confused with other aspects of our social practices regarding responsibility, such as being liable to overt blame or to some form of punishment. BPC is primarily about blameworthiness in this judgmental sense, not about overt blaming or imposing sanctions.

Whether one is not blameworthy or is merely less blameworthy depends on the extent of the deficiency in one's cognitive capacities; it is a matter of degree. For example, one would not be blameworthy for participation in the Holocaust if being socialized in German political culture caused such serious deficiency in one's cognitive capacities that it is impossible for one to question the moral permissibility of killing Jews or to refrain from active participation in the killing. For example, one may have developed with a sense of personal identity and standards of self-respect that are based on the conviction that the pervasive anti-Semitic beliefs and values of one's culture are evidently true and incontrovertible; consequently, one has no capacity to see Jews as defenseless fellow human beings who do not deserve to be killed. By contrast, one would be merely less blameworthy if one only found it difficult, rather than impossible, to realize that killing Jews was wrong and to refrain from participating in killing.

Lacking Capacity Responsibility versus
Being Not Blameworthy (Blameless)

According to the theory of responsibility defended in part 1, a necessary condition of moral blameworthiness for wrongdoing is possessing the basic powers of agency that constitute capacity-responsibility, namely, (1) cognitive powers that enable one to know the nature of one's acts, that they are right or wrong and the likely consequences of performing them; (2) powers of deliberation that enable one to make informed choices in the light of one's most deeply held goals and priorities, while taking into account available evidence concerning the most effective means of achieving them; and (3) powers of self-control that enable one to carry out one's choices in action effectively.[5] I assume that possession of each of these powers is a necessary condition for a person to have capacity responsibility. It is a defeasible presupposition of our social and legal practices that possession of these powers is what makes one a responsible person in the sense of being answerable for one's conduct; one is properly held accountable for one's conduct and is thus *eligible* for praise and blame, reward and punishment. By contrast, infants, very young children, and people with certain kinds of debilitating mental illness, who either do not have these powers at all or have one or more of them in a seriously deficient form, are *ineligible* for being held accountable; they are not responsible (answerable) at all. They are not fit subjects of moral judgment or legal punishment. We can call such individuals *nonresponsible*.[6]

When nonresponsible individuals do something wrong (by act or omission) we say that they are not to blame because they "could not help it," "it was beyond their control," or they "could not do otherwise." These ways of reacting to untoward behavior by nonresponsible individuals accurately reflect the role that possession of powers of agency plays in our social and legal practices; people are eligible for praise and blame, reward and punishment only if they are cognizant of the world around them, realize what they are doing, and are able to make informed choices and control their behavior. Being responsible (possessing powers of agency) gets one in the moral game, so to speak; once one is in the game and eligible, one can be held responsible (praiseworthy, blameworthy, deserving of reward, or liable to punishment, etc.) for one's exercise of those powers. However, responsible persons are sometimes not blameworthy for particular wrong acts because they have a justified excuse. For example, a person who kills someone accidentally and nonnegligently is not to blame.

The distinction between (1) a fully competent, responsible person who is eligible for blame but is justifiably excused as not blameworthy for a particular wrong act and (2) a nonresponsible individual deemed ineligible for blame in general (and therefore also "blameless") because he or she lacks powers of agency is clear and is not likely to lead to confusion . However, the relationship between justified excuses and diminished responsibility is more complex and deserves further comment.

Diminished Capacity Responsibility, Excuses, and Blameworthiness

People with diminished responsibility fall somewhere between being nonresponsible (lacking sufficient powers of agency) and being fully responsible (possessing sufficient powers of agency). Since BPC identifies diminished responsibility as a deleterious effect of bad political culture, it must receive close attention. Diminished capacity may sometimes involve a deficiency in all three powers of agency (cognition, deliberation, and self-control), but this happens only infrequently. Most instances involve an insufficiency in only one power; for example, people with addictions sometimes have adequate cognitive and deliberative powers, but they are severely deficient in powers of self-control. The example of diminished capacity that is used most often in discussions of the effects of bad political cultures is a deficiency in the cognitive power to tell right from wrong, coupled with insufficient power of deliberation. Unlike nonresponsible individuals, people with diminished capacity do not have a general exemption from praise and blame, reward and punishment; they can still be accountable to some degree for a wide range of their behavior. And even with respect to those areas of their behavior directly affected by their diminished capacities, they may not be totally immune to blame and punishment. Consequently, most people with diminished responsibility can be correctly described as blameworthy for some (perhaps most) of their wrongdoing, as well as praiseworthy for their good deeds.

We need to be careful, however, when we are considering instances in which people with diminished capacity are deemed not blameworthy for some particular act because they have a justified excuse. It is helpful to distinguish three different ways in which an excuse can be related to a specific deficiency in a power of agency that constitutes an individual's diminished capacity. First, in some cases the excuse is completely independent of the deficiency because the occurrence of the wrong act being excused does not depend on any performance (defective or otherwise) on the part of the actor. For example, a person who suffers from weakness of will due to alcoholism might kill a pedestrian while driving, not because he or she is drunk behind the wheel (let us assume that the person is uncharacteristically sober) but because the car's brakes failed. Second, sometimes the performance being excused is independent of the specific deficiency that constitutes the individual's diminished responsibility, although the occurrence of the wrong act being excused does depend on a defective performance by the actor. For example, the weak-willed (but sober) alcoholic might be distracted and unable to control the car because he or she has been stung several times by an angry hornet inside the car.

Third, in regard to examples covered by either category mentioned above, the justification of the excuse is independent of the specific deficiency that constitutes the individual's diminished capacity, so the fact that the actor has diminished capacity is essentially irrelevant. For this reason, cases like these are not of concern to me as I evaluate the central claim of BPC. Instead I focus on cases in which the specific cognitive and deliberative deficiencies that are the effect of a bad political culture and constitute individuals' diminished capacity also constitute the excusing conditions that make them not blameworthy (or less blameworthy) for their wrongdoing. For example, when BPC is applied to perpetrators of the Holocaust, the focus is on specific deficiencies in their cognitive capacity to realize that killing Jews is wrong and in their deliberative capacity to choose not to participate, since these are held to be the specific effects of being socialized in German political culture. If these deficiencies make it impossible for the person to avoid or to change the mistaken beliefs and wrong choices, they constitute a justified excuse that renders the person not blameworthy; if they make it difficult rather than impossible, they constitute a mitigating factor that reduces blame.

A Definition of Bad Political Culture

Defenders of BPC tend to state their thesis in broad terms that do not refer specifically to political culture. For example, Susan Wolf merely mentions "social pressure and norms." In an earlier article she referred to people who "act in ways strongly encouraged by their societies."[7] Another example is Ervin Staub, who usually refers to German culture in general: "Nazi ideology matched basic aspects of German culture." "Even absorbing an ideology that helps one to comprehend a chaotic world can be largely nonreflective. Some cultures and modes of socialization enlarge the capacity to bring such nonreflective processes into awareness. German culture and especially German child-rearing practices did not."[8] However, it is reasonable to assume that, at least in their references to the Nazis and Nazi ideology, these authors have in mind primarily the political crimes, such as wars of aggression and the Holocaust, committed by Germany as a matter of state policy. If this is correct, then it is primarily (though not exclusively) features of German political culture that are relevant for arriving at a more precise formulation of BPC.

It is not possible to provide a definition of bad political culture in the strict logical sense of a set of conditions that are individually necessary and jointly sufficient; what I do is provide a working analysis that includes the principal bad-making characteristics of political culture. The criteria of evaluation on which the working analysis is based are familiar from the mainstream tradition of political liberalism and democratic theory. Although these criteria are philosophically justifiable, no attempt is made to provide that justification here. I begin by setting forth some of the principal criteria for a good political culture; from these can be derived the main features that belong to paradigm cases of bad political culture. As I explicate these features, I also indicate how they were exhibited in German political culture in the years before the Holocaust and during the Holocaust.

Political culture, which includes certain values, attitudes, knowledge, and beliefs shared by members of a political community, should not be confused with the political system itself, which is composed of not only the formally defined institutions of government and public administration but also political parties, structures of power and influence, and interaction between them.[9] Political culture provides the specific attitudes and orientations that members of the community have toward the political system, its processes, and their role in it.[10] In the tradition of democratic liberalism, a *good political culture* has (at least) five good-making characteristics.[11] First, respect for the rule of law. Citizens have the civic virtue of respect for the rule of law, which includes a strong disposition to refrain from the use of violence themselves and to oppose and condemn its use by others. Second, citizens strongly value and support the central features of constitutional democracy, such as equality of citizenship, an independent judiciary, protection of civil liberties, and electoral accountability of the government. Third, citizen participation. Citizens are disposed (1) to participate actively in various levels of government (e.g., by voting) and in nongovernmental associations and civic organizations, and (2) to participate passively by keeping informed about public affairs, the programs of political parties, and so on. Fourth, solidarity, trust, and tolerance. In addition to respecting equality of legal citizenship, citizens have mutual respect and tolerance toward each other; the electorate is not severely polarized by narrow conflicts of interest. Fifth, political parties share a commitment to the public good. Although political parties ordinarily have serious conflicts over particular issues, they share a commitment to compromise for the public good when necessary; the political process is not viewed as a zero-sum game; and parties tend to be pragmatic rather than committed to dogmatic ideology or utopian goals.

From this can be derived some of the main characteristics of a bad political culture, since a lack (or a serious deficiency) in any of these good-making characteristics constitutes a bad-making characteristic; the more of these a political culture has the worse it is. Moreover, each of these characteristics can vary in strength or the degree in which it is present in a particular culture. There is evidence that German political culture before and during the Holocaust had each of these characteristics in a fairly strong form.[12] First, lack of respect for the rule of law. Immediately after World War I, Germany experienced several abortive revolutions from both the right and the left, primarily because most Germans did not accept the legitimacy of the Weimar Republic and wished to see it replaced by a more traditional, authoritarian regime. Throughout the 1920s Germany was beset by street violence among rival paramilitary groups, including the Free Corps, which was composed mostly of alienated veterans; there were also frequent pitched battles between armed Communists and Nazis.

Moreover, there was no public protest against the extralegal assassination of Ernst Roehm and over one hundred other Germans in July 1934, assassinations that were ordered by Hitler and carried out by the SS. Second, little or no support for constitutional democracy. Germany had a strong tradition of political authoritarianism, and in the late nineteenth and early twentieth centuries most Germans came to reject the ideals of the Enlightenment, individualism, constitutionally guaranteed civil rights, and democracy. They had had very little experience with democracy, and much of it, including the years of the Weimar Republic, had been unsuccessful. As a consequence, most Germans welcomed the end of parliamentary government and the suspension of civil liberties that occurred when Hitler and the Nazis gained control in 1933. Third, lack of active citizen participation. Perhaps the principal effect of German authoritarianism was to keep most Germans at what Almond and Verba call the "parochial" and "subject" stages of development of political culture right up through the 1920s. There was an increase in populist sentiment and growing participation in public demonstrations. Despite the very intense interest in political issues and high levels of voting, participation in the political process (as opposed to extralegal violence) still tended to be passive rather than active.[13] Fourth, low levels of solidarity, trust, and tolerance. Germans were highly polarized politically along lines of class and ideology; most of the major parties defined themselves in terms of the narrow interests of their constituents; and the great majority of Germans, whether liberal or conservative, working class, middle class or elite, were to some degree religious and/or racial anti-Semites (most of them strongly so). Fifth, political parties do not share a commitment to the public good. Most political parties in Germany were highly ideological, often proclaiming unrealistic goals and utopian ideals even as they pursued short-term advantages for their constituents. Parties were not inclined to compromise for the common good and it became increasingly difficult to form working coalitions in the Reichstag; beginning in 1930, the chancellor had to be appointed by the president (in accordance with a provision in the Weimar constitution) instead of through elections. When Hitler was appointed chancellor, German parliamentary democracy was already moribund.

   In addition to these bad-making characteristics, each of which represents a lack or deficiency, is a characteristic found in German political culture that is itself positively bad, sixth, an extreme form of nationalism as an overriding value. Many historians and other scholars have noted the exaggerated form that nationalism took in Germany during the nineteenth and early twentieth centuries. Germans thought of themselves as a superior people having the right to rule over others. Germans also believed that they were surrounded and besieged by enemies, which caused many of them to be very paranoid and to have a continuing sense of unfulfilled greatness and present unfairness. Consequently, the German political process tended be geared toward militarism and wars of imperial conquest.[14]

A Psychological Hypothesis Regarding the Causal Relation
between Bad Political Culture and Diminished Capacity

In order to be at all plausible, BPC must include an account of the way in which these characteristics of German political culture are supposed to have caused diminished capacity in individuals who were socialized in it. Such complicated social processes are understood only incompletely, but some theories in current psychology help us make an educated guess. Staub draws on his own empirical psychological research to provide a fairly detailed explanation of the way in which some aspects of the process are supposed to take place.[15] If political culture ever does in fact cause diminished capacity in individuals, it seems reasonable to suppose that it does so in ways like those that Staub's hypothesis suggests. The hypothesis is meant to explain how being socialized in the bad political culture in Germany caused individuals to develop with the specific deficiencies that constituted their diminished capacity, namely, a deficient cognitive capacity to know that killing Jews was wrong and a deficient deliberative capacity to choose not to participate in the killing. (I am presenting this hypothesis in order to clarify the meaning of the BPC thesis and thus evaluate it more effectively. Consequently, I am postponing other empirical questions such as whether socialization in German political culture affected all or only some Germans and whether all those who were affected were affected in the same way and in the same degree. I also leave until later the closely related ethical question of whether the effects of such socialization always constitute diminished capacity that renders one not blameworthy or less than fully blameworthy for some of one's wrong acts and omissions.)

Staub's hypothesis is that individuals who are socialized from birth to believe in anti-Semitism, authoritarianism, and nationalism (three salient values of German political culture) are very likely to be deficient in the cognitive capacity to know that killing Jews is wrong and in the deliberative capacity to choose not to participate in the killing. The argument in support of this hypothesis rests primarily on the premise that these three values are mutually supportive when they are successfully instilled in a person through socialization; their combined effect is the set of specific deficiencies in the person's cognitive and deliberative capacities to judge the morality of killing Jews.

Anti-Semitism

One is socialized to believe that Jews are inherently foreign, dangerous, criminal, and debased and that the German nation therefore faces a serious "Jewish problem" that must be solved in one way or another. To say that one is socialized to have these beliefs means that they become essential elements of one's sense of personal identity. By example, exhortation, praise, blame, and all the other means of moral training and education, one's parents, teachers, and ministers convey the message that being a good Christian and a true German depend on unquestioning acceptance of these beliefs and acting accordingly. If the socialization is successful, being a good anti-Semite becomes a principal source of one's self-respect; correspondingly, to doubt or question these beliefs or to violate them in action causes feelings of guilt and shame. The more one is convinced of the truth of anti-Semitism, the weaker become one's cognitive and deliberative capacities to critically evaluate it in the light of contrary evidence, including one's own direct experience with Jews (if any). Consequently, one may find it extremely difficult (or even impossible) to doubt, critically evaluate, or reject one's anti-Semitic beliefs or contravene them in action.

Authoritarianism

A relatively new psychological scale for measuring authoritarianism as an individual trait has been developed by Bob Altemeyer. His scale measures the trait of authoritarianism, which consists of three attitudes: (1) submission to authorities perceived to be established and legitimate; (2) aggressiveness, viewed as sanctioned by the authorities, toward permissible targets who are believed to be "troublemakers," "immoral," "criminal," or "unpatriotic"; and (3) conventionalism, "a high degree of adherence to conventions that are perceived to be endorsed by society and its established authorities."[16] Germans who were socialized in the political culture of the 1920s and 1930s clearly tended to exhibit these attitudes, especially aggressiveness toward a wide variety of "undesirables" such as liberals, Communists, Gypsies, homosexuals, and Jehovah's Witnesses. Jews served as the paradigmatic target of hostility, with both religious and racial anti-Semitic ideology fostered by clerical and political elites providing supporting rationalizations. Germans, like all authoritarians, tended to be both hostile and self-righteous, with little or no motivation to be self-critical of their own beliefs, which in any case tend to be identical with those of their authorities. Being socialized to accept authoritarian values involves the acquisition of such traits as deference and obedience, and the deliberate blocking of tendencies toward independent thought, reflection, or criticism. Thus, to be a good authoritarian, one must reject liberal values such as individual autonomy and practices such as reasoned public discussion of political issues. Moreover, the stronger one's authoritarianism, the weaker one's cognitive and deliberative capacities to critically evaluate the morality of anti-Semitic policies, including genocide, and to choose not to participate in them. People with strongly authoritarian personalities find it extremely difficult (or even impossible) to doubt, much less change, their political beliefs.

Nationalism

The extreme form of German nationalism, exemplified as a psychological trait of individuals, took the form of an exaggerated patriotism. From an early age, Germans were socialized to take pride in the belief that they belonged to a unique and superior people having the right to rule others; as a consequence, their sense of personal identity and self-respect was constructed to give primacy to the fact of being German and the culturally attributed superiority that went with it. Moreover, they were strongly inclined to support wars against other nations perceived to be both hostile and inferior. Since this exaggerated patriotism was combined with the paranoid anti-Semitic belief that "the Jew" was a mortal threat to the nation, and with the authoritarian tendency to vent one's hostility on victims identified as legitimate targets by respected authorities, many Germans became "willing executioners" in the Holocaust.[17] The stronger one's nationalism, the weaker one's cognitive and deliberative capacities to see and appreciate that it was morally wrong to kill Jews, making it either extremely difficult or impossible to doubt, critically evaluate, or change one's belief that it was morally right, even a duty, to kill Jews.

It is extremely important to see that BPC is not just making the (noncontroversial) claim that Germans were taught to hold these mistaken beliefs and values. BPC also includes the much stronger claim that because of the manner in which Germans were socialized, they not only acquired these mistaken beliefs, but they were also *lacking (or seriously deficient in) the cognitive and deliberative capacities to avoid, question, or change them.* The anti-Semitic beliefs and values became an essential element of their personal identity and a basis for self-respect; consequently, they found it psychologically impossible or extremely difficult to doubt or critically evaluate those beliefs and values, or to act in violation of them (or both). These ongoing cognitive and deliberative deficiencies, in turn, guaranteed that they would not be able to avoid particular mistaken beliefs and wrong choices about how to treat Jews. In effect, BPC argues that being socialized in a bad political culture caused a kind of nonculpable ignorance.

In ethics and in law, ignorance does not necessarily excuse or mitigate blame; when it does, it has to be nonculpable ignorance. Persons with adequate powers of cognition and deliberation can nevertheless arrive at mistaken beliefs and make wrong choices because they fail to exercise their powers or because they do not exercise them carefully.[18] When they fail in this task, their ignorance is culpable. It is precisely because they have the capacity to avoid or correct their mistakes that they are fully answerable for having made them. However, if BPC is correct, Germans socialized in their bad political culture were not answerable (or at least not fully answerable) for their participation in killing Jews, since they found it impossible (or extremely difficult) to avoid having mistaken beliefs and making wrong choices in regard to their beliefs, values, and actions involving Jews; they could not help themselves. Or so the hypothesis holds.

The Critical Evaluation of BPC

This critical evaluation of BPC is organized around the following four questions that can be asked about the hypothesized effects of socialization into German political culture that are supposed to constitute diminished capacity:

1. What was the scope of socialization?
2. What was the incidence of diminished capacity among those socialized?
3. Did individuals play an active or a passive role in socialization?
4. To what extent did individuals who played an active role engage in activities of motivated irrationality such as purposeful self-deception?

Obviously, it is impossible to provide definitive answers to these questions here; instead, the discussion of each question only indicates some of the main reasons for thinking that a particular answer is correct (or most likely correct). The answers proposed, when taken together, support a conclusion that diminished capacity most probably played a minor role in the perpetration of the Holocaust and therefore can have only a marginal effect, overall, on the assessment of the blameworthiness of individual Germans for their role in the Holocaust.

What Was the Scope of Socialization?

Were all Germans subjected to the kind of socialization into the political culture described in the hypothesis, or only some of them? It is almost certainly false that all Germans were subjected to a process of socialization aimed at making them convinced anti-Semites, authoritarians, and ultranationalists. This is not to deny that these values were salient in the majority political culture and that many (perhaps most) Germans were socialized in the way required by the hypothesis. However, no society has the ability to uniformly socialize all of its members. Even small, isolated, and homogeneous societies end up with some nonconformists, deviants, and innovators. The scope of socialization would have to be even more restricted in a large, cosmopolitan society like that of Weimar Germany, which has been called a "cradle of cultural modernity."[19] Germans who were not anti-Semites, authoritarians, or nationalists may have been in a minority, but it was a sizable minority that included millions of people. It seems reasonable to conclude that the scope of socialization into the majority political culture of Germany fell far short of being universal.

What Was the Incidence of Diminished Capacity among Those Socialized?

If being socialized in a bad political culture were causally sufficient for developing with diminished capacity, there would be a perfect correlation between them. However, formulations of BPC tend to lack precision, and it is not easy to be confident about the causal relations being asserted. As far as I am aware, no BPC defender makes the strong claim that socialization is causally sufficient. Of course, it would be easy to formulate a truism immune to empirical refutation: All individuals subjected to genuine (true) socialization in German political culture developed with diminished capacities. This would only prompt the additional question: What was the incidence of genuine socialization? It is very likely that the only way to answer this new question would be to ascertain the incidence of diminished capacity. Such vacuous circularity can be avoided (and the critical discussion simplified) by making the assumption that BPC asserts only a correlation between socialization and diminished capacity, with "socialization" referring only to the process of being subjected (exposed) to various methods of moral training and education, regardless of the outcome. Our question then becomes: *How strong was the correlation between socialization and diminished capacity?*

It is impossible, of course, to get an exact number for the strength of the correlation; a rough estimate of the degree of correlation is the best that can be done. A thought experiment might produce a rough answer to the question. What counts as the relevant kind of diminished capacity must be kept in mind. Constructing an example that is both clear and historically plausible can help make this vivid. Let us take as our example children born in a peasant village in rural Germany, whose parents, like almost all the other pious Christians in the village, are anti-Semitic, authoritarian, and nationalistic. Let us suppose that these parents, who are Catholic, hold a divine command view of morality (like most peasants, including the priest, they are ignorant of the Thomistic subtleties in official Vatican teachings). The children receive little or no formal education, and they spend their lives entirely in the vicinity in which they were born. Political activity, such as it is, is virtually restricted to voting as the parish priest tells them to vote.

It seems reasonable to suppose that children reared in circumstances like these might grow up with the specific kinds of deficiencies in cognitive and deliberative powers hypothesized by BPC. They do not just happen to have mistaken beliefs about Jews that they might have avoided or that they might now change in the light of new experience. It was inevitable that they would have these beliefs and that they would find it extremely difficult, or even impossible, to doubt or change them. Moreover, it would never occur to them to wonder whether they should treat the handful of Jews who live in their village differently than they have been taught to do; or if the thought should occur to them, they will be utterly incapable of the kind of deliberation that is needed to make such a choice (which for them would be a radical change). Thus it seems very plausible to conclude that they might suffer from diminished capacity of the kind hypothesized in BPC.

However, if we ask ourselves why it seems plausible that children reared in these circumstances would suffer from diminished capacity, we see immediately that we have built into our hypothetical example precisely those factors that, taken together, virtually guarantee the result. The environment in which the socialization takes place includes not only a bad political culture but also social isolation, cultural homogeneity, and lack of education. It is not as though our hypothetical example is totally unrealistic, however, since peasants like the ones imagined existed (and still do exist) in Germany and all over Europe. (The Polish peasants interviewed by Claude Lanzmann in his documentary *Shoah* come to mind.) The problem is that although the example does reflect what some Germans were like, it does not represent Germans in general. And there are good reasons to doubt whether very many other Germans who were socialized in German political culture also developed with the specific deficiencies in capacity that afflict our imaginary (but realistic) peasants. Most Germans lived in cities; they were well educated (many highly so); they interacted with people from different religions, including Jews; they read newspapers and books; and they traveled. In short, even if many Germans were socialized in the majority political culture, there is little reason to think that they would be likely to develop with the specific deficiencies in capacity hypothesized by BPC, unless that socialization took place in an isolated and restricted environment similar to that in our example.

Of course, many (perhaps most) Germans who were socialized in the majority political culture did acquire some anti-Semitic beliefs and values, but (as I noted before) that is a different matter. Having mistaken beliefs and values by itself does not constitute diminished capacity. A person could be anti-Semitic, for example, but nevertheless choose not to participate in killing Jews when faced with the choice. Indeed, studies of those who rescued Jews during the Holocaust uniformly report that some rescuers were anti-Semitic. Some did it for pay, but just as many rescued out of principle. For example, some anti-Semitic Catholic rescuers in Poland believed that Jews should be converted, not killed.[20] There is a great deal of additional evidence that holding anti-Semitic beliefs and values by itself does not constitute diminished capacity. For example, a number of historians have noted that Germans who were silent bystanders in the persecution of Jews engaged in public protest against the so-called euthanasia program because it involved the secretly authorized legal killing of German citizens who were not Jewish. These Germans had sufficient capacity to see and appreciate the immorality of killing defenseless people solely on the ground that they were "life unworthy of life" (i.e., handicapped, elderly, deformed, and the like).[21] It begs the question to assume that Germans who protested the "euthanasia" program lacked the capacity to see and appreciate the immorality of the genocide against the Jews. Thus there is no good reason for thinking that the correlation between socialization and diminished capacity was strong.

Did Individuals Play an Active or a Passive Role in Socialization?

The deficiencies that constitute diminished capacity can vary in degree, in some cases making it impossible for the individuals to avoid or change their mistaken beliefs, values, and choices, and in others making it difficult to one degree or another.

Wrongdoing caused by the first kind of deficiency renders the person not blameworthy, whereas that caused by the second kind only mitigates blame. I shall call the first kind of diminished capacity *exculpating deficiency* (in effect, the deficiency serves as an excusing condition) and the second kind *mitigating deficiency* (the deficiency is a mitigating factor).The first kind, having an exculpating deficiency, exculpates one from wrongdoing only if one could not help having the deficiency. For example, suppose a child is exposed from infancy to intense and continuous socialization into the kind of isolated peasant culture described in the hypothetical example; there is never a point in such a child's development when it has the chance to develop the critical cognitive and deliberative capacities needed to avoid the mistaken beliefs and wrong choices it will make as a grown-up. In that case, the person is blameless for having the exculpating deficiency, which in turn makes him or her blameless for the wrongdoing that the deficiency brings about. The person could not help having developed with the deficiency, and as an adult he or she cannot avoid or change the mistakes in belief and choice caused by the deficiency. However, matters are not so clear when an individual is exposed to socialization that begins later in life, is less intense, or is interrupted (or all of these). In particular, I want to consider methods of socialization that assign or allow an active role for the learner in the process, especially when they occur in an environment radically different from the peasant culture sketched above. The next question raises that possibility, which I have ignored up to now.

The second kind, wrongdoing caused by a mitigating deficiency, lessens the degree of the individual's blameworthiness. But mitigating deficiencies vary in severity, and so does the degree to which they lessen blameworthiness. However, just as with exculpating deficiencies, a deficiency mitigates blameworthiness only if the individual could not help having it. If a mitigating deficiency results from early, intense, and continuous socialization similar to that sketched above, then the individual had no chance to avoid the deficiency; he or she is not to blame for it. However, it is also possible for a mitigating deficiency to result from socialization that is to some degree casual or superficial, occasional or interrupted, which occurs in a social environment unlike the peasant society. If the learner is assigned or is allowed to take an active role in socialization, there emerges the possibility that the learner may be partly to blame for the deficiency. In addition, because a mitigating deficiency does not make it impossible to avoid or change particular mistaken beliefs and wrong choices that result from it, there is room for individuals to play an active role by using their other powers of agency to compensate for and control these bad effects of the deficiency.

To What Extent Did Individuals Who Took an Active Role Engage in Activities of Motivated Irrationality Such as Purposeful Self-Deception?

Two principal ways in which individuals exposed to socialization can play an active role are (1) in construction of the self, including personal identity and the bases of self-respect, and (2) in using their other powers of agency to compensate for and control the bad effects of diminished capacity.[22]

Active Construction of the Self. Socialization is never an entirely one-way relation of active socializers to passive learners, not even in the extreme case described in the hypothetical example of peasant culture, in which the room for active maneuvering seemingly approaches zero. The model of the passive learner needs to be replaced with a model of the active learner engaged in a process that includes selective adaptation to the prevailing culture as presented through socialization. To illustrate how individuals might actively participate in the construction of their own selves (i.e., the self that each of them acquires), I shall use an example of a person being socialized in German political culture, but stipulating that the person lives in an urban area, gets a good education, and so on, in order to reflect the fact that most Germans were not rural peasants.

The central task in the construction of the self is to acquire a sense of personal identity, which consists of a set of basic commitments, beliefs, values, and goals that define who one takes oneself to be; personal identity is how an individual thinks of himself or herself (as distinct from social identity, i.e., one's identity as conceived by others in the community). The construction of personal identity is almost certainly not causally independent of culture; indeed, most socialization is aimed at making personal identity as similar as possible to social identity. The virtue of the model of the active learner engaged in selective adaptation to culture is that it draws attention to the fact that the individual being socialized usually has as much to do with making personal identity converge with the values of the political culture as the "socializers" do. What follows is a sketch of the way in which an individual might actively engage in the construction of the self by using, among many other activities, tactics of purposeful self-deception in order to become a "good German," that is, a convinced anti-Semite, a strict authoritarian, and a fervent nationalist.[23] Moreover, I shall assume that the socialization to which he or she was exposed would not by itself have been sufficient to achieve this particularly strong identification with cultural values; the individual's active collaboration was a necessary condition. This example of psychological development is used precisely because it is not very unusual, but rather quite common.

During childhood, socialization in the family, neighborhood, church, school, and so on, provides the basic content for a viable concept of personal identity, including anti-Semitic, authoritarian, and nationalistic beliefs and values. At this stage of moral development, the child lacks developed critical capacities and is motivated primarily by love for its parents, a desire to please them by conforming to their wishes, and a prudential concern to avoid their disapproval and punishment.[24]

In later childhood and early adolescence, the young person encounters increasing cognitive dissonance caused by new experiences and information that conflicts with his or her anti-Semitic beliefs and values. For example, Jewish friends at school seem nice and have ordinary human qualities, hatred of Jews is inconsistent with basic Christian teachings (love your enemy; do good to those that hate you), with moral precepts such as the wrongfulness of harming others, and with the fact that scientific evidence does not support racist ideology. These and other experiences also cause cognitive dissonance in relation to the young person's authoritarian and nationalistic beliefs and values.

As the extent and strength of cognitive dissonance increases, the young person experiences more and more psychological conflict and anxiety, including feelings of guilt and shame; he or she becomes strongly motivated to alleviate or avoid these subjectively stressful experiences by engaging in various tactics of purposeful self-deception—a species of motivated irrationality.

Some additional motives the young person has for engaging in tactics of self-deception include a desire to retain parental approval, a sense of integrity to maintain self-respect, a desire for peer approval, and a desire to avoid existential anxiety about the meaning of life (including, of course, the meaning of his or her own particular life). The tactics of self-deception are irrational in a narrow sense. They involve (among other things) systematic avoidance of relevant evidence that might confirm suspicions that one finds threatening (e.g., that one's parents are narrow-minded bigots). Sometimes engaging in self-deception, although it may be irrational in this narrow sense, is not irrational, everything considered (e.g., believing, against the preponderance of available evidence, that one will not die from a cancer sometimes is causally efficacious in motivating one to seek and find a cure). Most of the time, however, engaging in self-deception in order to evade acknowledging morally relevant facts or to avoid making a difficult moral choice is both irrational and blameworthy, everything considered. The individual can choose what kind of person he or she wants to be and has the capacity to choose not to become a convinced anti-Semite, a submissive child, or an ardent nationalist. There is nothing inevitable about choosing to engage in self-deception in order to avoid the psychological stress of calling into question one's culturally defined identity. (In chap. 6 I discuss the example of Adolf Hitler, who used self-deception to construct a self-identity that rejected most of the culture in which he was reared.)

The young person is motivated to engage in one or more of a variety of psychological tactics of purposeful self-deception, the overall aim of which is to evade conscious acknowledgment of the experiences and information that cause cognitive dissonance with his or her developing sense of personal identity. Socialization creates one set of incentives for the young person, and his or her independent experience creates another set; neither source by itself necessarily provides sufficient motives to cause the young person to act one way or the other. Ideally, the young person should make a conscious choice after deliberation. In fact, some young people avoid making the choice by psychological tactics of procrastination; others, like the young person in our example, choose instead to engage in tactics of self-deception. Several tactics may be used, including *avoidance* of any action, inquiry, investigation, or conversation that might lead to information that one suspects would further undermine or challenge one's sense of personal identity. This constitutes acceptance of a state of willful ignorance, a refusal to think about one's suspicions, and avoidance of self-reflection. *Biased interpretation of relevant evidence* includes selective use of evidence, rationalizing, making excuses, and denigrating the source; *purposeful forgetting* disposes of unwanted or threatening information. *Denial* is an automatic, unthinking refusal to accept unwanted information. *Blocking emotions* facilitates engaging in pretense, and using *convincing tactics of presentation of oneself to others,* for example, assures others that one is a fanatical anti-Semite so that they respond accordingly. The individual can then use their reactions as independent evidence that he or she is indeed an anti-Semite.[25]

With time, engaging in a sustained project of purposeful self-deception creates mental habits of attention, noticing, reasoning, imagination, and fantasy that together constitute an *anti-Semitic cognitive style,* which functions to stabilize one's sense of personal identity and to avoid cognitive dissonance. It can become so thoroughly habitual and "second nature" that one finds it impossible to doubt or change one's mistaken beliefs and wrong choices. The individual, by taking an active role in socialization, has brought about deficiencies in his or her own powers of agency that constitute diminished capacity. However, because the person chose to construct the self in the image of conventional anti-Semitism, purposefully subverting his or her own agency in the process, he or she is to some extent blameworthy for having the deficiency. He or she may also be blameworthy to some extent for making the particular mistakes and wrong choices that the diminished capacity promotes.

Using Powers of Agency to Compensate for and Control the Bad Effects of Diminished Capacity.   In addition to the active role one can play in the construction of the self, there are opportunities to use one's other powers of agency to compensate for and control the bad effects of one's diminished capacity. The only proviso is that the diminished capacity must be due to a mitigating deficiency, one that makes it difficult but not impossible to avoid its bad effects. Mitigating deficiencies vary greatly in severity. Some may be quite severe, requiring the persons afflicted to display extraordinary levels of cognitive awareness, deliberative reflection, and self-control in order to avoid the mistakes to which their deficiency makes them prone. Most mitigating deficiencies, however, range somewhere between severe and slight, which means that many people with diminished capacities would not find it too difficult to avoid the mistaken beliefs and wrong choices by actively using their other powers of agency. For some, it might be quite easy. Altemeyer notes that many American and Canadian subjects who initially score high on his authoritarian scale are quite surprised and embarrassed when they learn their high score. He also notes that authoritarian scores consistently drop as levels of college and university education rise.[26]

This means that even if many people develop with diminished capacity as the result of socialization in a bad political culture, most of them will be afflicted with a deficiency whose bad effects they have the capacity to counter and control, at least to some extent. Consequently, it is a reasonable moral expectation for them to use their powers of agency to avoid the mistakes and wrong choices to which they are prone, and it is fair to judge them blameworthy if they make no attempt to do so. If they genuinely try and fail, however, they may well be blameless.

Many people with a mitigating deficiency, not content with merely failing to use their powers of agency to compensate for and control the bad effects of their deficiency, instead engage in tactics of purposeful self-deception in order to maintain the basic commitments, beliefs, and values that constitute their personal identity. Active engagement in a sustained project of self-deception is a very common method used to construct a self that is compatible with the values of the culture into which one is being socialized. However, such projects are not always completely successful, and the person ends up with a self that is conflicted and not psychologically well integrated, although it is compatible with the culture. In such cases, there is a continual need for damage control as one's favored beliefs and values are repeatedly threatened, a need that is met by using the same tactics of purposeful evasion noted in the discussion of the active construction of the self. Clearly, if it is blameworthy to fail to use one's powers of agency to compensate for and control the bad effects of a deficiency, it is even more blameworthy to use them to actively protect and sustain the deficiency by a project of self-deception.

Finally, people commonly have strong prudential and selfish motives for conforming to the majority's political culture, motives that have little to do with moral or political principles. Such prudential and selfish motives include a desire to curry favor with others, opportunism, ambition, greed, fear, and cowardice. However, being selfish, ambitious, or greedy does not necessarily make one an amoral sociopath; indeed, many competent people are motivated by these nonideological motives to engage in self-deception in order both to maintain minimal self-respect and to impress others. There is every reason to suppose that many Germans who were not convinced anti-Semites or rigid authoritarians but had selfish motives like these engaged in self-deception so that they could maintain a reputation as "good Germans." These Germans were to some degree blameworthy for exercising their powers of agency in these selfish ways.

Summary

The scope of socialization into the majority political culture of Germany in the years before and during the Holocaust fell far short of being universal, and the correlation between socialization and diminished capacity was not strong. The model of the learner as largely passive that seems to be presupposed by proponents of BPC does not fit in all cases. It needs to be replaced, or at least supplemented, by the model of the active learner as engaged in a project of constructing his or her self and selectively adapting to the majority political culture as presented in socialization. I identified two main ways in which persons can play an active role in relation to the process of socialization and its bad effects: (1) in the construction of the self and (2) in using their other powers of agency to compensate for and control the bad effects of mitigating deficiencies. People are blameworthy to the extent that they use their powers of agency to engage in purposeful self-deception in order to construct a self with deficient capacity or in order to avoid compensating for or controlling their deficiencies. Many people have strong prudential or selfish motives for engaging in purposeful self-deception in order to keep their self-respect and reputation; they are also to some degree blameworthy. If these particular conclusions are correct, then it seems reasonable to infer that diminished capacity probably played a minor role in the perpetration of the Holocaust; therefore, it can have only a marginal effect, overall, on the assessment of the blameworthiness of individual Germans for their role in that catastrophe.

Notes

1. Susan Wolf, "Sanity and the Metaphysics of Responsibility," in *Responsibility, Character, and the Emotions: New Essays in Moral Psychology,* ed. Ferdinand David Schoemann (New York: Cambridge University Press, 1987), 46–62; Susan Wolf, *Freedom within Reason* (New York: Oxford University Press, 1990); Ervin Staub, *The Root of Evil: The Origins of Genocide and Other Group Violence* (New York: Cambridge University Press, 1989).

2. Wolf, *Freedom within Reason,* 121–122.

3. Staub, *Roots of Evil,* 148.

4. Wolf, "Sanity and the Metaphysics of Responsibility," 445.

5. H. L. A. Hart, *Punishment and Responsibility* (Oxford: Clarendon, 1968), 227–230.

6. Hyman Gross, *A Theory of Criminal Justice* (New York: Oxford University Press, 1979), 306–313.

7. Wolf, "Sanity and the Metaphysics of Responsibility," 422.

8. Staub, *Root of Evil,* 100, 148.

9. Gabriel Almond and Sidney Verba, *The Civic Culture: Political Attitudes in Five Nations* (Princeton, N.J.: Princeton University Press, 1963), 73.

10. Almond and Verba, *Civic Culture,* 13–15.

11. Almond and Verba, *Civic Culture,* 17–20; Robert D. Putnam, *Making Democracy Work: Civic Traditions in Modern Italy* (Princeton, N.J.: Princeton University Press, 1993), 33–38, 86–116; John Rawls, *Political Liberalism* (New York: Columbia University Press, 1993), 54–58; David H. Jones, "A Pragmatic Defense of Some Liberal Civic Virtues," *Southern Journal of Philosophy* 30, no. 2 (1992): 77–92.

12. Jackson J. Spielvogel, *Hitler and Nazi Germany: A History* (Englewood Cliffs, N.J.: Prentice-Hall, 1992), chaps. 1–3.

13. Almond and Verba, *Civic Culture,* 24.

14. Staub, *Roots of Evil,* 104–108.

15. Staub, *Roots of Evil,* 100–111.

16. Bob Altemeyer, *The Authoritarian Specter* (Cambridge: Harvard University Press, 1996), 6–12.

17. Daniel Jonah Goldhagen, *Hitler's Willing Executioners: Ordinary Germans and the Holocaust* (New York: Knopf, 1996).

18. Wolf, "Sanity and the Metaphysics of Responsibility," 444.

19. Spielvogel, *Hitler and Nazi Germany,* 17–19.

20. Nechama Tec, *When Light Pierced the Darkness: Christian Rescue of Jews in Nazi-Occupied Poland* (New York: Oxford University Press, 1986), 53–63, 99–112; Eva Fogelman, *Conscience and Courage: Rescuers of Jews During the Holocaust* (New York: Doubleday-Anchor, 1994), 176–177.

21. Goldhagen, *Hitler's Willing Executioners,* 111; John Weiss, *Ideology of Death: Why the Holocaust Happened in Germany* (Chicago: Ivan R. Dee, 1996), 350–351; Spielvogel, *Hitler and Nazi Germany,* 258–259.

22. Lawrence C. Becker, *A New Stoicism* (Princeton, N.J.: Princeton University Press, 1998), 93–111.

23. David H. Jones, "Pervasive Self-Deception," *Southern Journal of Philosophy* 27, no. 2 (1989): 217–237.

24. Jerome Kagan, *The Nature of the Child* (New York: Basic, 1994).

25. Mike W. Martin, *Self-Deception and Morality* (Lawrence: University Press of Kansas, 1986), chap. 2.

26. Altemeyer, *Authoritarian Specter,* 85.

Suggestions for Further Reading

Altemeyer, Bob. *The Authoritarian Specter.* Cambridge: Harvard University Press, 1996. The empirical psychological evidence for the existence and extent of the trait of authoritarianism.

Becker, Lawrence C., ed. *Encyclopedia of Ethics.* New York: Garland Publishing, 1992. Articles on moral development, moral psychology, psychology, and social psychology, among others.

Gross, Hyman. *A Theory of Criminal Justice.* New York: Oxford University Press, 1979. See especially "Diminished Responsibility" (pp. 310–316).

Kohlberg, Lawrence. *Essays on Moral Development.* 2 vols. New York: Harper & Row, 1981, 1984. An influential stage theory of moral development emphasizing moral judgment.

Putnam, Robert D. *Making Democracy Work: Civic Traditions in Modern Italy.* Princeton, N.J.: Princeton University Press, 1993. Empirical study of the role of political culture in the working of democratic government; chapters 5–6 are especially relevant.

Rawls, John. "The Sense of Justice." *Philosophical Review* 72 (July 1963): 281–305. A psychologically plausible and philosophically sophisticated sketch of moral development.

Spielvogel, Jackson. *Hitler and Nazi Germany: A History.* Englewood Cliffs, N.J.: Prentice-Hall, 1992. See chapters 1–2.

Staub, Ervin. *The Roots of Evil: The Origins of Genocide and Other Group Violence.* New York: Cambridge University Press, 1989. A psychological and cultural investigation of four case studies: the Turkish genocide against the Armenians, the Nazi Holocaust, the Cambodian genocide, and the "disappeared" in Argentina.

Chapter 6

The Principal Perpetrator: Adolf Hitler

A Brief Historical Overview of the Holocaust

In order to comprehend Adolf Hitler's role as the prime mover in initiating and implementing the Holocaust, we need a fairly accurate picture of the historical setting in which it occurred and an appreciation of its scope and complexity. What has come to be known as the Holocaust included the extermination of 5–6 million Jews, Gypsies, and other "undesirables" by the Germans, with substantial help from some of their allies and non-German volunteers. The systematic killings were carried out as a matter of official German state policy during World War II, from 1941 until very nearly the end of the war in May 1945. They were ordered by Adolf Hitler, the fanatical, anti-Semitic ruler of Germany for whom exterminating the Jews, in particular, was an essential ideological goal equal in importance with securing living space (*Lebensraum*) for Germany by the conquest of the Soviet Union.[1]

It is important to keep in mind that the Holocaust commenced after an eight-year period in which Hitler and the Nazi regime enjoyed spectacular successes in both domestic affairs and foreign policy, including a string of military victories that left Germany the unchallenged master of most of Europe. By 1938, well before the beginning of World War II, the charismatic Hitler had become a revered leader of his nation. Only five years before, when he became chancellor (1933), a significant portion of the German electorate (principally Social Democrats and Communists) had opposed the Nazis. Hitler and his regime early on silenced much of this potentially dangerous opposition by the use of force and police terror. But Hitler could never have achieved his status as a beloved and respected leader by brute force alone. A majority of Germans, mostly from the political right and center, eventually gave him their wholehearted support. In a few short years he had revived their pride as a nation and kindled their hopes for a better future. This substantial majority was composed of people from every class and profession, including a significant portion of the working classes, which had initially been mostly hostile.[2] Hitler achieved this high level of popular support by restoring political stability after years of chaos, ending the disastrous unemployment caused by worldwide depression, and, in effect, undoing the humiliating World War I defeat of 1918 with a series of bold steps such as pulling out of the League of Nations, reoccupying the Rhineland, and annexing both Austria and Czechoslovakia without resort to war. One German historian has stated that if Hitler had died in 1938, he would have become known as "Adolf the Great, one of the outstanding figures in German history."[3]

When Hitler started World War II with the invasion of Poland in 1939, most Germans did not want war, but most of them overcame their apprehension as German forces achieved a relatively low-cost victory in a few weeks. By the summer of 1940 Hitler had gone on to conquer Norway, Denmark, the Netherlands, Belgium, and France, again with relatively low casualties. After signing an armistice with the French, he returned to Berlin in triumph. The period between the summer of 1940 and the summer of 1941 (with the invasion of the Soviet Union) saw Hitler's popular prestige and power grow ever greater and remain so until after the defeat at Stalingrad in February 1943.[4] Significantly, the Holocaust was planned and initiated, and most of the millions of killings were completed, during the period of Hitler's (and his regime's) maximum prestige and power. This means that the great majority of Germans who participated in the Holocaust from 1941 to 1943 were almost surely very loyal to Hitler, highly supportive of the regime, and patriotically motivated to participate willingly in achieving the ideologically defined goals of the war. I call this surge of patriotic motivation "triumphant nationalism." By 1941, the regime's goals were publicly known to include the conquest of vast new territories in the Soviet Union and the subjugation and enslavement of millions of people who lived there. This aggression was justified on the grounds that Germany had a sacred duty to preserve Western civilization from the "Asiatic" hordes and to protect Germany from "Jewish bolshevism."[5] In fact, ordinary German soldiers fought savagely and unrelentingly against the Soviet Union, committing atrocities against soldiers and civilians alike.[6]

As it turned out, the ideologically defined goals of the war also included genocide against all Jews and most Gypsies, who were deemed racially unfit to live in a purely Aryan society. It seems reasonable to suppose that the same strong and pervasive triumphal nationalism that motivated Germans to participate willingly in achieving the other radical wartime goals of the regime was also salient among the motives that prompted them to participate willingly in the Holocaust. (Although most explanations of why ordinary Germans in police battalions willingly participated in genocide either ignore or discount the role of patriotic nationalism; see chap. 7.)

Anti-Semitic Policies Preceding the Holocaust

The anti-Semitic policies of the Nazi regime between 1933 and 1941 (before the Holocaust actually began) can be divided into three phases. The first phase, from 1933 to 1935, saw relatively little violence against Jews; it consisted of an abortive boycott of Jewish businesses, followed by laws that excluded Jews from the civil service, the legal profession, judgeships, the medical profession, teaching positions, entertainment, and the press, together with quotas on the number of "non-Aryans" who could attend secondary schools and universities. There was a lull in anti-Semitic activity until March 1935, when a second phase was ushered in by a wave of violence and a new boycott against Jewish businesses. Hitler and some of his economic advisers feared that these spontaneous actions might get out of control, so anti-Semitic activity was channeled into law by Hitler's announcement of the Nuremberg Laws at a party rally on September 15, 1935. This set of laws and implementing decrees stripped Jews of their citizenship and all political rights, outlawed marriage and sexual intercourse between Jews and "subjects of German and kindred blood,"and defined a Jew as "anyone descended from at least three grandparents who are fully Jewish as regards race." There followed another lull until 1938. Renewed violence broke out in July, a special identification card for all Jews was introduced, and, most disturbing of all, a two-day pogrom occurred on November 9–10, which came to be known as *Kristallnacht* (the night of broken glass). Orchestrated by the Nazi Party, the orgy of violence was ostensibly a "spontaneous" reaction to the assassination of a German diplomat in Paris by a young Jewish man. Throughout Germany synagogues were burned, Jewish businesses and homes were destroyed, one hundred Jews were killed and thousands assaulted, and 20,000 Jewish males were arrested and sent to concentration camps. The Nazis then proceeded to exclude Jews form all aspects of social and economic life and vigorously pursued a policy of forced emigration, which remained the official policy until the fall of 1941.[7]

The Scale and Complexity of the Final Solution

It is not my purpose to give a complete account of all aspects of the process of genocide that the Germans referred to as the "final solution of the Jewish question." However, several principal categories of perpetrators can be identified by focusing on some salient aspects of the process. A perpetrator is any person who knowingly took part in the process of destruction of the European Jews, whether by (1) ordering, authorizing, or planning the killing, (2) directly participating in the killing itself, or (3) knowingly making an essential contribution to the killing.[8]

Planning and Decision Making by German Leaders

The decision to exterminate the Jews most probably was made by Hitler sometime in early 1941; SS chief Heinrich Himmler had overall charge of planning and carrying out the decision in conjunction with the invasion of the Soviet

Union. The widened war would provide the necessary cover for the huge destructive process, and eventually the elites in every major German institution would become involved in the planning and implementation.[9] The prime example of a perpetrator drawn from this category is, of course, Adolf Hitler himself, the main subject of this chapter.

Outdoor Killing Operations

Specially trained genocidal units of the SS, Einsatzgruppen (special task groups), German police battalions, and non-German police auxiliaries made up of volunteers primarily from the Baltic states and the Ukraine, killed about 1.3 million victims, primarily Jews, in Poland and the territories of the Soviet Union. The principal method used was mass shooting of victims next to prepared open pits; the dead or dying victims would fall into the pits and be buried. The second example of perpetrators is drawn from this category (discussed in chap. 7): the men in the German police battalions that operated primarily in Poland. These men have been the subject of increased scholarly study in recent years.[10]

Killing Center Operations

The methods used to kill victims face-to-face in the field were psychologically disturbing to the perpetrators, which raises an important question: Were the perpetrators suffering from physical revulsion or did they have moral qualms? The open-air methods were inefficient as well as disturbing, and planners began almost immediately to search for different and "better" methods of killing. One method adopted was the mobile gas van, first as a replacement for open shooting and then as a component of the killing process at Chelmno (Poland), the first killing center to be put in operation. The principal killing method, gas chambers in conjunction with crematoria, was used in all of the remaining centers, including three in Operation Reinhard (Belzec, Sobibor, and Treblinka) in eastern Poland, one near Lublin (Majdanek), and the infamous killing center near Oswiecim (Auschwitz). Together, these killing centers accounted for about three million victims.[11] The perpetrators who served in the killing centers are not considered separately as a principal example, although killing victims face-to-face outdoors is compared with working in a killing center.

Institutions Providing Logistical Support

In addition to the perpetrators who were directly involved in killing the victims, there were many who contributed indirectly by fulfilling essential tasks without which the Final Solution would have had neither its enormous, continent-wide scope nor its efficient deadliness. Lawyers and judges had to write and enforce laws that defined what a Jew was, Catholic and Protestant churches had to cooperate in identifying Jews and Aryans, police had to round up and guard Jews in the cities and countryside, the railroads has to transport them (first to ghettos and then to killing centers), bureaucrats had to legally confiscate Jewish property, and so on. Virtually all of the people who participated in the Final Solution in these indirect but essential ways were fully aware that Jews (and Gypsies) were being systematically killed by their own government, and therefore they were perpetrators. I refer to perpetrators in this diverse category as "impersonal bureaucrats" (the so-called desk murderers). Although impersonal bureaucrats outnumbered perpetrators directly involved in the killing, they are not discussed as a separate example; however, I discuss issues of their blameworthiness along with that of perpetrators directly involved in the killing.

The Germans received substantial help in the genocidal killing from large numbers of non-German volunteers and from foreign governments, among them their allies Italy, Bulgaria, Romania, and Hungary, as well as satellite states Slovakia and Croatia. The involvement of so many non-German individuals and governments might suggest that focusing on the role of German perpetrators is unjustified. Raul Hilberg, in the preface to *The Destruction of the European Jews,* gives his own reply to this objection:

> Still, the act of destruction was German, and the primary focus in this portrayal is therefore placed on the German conceptualizers, initiators, and implementers of the deed. *They* constructed the framework within which collaborators in Axis and occupied countries made their contributions to the operation, and *they* created the conditions that confronted Jewry in a closed ghetto, the roulette wheel of a roundup, or at the entrance of a gas chamber. To inquire into the structure of the phenomenon is to ask the question about the Germans first.[12]

The Principal Perpetrator: Adolf Hitler

Assessing Hitler's Blameworthiness

The glaringly immoral and evil nature of Hitler's deeds may seem so self-evident that engaging in a careful ethical investigation of the moral blameworthiness that he incurred for his central role in the Holocaust may seem to be a waste of time. However, a general principle in the theory of responsibility states that the fact that someone has done something wrong by itself does not establish his or her blameworthiness for doing it. It is not enough to vilify him without also truly understanding the reasons for that vilification. It is important to avoid the facile (and false) view that he was some kind of inhuman "monster" or cruel psychopath who enjoyed inflicting pain and death for its own sake. For one thing, categorizing Hitler entirely in psychiatric terms runs the real danger of absolving him of responsibility, since his actions might then be viewed as symptoms of mental illness that were beyond his control. There is no doubt that Hitler was very neurotic and that he had a defective and vicious moral character, but he was not insane. He had more than adequate powers of cognition, deliberation, and self-control to make him answerable for his actions. We have an obligation to investigate carefully how he used and misused his powers of agency to, among other things, construct a self that was capable of perpetrating some of the most horrendous acts in history.

In this chapter I apply the theory of responsibility developed in part 1 to the deeds Hitler perpetrated as the prime instigator of the Final Solution. There is a series of questions that need to be answered in order to assess his blameworthiness. (1) What did he do? Specifically, what were the wrong actions and omissions for which he is allegedly accountable? (2) Since the seriousness of a wrong act increases the agent's blameworthiness (everything else being equal), it is necessary to assess how bad his deeds were. (3) Were the elements of full blameworthiness for wrongdoing present? Did Hitler act knowingly and intentionally? If he was ignorant in some relevant way, was his ignorance culpable or nonculpable? Did he suffer from diminished capacity? Did he have any other kind of justified moral excuses such as a lack of ability or opportunity to do otherwise? Were there any mitigating circumstances that make him less blameworthy?

What Did He Do?

Since Hitler was the chief perpetrator of the Holocaust, what wrong acts did he perform for which he is prima facie blameworthy? A partial list of the relevant acts Hitler performed is more than adequate for our purposes. All of these acts were performed in his official role as Führer and Reich Chancellor, which from 1934 to 1945 included being the head of the government and the National Socialist Party, and (after 1938) commander of the armed forces as well; indeed, Hitler was an absolute dictator.[13]

First, Hitler ordered the enactment of laws and pursued a set of domestic anti-Semitic policies from 1933 to 1941 that (in the end) deprived German Jews of all rights of citizenship, excluded them from all economic activities and professions, isolated them from the rest of German society in a state of poverty and helplessness, and forced as many of them as possible to emigrate. Thus Jews who remained in Germany in 1941, together with those rounded up in ghettoes in conquered Poland, were completely defenseless against the genocidal actions that followed.

Second, in 1940–1941 Hitler ordered army generals and SS leaders to regard the coming invasion of the Soviet Union as a "war of annihilation" in which their troops would have to kill all Soviet political commissars and "Jewish-Bolshevik intelligentsia."[14] When fully implemented, these orders resulted in both the SS Einsatzgruppen (supplemented by police battalions) and (later) units of the Wehrmacht initiating the genocide against the Jews of eastern Poland and the Soviet Union.

Third, in 1941 Hitler decided to implement an official policy of genocide regarding all Jews and Gypsies in Germany and German-occupied Europe, a policy that came to be called euphemistically "the final solution of the Jewish Question." As a result, 5–6 million Jews, and at least 200,000 Gypsies, were killed between 1941 and 1945.[15]

How Bad Were His Actions?

Hitler's actions were wrong, in the first place, because they violated the basic prima facie duty not to kill others, which is in the core content of morality. Hitler himself did not directly kill any Jews, but as the absolute dictator of Germany, he authorized the genocidal policies that led to the deaths of millions of Jews and Gypsies (among millions of others killed as combatants and civilians as the result of the military campaigns he directed). In both ethics and law, superiors who order those under their authority to kill are deemed to have caused the deaths that result; this applies to military commanders as well.[16] This is nothing more than a clear application of the notion of role responsibility. Consequently, one is justified in saying that through his actions as wartime dictator, Hitler caused the deaths of millions of people. Everything else being equal, the most serious harm that one human can inflict on another is to cause his or her death; for this reason the most stringent prima facie moral duty is the prohibition against killing others. Again, everything else being equal, it is more serious to kill two people than to kill one, and more serious to kill three than to kill two, and so on. Therefore, Hitler's actions, which caused millions of deaths, are among the most serious breaches of a basic moral duty that can be imagined; not only were they wrong, but they were exceedingly bad and evil.

In addition, Hitler's decision as the wartime dictator of Germany to pursue an intentional policy of genocide against all Jews, wherever they existed, was an act of unprecedented immorality because of the enormity of its goal: that an entire people should cease to exist. This is the chilling implication of the expression "the final solution of the Jewish question." Hitler set out to achieve nothing less than an end to Jewish history, culture, and any prospect of a Jewish future. This makes his action different in kind from mass murder (of individuals). As bad as the mass murder was, the attempt to literally kill a people was even worse.[17]

Which of the Elements That Make Wrongdoing Unquestionably Blameworthy (If Any) Were Present in Hitler's Performance of These Wrong Actions?

In this section I try to answer each part of the question by looking only at relevant factual evidence. What counts as relevant evidence is determined by the ethical criteria that underlie the justification of judgments of blameworthiness, including the validity of excuses. Keep in mind that facts alleged as excusing conditions must be objectively true in order for the excuse to be morally justified.

Knowledge. Did Hitler know the nature of his acts? Did he fully realize what he was doing? There can be no doubt that he knew that the implementation of his genocidal policies brought about the deaths of millions of people, since that was his intended goal. However, it is doubtful that Hitler genuinely understood much more than that about the objective nature of his actions. For example, if the question is whether he realized that he was killing perfectly harmless and defenseless men, women, and children who had done nothing wrong and consequently did not deserve to be put to death, the answer must surely be that he did not realize these aspects of what he did. To the contrary, he was convinced that all Jews were incredibly dangerous beings who had already inflicted great harm on Germany and on civilization in general and that their continued existence posed a mortal threat to the nation. If the question is whether Hitler knew that his actions were seriously wrong and evil, the answer is obviously that he did not; he sincerely believed that he was fully justified in ordering the mass killings. Thus the overall conclusion must be that Hitler lacked relevant knowledge; he did not fully realize the nature of his horrendous actions or their deeply immoral nature. He acted in considerable ignorance. (Later I address the important question of whether his ignorance was nonculpable.)

Intention. Hitler certainly initiated, authorized, and pursued his genocidal policies intentionally; he did not pursue them accidentally, by mistake, or in a fit of negligent absentmindedness. So it is reasonable to conclude that he intentionally ordered the killing of millions of people. However, since he did not know that his victims were harmless and he did not think that his actions were wrong (indeed, he thought they were right), it follows that he did not have (and logically could not have) the intention to kill millions of defenseless people or do anything he consciously believed to be morally wrong. Although what he did was objectively wrong, he did not do it either because it was wrong or in spite of knowing that it was wrong. In short, Hitler did not intentionally do wrong; rather, he intended to do what he sincerely thought was right.[18]

Ability and Opportunity to Do Otherwise. The expression "could have done otherwise" can be understood in two different ways: It can have a purely factual/descriptive meaning or it can have a normative/ethical meaning. Viewed objectively, Hitler had the physical ability and mental capacity to do otherwise; that is, had he so desired, he would have been able to refrain from initiating the genocidal policies. All that was required of him was to do nothing in this regard. The fact that he held strongly anti-Semitic beliefs meant that, as a matter of fact, he did not desire to desist from those policies. But these facts do not show that he lacked the physical and mental ability to desist. Lack of desire must not be confused with lack of ability. A person can have a desire to do X but lack the ability (e.g., run a mile in four minutes or stay on a diet) or can have the ability to do X but lack the desire (e.g., do a good imitation of Elvis Presley or cheat on an examination). From an objective point of view, Hitler also had the physical and institutional opportunity to desist from his genocidal policies; he was not physically constrained or institutionally hampered in his pursuit of the policy of genocide against the Jews and Gypsies. Indeed, Hitler himself would have agreed with these conclusions about his physical ability and opportunity to do otherwise. In this sense, he acted freely and voluntarily.

The question of whether Hitler had the ability and opportunity to do otherwise in the normative/ethical sense of those expressions is more complicated. Would it have been reasonable and fair to require him to desist from his genocidal policies, given the objective risks, costs, and harms that he would thereby have incurred in the circumstances in which he was acting? From an objective point of view it seems clear that Hitler did have a fair opportunity to do otherwise; there were no risks, costs, or harms that he would have incurred by refraining from his genocidal policies that would have made it unreasonable to require him to desist. On the contrary, there was an incalculably good benefit, the saving of millions of lives, that would have resulted from his refraining. So there is no objective reason to think that Hitler "could not do otherwise." Of course, this objective analysis leaves out the way in which Hitler looked at the situation in which he was acting. He believed that he could not do otherwise than kill all the Jews; he truly believed that he had no choice. Why did Hitler believe this? Because for him the very survival of Germany and civilization were at stake; the subversive and dangerous worldwide "Jewish conspiracy" had to be crushed. In addition, Hitler was convinced that he alone was capable of successfully waging the war against this conspiracy.[19] Finally, he was convinced that the opportunity to act would not last very long; from 1938 on, Hitler feared that he would not live long enough to finish his monumental task.[20] Thus Hitler sincerely (but mistakenly) believed that he had no choice but to go to war and to order the genocide of the Jews; he was convinced that "he could not do otherwise."

Bad Motives.   From an objective point of view, Hitler was full of hatred for Jews as well as many other peoples such as Slavs and Gypsies whom he regarded as inferior to Aryans. His hatred would be unequivocally bad from an ethical point of view if it stemmed from vicious character traits such as cruelty and sadism. There is a lot of evidence that throughout his life Hitler was in fact ruthless, vindictive, faithless, and cruel in his dealings with people.[21] Consequently, if his hatred of the Jews was just another expression of his underlying cruelty, then he acted from a morally bad motive, which makes him more blameworthy for the killings than he might otherwise have been. In opposition to this assessment there is the fact that Hitler believed that the Jews had in fact done immeasurable harm to Germany and civilization, that because of their alleged "corrupt blood" they had a biologically determined criminal nature, and that they were bent on destroying "good German blood."[22] So at least part of the explanation for his hatred of the Jews lies in his ideological beliefs about them. Since he was convinced that these beliefs were true, his hatred did not come entirely from the cruel streak in his character. Moreover, from his point of view, his hatred of the Jews was fully justified and appropriate; he did not see himself as being cruel or sadistic but rather as a good German willing to make great sacrifices to do his duty to save his country.

In summary, when Hitler's beliefs about the nature of his acts and the reasons he had for doing them are taken into account, a conclusion can be drawn that he was *not blameworthy* for them. He was to a great extent ignorant of the true nature of what he was doing, including that it was almost inconceivably evil. Quite to the contrary, he believed that what he did was right and fully justified. Moreover, he believed that he had no choice and that he could not have done otherwise. Finally, his motives were not exclusively bad and included the ordinarily admirable motives of a sense of duty and a willingness to sacrifice.

This conclusion, which most people would find totally unacceptable, is the result of postponing the question of whether Hitler's ignorance (upon which the conclusion that he is not blameworthy depends) is culpable or nonculpable. Taking Hitler's own view of his actions and reasons leads to agreeing with him that he was blameless. It is time now to look critically at Hitler's beliefs, inquire into how he came to hold them, and attempt to assess his blameworthiness for his own ignorance.

Did Hitler Suffer from Diminished Capacity Responsibility as a Result of Being Socialized into the Bad Political Culture of Austria?

Diminished capacity probably played a minor role in the perpetration of the Holocaust because most Germans were not subjected to early, intense, and continuous socialization into anti-Semitism, authoritarianism, and nationalism (three salient traits of German political culture). Consequently, even if most German perpetrators were exposed to the bad political culture of their time, in the great majority of cases this did not deprive them of sufficient cognitive ability to realize that genocide was immoral or cause them to have inadequate deliberative powers to refrain from participating. Therefore, these German perpetrators could not excuse themselves for their participation by appealing to the alleged effects of socialization. Barring some other excuse or mitigating circumstance, they were to some extent blameworthy for their wrong actions.

However, Hitler was born and reared in Austria and did not move to Germany until he was twenty-four years old. During this period Austrian political culture was very similar to that of Germany and was even more strongly anti-Semitic.[23] Was the young Hitler subjected to early, intense, and continuous socialization into Austrian anti-Semitism and authoritarianism that might excuse his ignorance? The available evidence indicates fairly strongly that he was not; quite the contrary, it would be more accurate to describe the young Hitler as having been "undersocialized." For example, Hitler did not acquire any of the middle-class values that his authoritarian father strove to instill in him. He was lazy and shirked work; he was a poor student and hated most of his studies; and he deliberately set out to lead a life as an artist, as far removed as possible from the civil service career that his father wanted him to follow. Like virtually all young Austrians, Hitler was confirmed in the Catholic faith, but he was never religious and as an adult became strongly anti-Christian.[24] These facts lead to the conclusion that Hitler was not a passive subject of cultural socialization; he stands out as someone who resolutely resisted the role of a young man aspiring to become a successful member of the Austrian middle class. No doubt, he had his share of middle-class pretensions and a sense of superiority toward people in the working classes, together with some conventional anti-Semitic attitudes, but there is no evidence that he acquired his adult fanatical anti-Semitic beliefs early in life as the result of socialization. Indeed, Hitler himself claims that his own family frowned upon anti-Semitism as evidence of backwardness and lack of education.[25] It seems reasonable to conclude that Hitler did not suffer from diminished capacity responsibility as the result of being subjected to early, intense, or continuous socialization in the bad political culture of Austria. Thus his ignorance cannot be excused on that ground.

A Psychological Hypothesis about the Active Role Hitler Took in Constructing His Own Self and the Tactics of Self-Deception He Employed in Doing So

Although it is fairly certain that Hitler's ignorance was not caused by early and intense socialization, there is not enough evidence available to establish an alternative explanation with certainty. Most of the evidence supports the conclusion that Hitler played an extremely active role in constructing his own self from a very young age and that from the beginning of this project he made extensive use of various tactics of motivated irrationality, especially self-deception. It was many years before he attained a relatively stable sense of personal identity. When he was thirty years old, he arrived at a conception of himself as a political leader with a "divine mission" to save his nation. That conception was in turn heavily dependent on the ideological beliefs he acquired as an adult that Jews were a mortal threat to Germany and that genocide was necessary and justified. Consequently, his ignorance of the true nature of his immoral actions was largely the result of his own active construction of his self—of the way in which he had come to conceive himself and the purpose of his life.

The First Attempt at Constructing a Personal Identity: The Artist.   Hitler did not finish *Realschule* (secondary school), which he attended for four years in the provincial cities of Steyr and Linz. Since the winter of 1905 he had been living at home with his mother and sister (his father had died in 1903). He quit school for good in the fall, at the age of sixteen. He spent the next two years with no definite plans of any kind. When he was asked what he wanted to be, he would reply, "A great artist." He spent his time at home during the day "reading, drawing, and dreaming" and in the evening would often go to the opera. He especially enjoyed Wagner.[26] During this time his fantasy life shifted between dreams of becoming a great painter and grandiose plans for rebuilding Linz when he became a master architect. In the spring of 1906 Hitler's mother financed a one-month stay for him in Vienna, where his imagination was fired by the monumental buildings of the capital city.[27]

In early 1907 Hitler's mother was found to have cancer, and this may have precipitated his decision to move to Vienna in the fall in order to apply for the painting course at the art academy. He probably began to realize that he might have to start taking charge of his own life. The move to Vienna showed how psychologically independent (and alienated) Hitler was at eighteen, and also how unrealistically confident he was: He moved to Vienna before he knew whether he could gain admission to the art academy. In *Mein Kampf* Hitler admits that he was devastated when he was rejected by the academy: "It struck me as a bolt from the blue."[28] But Hitler did not give any serious consideration to doing something else with his life besides becoming an artist. Instead he seized upon some consolatory remarks made by the director of the academy, from whom he had sought an explanation for his rejection for admission to painting. When the director told him he should concentrate his efforts on studying architecture because his talents in that field were greater than his aptitude for painting, Hitler abruptly shifted to considering this new possibility. "In a few days I myself knew that I should some day become an architect."[29]

However, Hitler did not take any of the necessary steps to attain this new goal. For example, he would have needed a secondary school certificate in order to take the preparatory courses for the program in architecture. However, he did not return to school, and it is very likely that he had never had any intention to do so. This episode illustrates Hitler's already deeply ingrained tendency to evade harsh realities by retreating into comforting but unrealistic fantasies. "His solution to rejection by the Academy was to go back to the Stumpergasse [the boarding house in which he was staying] and settle down as if nothing had happened. In this sanctuary, he resumed what he grandly called his "studies," doodling and reading, with excursions around town or to the opera."[30]

When Hitler's mother died in December 1907, he returned to Linz for a two-month stay to settle her affairs. He had been very close to his mother and her death devastated him. In February 1908 he returned to Vienna and lived there for the next five years, completely cut off from his remaining family. A boyhood friend from Linz, August Kubizek, had joined him and during much of the first year provided some companionship in a relationship dominated by

Hitler.[31] In October 1908 Hitler applied a second time for admission to the art academy, this time to study architecture; he was not even allowed to take the test, presumably because the sample pictures he submitted were judged to be too poor to qualify him for the examination. This was the end of Hitler's attempts to follow a formal program of training in art, and it must have been a psychologically wrenching experience that severely tested his conception of himself as an artist. He was so demoralized and embarrassed that he abruptly changed lodgings without telling Kubizek where he had moved, thus ending the only personal relationship he had.

Hitler was now truly alone and emotionally adrift, yet there is no evidence that he questioned or modified his self-conception as an artist in any way. At first, his solitary life was fairly comfortable, but when the money left him by his father and mother finally ran out, he turned to making a living by painting postcards, which he and an acquaintance sold in cafes and bars. His life was exceedingly ascetic; he did not drink and only occasionally smoked a cigarette. Hitler evidently had no sexual experience. He deliberately abstained from any contact with women because he believed they were immoral and socially dangerous.[32] At one point Hitler was reduced to living in a shelter for the homeless. Finally, in May 1913, when he was twenty-four, Hitler left Vienna for Munich, in part because he wanted to avoid the Austrian draft.[33]

Just as Hitler developed his conception of personal identity in these years largely independently of the objective circumstances of his life, he also began to develop his political ideas, not so much as a practical guide for action but as an abstract and theoretical scheme that could supply meaning to his life. His method for gathering the materials for this worldview was to search for confirmation of his already well-established biases and attitudes. Foremost among these was his conviction, from which he never deviated, that his failures could not be his own fault; consequently, he was certain that the correct explanation for his failure was always to be found in some flaw or obstacle in the world around him or in the shortcomings or evil of others. As one historian has put it, among Hitler's negative characteristics was "a total lack of capacity for self-criticism."[34] However, there is no reason to conclude that Hitler's lack of capacity was anything but self-induced by his own motivated self-deception. His evasion of self-knowledge, a very common kind of motivated irrationality that protects one's self-respect, was evident throughout Hitler's childhood and by early adulthood had evolved into a character trait, the vice of self-deception.

The two pillars of Hitler's political outlook, which he acquired in this period (roughly between 1911 and 1913), were an especially virulent version of anti-Semitism on the one hand and Pan-German nationalism on the other. The "eastern" variety of anti-Semitism that he encountered in Vienna "was (and is?) endemic and murderous, directed not towards assimilation or integration but towards liquidation and extermination."[35] Hitler probably was attracted to this radical version of anti-Semitism because it used the abstract conception of "the

Jew" as a scapegoat to explain the social and economic ills that he had seen firsthand in Vienna. These conditions engendered in him strong feelings of resentment and anger, and his anti-Semitic ideology provided a ready target at which they could be directed. It also offered the inestimable advantage of not requiring him to engage in any self-criticism and holding out the promise of an effective solution for the world's problems, namely, the removal or liquidation of the Jewish people.

As for the attractions of Pan-German nationalism, Hitler thought of himself as a stranger in Austrian culture, which he had come to believe was contaminated by "foreigners and Jews." Consequently, he became strongly identified with German culture and nationhood, believing that all Germans should be united in one country. It is striking that each of these political conceptions is built on an abstraction; in the case of anti-Semitism, it is the mythical "Jew," whereas in the case of Pan-German nationalism it is the ideal of a future united German "Volk" (people).[36] Nonetheless, his belief in these abstractions provided Hitler with a way to satisfy his growing desire for vindication and revenge against a world that he believed was somehow unfairly stacked against him. That Hitler held these political views primarily as theoretical abstractions unconnected to real people is confirmed by people who knew Hitler at the time in Vienna. They testify to his cordial relationships with some individual Jews and Poles and with his friend, Kubizek, who was Czechoslovakian. But nearly all who knew him remark on his virulent tirades against Jews and others in boardinghouse "speeches" that he gave.[37]

Hitler's first attempt at constructing a personal identity as an artist was successful only in the sense that he was able to cling to it in the face of objective failure by engaging in systematic self-deception. Not surprisingly, Hitler's personal identity as an artist was quite fragile, and he had to engage in continuous self-deception to maintain it. The coming of World War I gave him the opportunity to forge a new identity, which, unlike his conception of himself as an artist, would be to some extent grounded in reality.

The Second Attempt at Constructing a Personal Identity: The Soldier. Hitler shared the joy and enthusiasm with which most Germans (and the citizens of other European countries) greeted the outbreak of World War I. Viewing himself as a German and not as an Austrian, he joined the Sixteenth Bavarian Infantry Regiment in Munich shortly after the war started. Later in *Mein Kampf* he described his feelings: "To me those hours seemed like a release from the painful feelings of my youth. Even today I am not ashamed to say that, overpowered by stormy enthusiasm, I fell down on my knees and thanked Heaven from an overflowing heart."[38]

Filled with patriotic fervor, Hitler saw the war as the means by which the German people would finally achieve real unity and greatness. His strong motivation showed itself in four years of exemplary service at the front as a courier. He did not just put in his time but displayed conscientiousness and courage. Awarded the Iron Cross Second Class early in the war, in 1918 Hitler also received a certificate for bravery as well as the Iron Cross First Class (rarely awarded to enlisted men). Although he was promoted to corporal, he was denied further promotion because he was thought to lack leadership qualities. Having already been wounded twice, he was caught in a gas attack that left him temporarily blinded just four weeks before the end of the war. Germany capitulated, the Kaiser abdicated, and the armistice was signed while he was recuperating in a military hospital away from the front.[39]

Hitler's military service in World War I is often, and correctly, singled out as the most important experience in his life.[40] The war served as Hitler's redemption in two related ways; first, as an opportunity for him to forge a new (and temporary) identity as an ordinary soldier and, second, as the catalyst for the development of his final and most radical identity—a political leader with a divine mission to save his nation.

After years of drifting and failure, Hitler welcomed the structured and meaningful life he found in the army. For the first time in his life, he had obligations that he took seriously and clear goals that he believed in. Moreover, army life was very impersonal, so he could lose himself in his role responsibilities as a courier and remain aloof from the other men with whom he served. In fact, most of them barely tolerated Hitler as an odd duck, and some of them were angered by his zeal and conscientiousness.[41] Nevertheless, Hitler's four years of army life afforded him the opportunity to construct a new personal identity that gave him a solid basis for self-respect and a rewarding sense of purpose that he took very seriously. Indeed, Hitler was an ideological "true believer" who staked everything on Germany achieving a resounding victory over its enemies and embarking on a new era of national greatness. His recently found sense of purpose thus depended on more than just his own personal success as a good and brave courier; it also required a successful outcome of the war, a resounding German victory. Despite the fact that Hitler's new identity was grounded in reality to some considerable extent, it also reflected his heavy dependence on abstract theoretical considerations and the low value that he placed on personal relationships. As one historian put it, Hitler's life was marked by "an exceptional intensity of political living and feeling alongside an exceptional meagerness of personal experience."[42]

Since the viability of Hitler's personal identity as a good soldier depended on a German victory, it was quite fragile; indeed, when Germany capitulated, the Kaiser abdicated, and the armistice was signed, he went into a deep depression. It was this new and very profound psychological crisis that led Hitler to construct yet another personal identity over the course of the next year.

The Third (and Final) Attempt at Constructing a Personal Identity: The Political Leader with a Divine Mission to Save His Nation. In *Mein Kampf* Hitler admits that when he learned of the German capitulation, the new government, and the armistice, he returned to his barracks, threw himself on his bed, and wept.[43] From his point of view, Hitler faced a catastrophic situation. First, his beloved adopted country was defeated and humiliated, so his hopes for an era of national greatness and unity for Germany were dashed; second, his sense of personal identity as an ordinary soldier with an honorable vocation was destroyed, and, third, he again faced the ugly reality that at nearly thirty years of age, he was still a marginal man in a bourgeois world that he hated. "He was no further along in meeting the problems of vocation and earning a livelihood. He had no training, no work, no goal, no place to stay, no friends. In that outburst of despair, when he wept into his pillow at the news of the defeat and the revolution, he was expressing more of a personal than a national sense of loss."[44]

Hitler spent a year after the armistice drifting and vacillating before deciding to go into politics. The truth is that he was very ambivalent about a career in politics even when the catastrophic events of 1918 pushed him in that direction, in part because his middle-class prejudices against political activity made it seem rather unsavory. Moreover, he still thought of himself as being an artist by temperament and saw going into politics as, at best, a necessary detour.

The psychological processes by which Hitler constructed his new identity include the familiar tactics of self-deception. Hitler needed a sense of personal identity that would allow him not only to keep his self-respect but would also provide him with a justification for going into politics. The major threat to his self-respect was the humiliation caused by Germany's military defeat. Like any ardent nationalist, he had to find a way to deny the fact that Germany had been too weak to prevail over its enemies. Along with millions of Germans, Hitler seized upon the myth of a "stab in the back" by Jews and other traitors who had conspired to bring about a negotiated end to the war just when the German army was poised to achieve a decisive victory. The slogan Hitler used during the years he struggled to take power, "never again a November 1918," was meant to reassure people that the Nazis would never negotiate an armistice with an enemy. Of course, the fallacy behind this way of thinking was that the armistice had caused the defeat. In fact, the defeat had caused the armistice.[45] Another myth that Hitler accepted was the great superiority of enemy propaganda in demoralizing the Germans. This myth played a double role in his mind, since it fed his need to explain away the defeat and confirmed his cynical view that a national leader would have to manipulate the masses in order to wage war successfully.[46]

The new identity Hitler constructed reflects his self-absorption and egotism on the one hand and his tendency to indulge in grandiose plans and goals on the other. He became convinced that only he could lead a revolution to restore the honor of the German nation by undoing the defeat of 1918, a goal that would require going to war again, once the people had been prepared psychologically through propaganda and education. There is little doubt that during this period Hitler conceived a long-range goal to seize power, undo the Treaty of Versailles, rearm, and go to war in order to gain *Lebensraum* (living space) in the East, primarily in territory of the Soviet Union.[47] He had no detailed conception of what a utopian Aryan society would be like; he only knew that it would have no place for Jews and, at best, provide only a slave status for inferior people like Slavs. As early as 1919 Hitler was thinking explicitly about the "removal" of Jews, as demonstrated in a letter he wrote on the subject:

> Anti-Semitism on purely emotional grounds will find its ultimate expression in the form of pogroms. The anti-Semitism of reason, however, must lead to the planned judicial opposition to and elimination of the privileges of the Jews. . . . Its ultimate goal, however, must absolutely be the removal of the Jews altogether. Only a government of national power and never a government of national impotence will be capable of both.[48]

Hitler joined what was to become the National Socialist German Workers Party (the Nazis) in September 1919 and a month later experienced his first resounding success as a public speaker. This was the beginning of what was to become his spectacular success as a charismatic leader. Many commentators have observed that Hitler was such a powerful and effective political demagogue precisely because he shared the burning shame of the defeat of 1918 and the deep resentment toward the victorious Allies who dictated the harsh terms of the Treaty of Versailles that most Germans felt.[49]

By the end of 1919 Hitler had constructed his new personal identity as a political leader with a divine mission to restore the honor of his country. He also had a plan for achieving this goal. But when the military coup in 1923 in which Hitler took part failed, he made one major change in his plan. While he was in prison, he came to the conclusion that he could not succeed by using force to seize power directly, so he switched to a strategy of gaining power legally through opposition politics. The rest, as the saying goes, is history.

Assessing Hitler's Blameworthiness for His Ignorance

There is a striking consistency that runs through the psychological processes by which Hitler constructed the three conceptions of his personal identity. All three display the following features: (1) a high degree of self-absorption and egotism, (2) a lack of critical self-examination, (3) highly biased and unrealistic perception of the world around him, (4) a lack of moral virtues, and (5) the presence of several serious moral vices. Indeed, one historian has remarked that "there is no development, no maturing in Hitler's character and personality. His character was fixed at an early age—perhaps a better word would be arrested— and remains astonishingly consistent; nothing was added to it."[50]

There is at least a possibility that the development of Hitler's character was "arrested" by harmful experiences or conditions within the family over which he had no control. If this were indeed so, then Hitler would not have been entirely to blame for having developed a poor moral character. For example, some accounts of his early life mention that his father beat him frequently,[51] and this might indicate that the young Hitler was subjected to physical abuse that caused him to develop with serious defects in his character. However, most accounts tend to describe Hitler's father as having been gruff, but more bluster than bite.[52] In addition, there is ample evidence (some of which has been cited above) that Hitler's mother doted on him and that in general he led a carefree and even pampered existence as a youth. Therefore, absent specific and clear evidence to the contrary, there is justification for the conclusion that the youthful Hitler was not scarred or traumatized by physical or other kinds of abuse in the family sufficient to deprive him of the cognitive and deliberative capacities to construct his sense of personal identity in ways other than those he in fact chose. Indeed, the weight of evidence is that Adolf Hitler was throughout his life a virtuoso active constructor of his own sense of personal identity and that he is accountable for the ways in which he used his powers of agency to subvert and destroy whatever potential he had for acquiring virtue or good character.

A High Degree of Self-Absorption and Egotism

Hitler's first identity as an artist was clearly narcissistic, and his last identity as the leader destined to save his country was megalomanic. His self-absorption was mitigated (at least to some degree) only in his transitional identity as a soldier, but even then he did not develop any personal relationships with his fellow soldiers. Viewed in light of the demand for some degree of selflessness that is made by the core content of morality, especially the basic rules not to harm others, the morally stunted nature of Hitler's personality is clearly evident.

A Lack of Critical Self-Examination

There is no evidence that as an adult Hitler ever accepted responsibility for having made a mistake or having done something immoral. It is possible that by the time Hitler became an adult, he had engaged in self-deception so continuously and for so long that he truly came to lack the capacity for self-criticism; even if this is a correct assessment, however, he did not start out lacking that capacity. It was something he had to achieve through a long process of concocting rationalizations to evade taking responsibility for his actions, a practice that eventually became an ingrained habit. A complementary tactic was to blame others, which led to denigrating them as well. It was a gradual but almost inevitable process, once he had chosen to initiate it.

A Highly Biased and Unrealistic Perception of the World around Him

Reality and factual information are obstacles to the self-deceiver. Hitler's mind was always fixed on achieving some remote and lofty goal that he was supposed to realize no matter what the odds. This meant that he had always to disregard much of reality in order to keep working to attain his goal. Recall that he applied twice for admission to the art academy in Vienna and was rejected both times, but he never took any realistic steps to prepare himself for these examinations. He just assumed that he was qualified. When he was rejected, the fault had to lie with the professors at the academy. Similarly, if his adopted country had been defeated in war by its enemies, this could not be because Germany was inferior (militarily or racially) to them; the correct explanation had to involve betrayal, "a stab in the back." The closed circle of reasoning that Hitler employed in all of his self-deceptive thinking is glaringly obvious from an objective point of view. It is almost a caricature of clinical paranoid thinking: "Only I and my interests count in the world; everything else is of secondary importance or of no value. There is no possibility that I or my chief interest, Germany (my adopted home), could be wrong or at fault. Still, it is a fact that I have not succeeded and that Germany has been defeated. Therefore, there must be a hidden truth that explains why we who are really the best and deserve to win have been defeated."

The Lack of Moral Virtues

The self-deceptive evasion of acknowledging some unpleasant truth is a species of motivated irrationality, which suggests two questions: What were Hitler's motives for engaging self-deception? Were these motives good or bad? Hitler's motives for engaging in self-deception as an adolescent were different from those he had as an adult. When he was an adolescent, Hitler had three strong conscious desires that dominated his life. He desperately wanted to escape the boredom and conventionality of provincial Austria, he wanted to become someone famous and important, and he was passionately absorbed with the arts, especially music, painting, and architecture. These three desires motivated his self-deceptive construction of his earliest sense of personal identity as an artist. As noted before, self-deception is not necessarily bad; many young people have seemingly unrealistic dreams of becoming successful and famous in a profession, and such dreams often provide the motivation for undertaking realistic steps to attain such lofty goals. Hitler's self-deception, however, was not accompanied by realistic actions to attain his goal; moreover, failure did not prompt him to question his goal. Instead, he blamed others. It is fairly certain that Hitler was motivated to engage in these self-deceptive tactics of evasion by a deep and unacknowledged fear of failure and loss of status (especially in relation to the working classes in Vienna). This is a good example of how innocuous conscious motives can lead to distorted moral reasoning when they occur together with unacknowledged narcissism and cowardice. This pattern of self-deception prevailed during his six years of failure and drift in Vienna, a time that also saw him acquiring the building blocks of his political ideology — Pan-German nationalism and anti-Semitism. These doctrines gradually came to have greater and greater appeal to him because he was developing an ever greater desire for vindication and revenge against the world.

Assessing Hitler's motives for engaging in self-deception makes one thing very clear — he was virtually devoid of any form of personal attachment to others such as love, affection, friendship or communal solidarity. And there is no evidence of the virtue of benevolence. Instead he developed a streak of cruelty and vindictiveness. Needless to say, he was also sadly lacking in practical wisdom.

His conscious motives for constructing his second personal identity as a soldier were fairly straightforward. He wanted very much to bring some structure and meaning to his chaotic life, which serving in the army provided. He strongly desired all Germans to unite as one people and dominate Europe, since a triumph of German nationalism was the only way to keep the "oriental hordes" from inundating civilization. The hatred that Hitler developed for Jews, Slavs, and other people whom he considered inferior represents the dark side of his nationalism. In addition, instead of becoming buddies with his comrades at the front, he maintained his solitary aloofness and never shows a hint of "soft traits" such as benevolence.[53] Hitler's only positive traits were conscientiousness and courage in relation to his role responsibilities as a courier. However, it is safe to assume that even in these cases his unacknowledged narcissism provided much of the motivation.

By the time Hitler constructed his final personal identity as a political leader, his self-deception had long ago become a trait of his character, that is, a vice. This accounts for his rigidity, dogmatism, cruelty, and fanaticism both as leader of the Nazi Party during the years of struggle to gain power and as Führer and Reich Chancellor from 1934 on. There were no new motives at work in the construction of this final personal identity, but his conception of himself had become incomparably more grandiose and megalomanic and his goals were now of world-historical magnitude. Thus the bad consequences of his utter lack of both benevolence and practical wisdom, plus the presence of hatred and cruelty, now became catastrophic. He single-mindedly and intentionally started World War II, in which millions of people died,[54] and he ordered the implementation of the Holocaust.

Hitler's lack of the virtues was demonstrated in his attitude toward the German people in early 1945, when they faced invasion, certain defeat, and occupation by the Soviet Union and the western Allies. True to his social Darwinist views, Hitler told Albert Speer that because the Germans had proven to be the weaker party in the war, he no longer had any obligation to worry about their welfare. Thus he ordered a scorched-earth policy to destroy all the remaining infrastructure so that it could not be used by the enemy.[55] This would have brought immeasurably great additional suffering on ordinary Germans. Hitler's "love for the German people" was finally revealed for what it had always been: not a humane concern for the well-being of individual persons but a love of power and the desire to use that power to wreak revenge.

The Presence of Serious Moral Vices

If this analysis of the way in which Hitler constructed his sense of personal identity over the course of a dozen years or so is even close to the truth, then it appears that he almost single-handedly used his powers of agency to subvert his own moral development to become one of the worst perpetrators of evil in human history. It may seem superfluous at this point to draw up a list of Hitler's vices, but it is necessary for an adequate appreciation of what his enormous project of self-deception accomplished. There was nothing inevitable about Hitler's awful development; rather, it was the cumulative result of particular wrong choices that he made over the years. As one historian has noted, the evil of the adult Hitler is not found in the adolescent. "Instead of evil there is groping futility, perhaps an occasional note of defiance, but predominantly a desire to escape the world of hard realities into a world of romance colored by majestic art and sonorous music."[56] Reasons have already been given for rejecting the view that Hitler lacked capacity responsibility (whether because of the alleged pernicious effect of socialization in a bad political culture or because of abuse in his family) as an explanation for his escapism and bad moral character.

Hitler's moral vices include, first, his monumental egotism and self-absorption. In terms of virtue ethics, Hitler's megalomania was a vice in relation to the virtue of justified self-respect; his biased assessment of his own importance and moral worth was totally unjustified. In order to maintain this distorted view of his own worth, he had to engage in continuous self-deception. The more his self-deception served to justify wrongdoing and bad character, the more it became a vice. That Hitler developed only a meager capacity for personal attachments of any kind is the most likely explanation for many observers' sense that his development was arrested in some way. However, his own active construction of his sense of personal identity accounts for so much that is vicious in him, especially his hatred. His cruelty was not just the absence of benevolence but a positively bad trait: finding satisfaction and intrinsic value in humiliating, hurting, or killing others (or in having them killed).

In conclusion, Hitler was to a very great extent blameworthy for his "ignorance" about the nature of his wrong acts as chief perpetrator of the Holocaust. This is because his ignorance was the result of his nearly lifelong project of self-deception in which he chose to engage rather than deal honestly with the unwelcome realities he faced. Hence his ignorance was culpable ignorance. Objectively, Hitler had no one to blame but himself.

Hitler's Blameworthiness for His Wrong Acts as Chief Perpetrator of the Holocaust

If Hitler's ignorance was culpable, then he had no excuse for his horrendously evil acts as the chief perpetrator of the Holocaust. We have returned to where we began, namely, with the commonsense moral intuition that Hitler was to blame for his wrong acts, but with a much better understanding why that intuition is indeed correct.

However, we should also appreciate why our initial intuition might have been mistaken. This is of equal importance because it is very likely that most people blame Hitler for his role in the Holocaust, not because they understand the reasons why he deserves blame but because they automatically assumed that he, like everyone else, had sufficient capacity to know right from wrong, that he knew that genocide was wrong but did it anyway. In other words, many people have an "intuition" based on a simplified cartoonlike caricature of Hitler that ignores or obscures most of what is known about him that makes him so puzzling and challenging to our moral understanding. The fact that the "intuition" happens to hit on the correct conclusion that he is blameworthy is thus very misleading because it does not really get to the heart of the matter: Hitler's responsibility for becoming the person he was through an active project of self-deception. The approach that I have used makes room for the possibility that someone who does wrong (even catastrophic wrong) may not be to blame for it. In the case of Hitler's perpetration of the Holocaust, this possibility can be reasonably rejected (or so I have argued). It is possible however, for the evidence to support the conclusion that a perpetrator is not blameworthy; in that case there are moral reasons for justified excuses.

There is little reason to view Hitler as a victim of mental illness or childhood abuse who had no control over the defects in his character. He was a very unhappy youth, an alienated and frustrated adult man, and his life ended as a complete disaster. But there are many good reasons for concluding that he brought nearly all of it on himself.

Notes

1. Jackson J. Spielvogel, *Hitler and Nazi Germany: A History* (Englewood Cliffs, N.J.: Prentice-Hall, 1992), chap. 9.
2. Spielvogel, *Hitler and Nazi Germany,* 116–120.
3. Spielvogel, *Hitler and Nazi Germany,* 123, quoting Helmut Heiber.

4. Ian Kershaw, *Hitler* (New York: Longman, 1991), chap. 6.

5. Spielvogel, *Hitler and Nazi Germany,* 218–221.

6. Omer Bartov, *Hitler's Army: Soldiers, Nazis, and War in the Third Reich* (New York: Oxford University Press, 1991), chaps. 2–3.

7. Spielvogel, *Hitler and Nazi Germany,* 270–274.

8. Daniel Jonah Goldhagen, *Hitler's Willing Executioners: Ordinary Germans and the Holocaust* (New York: Knopf, 1996), 164.

9. Spielvogel, *Hitler and Nazi Germany,* 274–276; Raul Hilberg, *The Destruction of the European Jews* (New York: Holmes & Meier, 1985), 2:398–407.

10. Ernst Klee, Willi Dressen, and Volker Riess, *The "Good Old Days": The Holocaust as Seen by Its Perpetrators and Bystanders* (New York: Free Press, 1988); Christopher Browning, *Ordinary Men: Reserve Police Battalion 101 and the Final Solution in Poland* (New York: HarperCollins, 1992); Goldhagen, *Hitler's Willing Executioners.*

11. Spielvogel, *Hitler and Nazi Germany,* 276–80.

12. Hilberg, *Destruction of the European Jews,* 1:ix–x.

13. Spielvogel, *Hitler and Nazi Germany,* 115–116.

14. Hilberg, *Destruction of the European Jews,* 1:281.

15. Gerald Fleming, *Hitler and the Final Solution* (Berkeley: University of California Press, 1984); Hilberg, *Destruction of the European Jews,* 3:1000.

16. Telford Taylor, *Nuremberg and Vietnam: An American Tragedy* (Chicago: Quandrangle, 1970), 52–53.

17. Steven T. Katz, *The Holocaust in Historical Context,* vol. 1, *The Holocaust and Mass Death before the Modern Age* (New York: Oxford University Press, 1994), chaps. 3–4; Berel Lang, *Act and Idea in the Nazi Genocide* (Chicago: University of Chicago Press, 1990), chap. 1.

18. Lang, *Act and Idea,* chaps. 1–2, defends the view that Hitler knew that killing the Jews was evil and ordered the genocide because it was evil.

19. Sebastian Haffner, *The Meaning of Hitler* (Cambridge: Harvard University Press, 1979), 17–19.

20. John Lukacs, *The Hitler of History* (New York: Knopf, 1997), 44.

21. Haffner, *Meaning of Hitler,* 7.

22. Spielvogel, *Hitler and Nazi Germany,* 140–143.

23. John Weiss, *Ideology of Death: Why the Holocaust Happened in Germany* (Chicago: Ivan R. Dee, 1996), chaps. 11–12.

24. Bradley F. Smith, *Adolf Hitler: His Family, Childhood, and Youth* (Stanford, Calif.: Hoover Institution, 1967), chap. 5, "Early Youth."

25. Smith, *Adolf Hitler,* 87–88.

26. Smith, *Adolf Hitler,* 100.

27. Smith, *Adolf Hitler,* 101–104.

28. Smith, *Adolf Hitler,* 109.

29. Smith, *Adolf Hitler,* 109.

30. Smith, *Adolf Hitler,* 110.

31. Smith, *Adolf Hitler,* 116–122.

32. Smith, *Adolf Hitler,* 142.

33. Smith, *Adolf Hitler,* 122–132.

34. Haffner, *Meaning of Hitler,* 7.

35. Haffner, *Meaning of Hitler,* 9.
36. Smith, *Adolf Hitler,* 147–150; Haffner, *Meaning of Hitler,* 8–10.
37. Smith, *Adolf Hitler,* 149–150.
38. Joachim C. Fest, *Hitler* (San Diego: Harcourt Brace Jovanovich, 1974), 64.
39. Fest, *Hitler,* 67–79.
40. Smith, *Adolf Hitler,* 9. One historian calls his chapter on Hitler's war years "Redemption by War" (Fest, *Hitler,* chap. 5).
41. Fest, *Hitler,* 68.
42. Haffner, *Meaning of Hitler,* 4.
43. Fest, *Hitler,* 78.
44. Fest, *Hitler,* 79.
45. Haffner, *Meaning of Hitler,* 12–13.
46. Fest, *Hitler,* 74.
47. Fest, *Hitler,* 607; Haffner, *Meaning of Hitler,* 12.
48. Fest, *Hitler,* 114.
49. Spielvogel, *Hitler and Nazi Germany,* 26–28.
50. Haffner, *Meaning of Hitler,* 7.
51. Weiss, *Ideology of Death,* 192.
52. Smith, *Adolf Hitler,* 44–45.
53. Haffner, *Meaning of Hitler,* 7.
54. Fest, *Hitler,* 607.
55. Fest, *Hitler,* 733.
56. Smith, *Adolf Hitler,* 8.

Suggestions for Further Reading

Fest, Joachim. *Hitler.* San Diego: Harcourt Brace Jovanovich, 1974. The best long biography of Hitler.

Haffner, Sebastian. *The Meaning of Hitler.* Cambridge: Harvard University Press, 1979. The best short biography of Hitler.

Hilberg, Raul. *Perpetrators Victims Bystanders: The Jewish Catastrophe, 1933–1945.* New York: HarperCollins, 1992. See especially "Adolf Hitler," pages 1–19.

Lukacs, John. *The Hitler of History.* New York: Knopf, 1997. A study of the many different ways in which Hitler has been viewed by historians.

Redlich, Fritz. *Hitler: Diagnosis of a Destructive Prophet.* New York: Oxford University Press, 1998. Redlich, a M.D. and forensic psychiatrist, argues that the available medical and psychiatric evidence on Hitler's health does not explain his personality or his evil deeds.

Rosenbaum, Ron. *Explaining Hitler: The Search for the Origins of His Evil.* New York: Random House, 1998. An excellent philosophically sophisticated study of the many different psychological theories about Hitler's personality and character.

Smith, Bradley F. *Adolf Hitler: His Family, Childhood and Youth.* Stanford, Calif.: Hoover Institution, 1967. Indispensable for the early years of Hitler's life.

Spielvogel, Jackson J. *Hitler and Nazi Germany.* 3d ed. Englewood Cliffs, N.J.: Prentice-Hall, 1996. Chapter 5, "The Dictator," an excellent psychological and intellectual portrait, is nevertheless marred by some speculative and reductive Freudian and Jungian theories.

Chapter 7

Perpetrators: The Men in Police Battalions

Ordinary Germans served in police battalions that (under the control of the SS) took part in the Final Solution, principally by conducting outdoor mass shootings of Jews in Poland and the Soviet Union. The men who served in these outdoor killing units present a challenge to our attempts to understand the motivation of perpetrators. Unlike the voluntary members of the Nazi Party and the SS, most of the men in the police battalions were draftees who had not been given intensive ideological indoctrination. When they were initiated into killing operations in the field such as that at Josefow in Poland in 1942, they had not been brutalized by prior combat. Yet the great majority of them took part in the killing willingly, inflicting cruelty and humiliation on their victims before they killed them. Indeed, these men repeatedly engaged in extensive and gruesome acts of mass killing over a period of several years during the Holocaust.[1] These brutal killings were clear and flagrant violations of what amounts to a virtual moral taboo: the basic moral prohibition not to kill defenseless and harmless people, especially women and children, without any provocation.

The men in police battalions have been the subject of several scholarly studies in recent years that have provided us with a great deal of information about them and their activities.[2] These studies do not cover all police battalions, and they should not be used to make generalizations about the men who served in these kinds of units. Nevertheless, they give us some important facts about the motives and actions of one major kind of perpetrator that can help us to gain a better understanding of the nature and complexity of the Final Solution. All references to the men in police battalions are meant to apply only to those who served in the particular battalions that were the subjects of these recent studies, most notably Police Battalion 101.

The psychological puzzle presented by the actions of these men may be highlighted by contrasting them with other perpetrators who came to the task as already convinced Nazi ideologues or having been given intensive ideological indoctrination and training, including SS men in Einsatzgruppen, SS men in the

145

killing centers, Hitler and other Nazi leaders, and ordinary Germans who served in institutions that provided logistical support.

All men who were selected to serve in the SS outdoor killing units (Einsatzgruppen) had initially joined the SS voluntarily. In addition to the normal ideological indoctrination given to all new members, they had received additional indoctrination and training to explain their special role (defined as killing "partisans, commissars, and Jews") in the planned invasion of the Soviet Union.[3] Although these SS men had to engage in the same kind of gruesome direct killing that the men in the police battalions performed, they were generally much better prepared psychologically because they had joined the SS voluntarily and had received extensive training. By contrast, despite being under the control of the SS, nearly all of the men who served in police battalions were draftees who received hardly any ideological training.[4]

The number of SS men who served in the killing centers was relatively small compared to the approximately 3,000 SS men who served in the Einsatzgruppen. Nevertheless, like their counterparts in the Einsatzgruppen, they received the normal amount of SS ideological training. They too can be contrasted with the men in police battalions, since they were also somewhat prepared by inclination and SS indoctrination to engage in direct killing.

In chapter 6 I took an in-depth look at Hitler's motivation and his central role as a perpetrator; a study of other Nazi leaders would yield similar results. They were mostly all fanatical anti-Semites who were true believers in the Final Solution. Since they did not engage in direct killing, they had no psychological problems such as physical revulsion to overcome, so there is no difficulty in believing that they could readily approve of and direct the genocidal operations.

Finally, there is no puzzle in understanding how the thousands of German perpetrators who did not engage directly in the killing were able to participate willingly. The great majority of these bureaucratic perpetrators were far removed from the actual killings, so even if they had some moral qualms about the enterprise in which they were engaged, at least they did not have the heavy psychological burden of participating in face-to-face killing in outdoor operations. Even if they served in a killing center like Auschwitz, they might well escape duty in the installations that housed the gas chambers and crematoria. For most of them, it was probably easy to use self-deception to evade the full truth about the genocide and their role in it. Of course, many of these "desk murderers" had no need for self-deception because they too believed that the Final Solution was justified; for example, if they belonged to the Nazi Party or the SS or they held deeply anti-Semitic beliefs as a matter of personal conviction, they very likely would have looked on their participation as a matter of moral duty.

The reasons for selecting the men who served in police battalions as the focus of this chapter on ordinary German perpetrators should now be clear. Most of them were draftees, not volunteers; they participated in killing before they had been brutalized by combat; they had not been given intensive ideological indoctrination, and yet they participated in directly killing large numbers of defenseless and harmless Jews in gruesome outdoor operations, thereby violating a basic moral prohibition. Although this discussion focuses on the men in police battalions, it includes relevant observations about the actions and motives of perpetrators in other categories for comparison and contrast. Such comparison is especially necessary in the evaluation of alternative explanations, since often a particular explanation that can be readily applied to one category, say, impersonal bureaucrats, is not at all applicable to shooters in outdoor, face-to-face killing operations.

Blameworthiness will be assessed after consideration of a number of competing hypotheses that are intended to explain the actions and motives of the men in the police battalions. A clear distinction must be made between factual/empirical questions about what the men did and why they did it, on the one hand, and ethical/normative questions about the wrongness of their acts and their blameworthiness for having done them, on the other. Our first task is to try to identify the explanation (or set of explanations) that is most likely to be true, given the available evidence. I will then propose a synthesis of several of the most likely explanatory factors that, taken together, explain the widest range of evidence. Only then will we turn to the ethical questions.

Two Kinds of Explanations for Actions: Situational and Dispositional

Historians and psychologists tend to use one of two explanations to analyze why an individual or a group acts in a specific way on a particular occasion. A *situational explanation* accounts for an action by appealing to characteristics of the situation in which it is performed. If it is a complete explanation, then the characteristics appealed to are sufficient to account for the behavior being explained; they constitute "the cause." For example, the genocidal killing performed by the men in police battalions might be explained solely by appealing to the fact that they were under coercion, such as facing dire punishment if they refused to follow orders. If this contention is correct, the participation of the men is fully accounted for by the situation in which they acted, namely, being on active military duty and under orders backed by a credible threat of punishment. Taken as a whole, the characteristics of this situation were sufficient to induce the men to obey; furthermore, any other group of psychologically normal men would behave in much the same way because the vast majority of men do not want to die and thus are extremely unlikely to refuse an order in those circumstances. The distinguishing feature of this kind of explanation is that it succeeds independently of any suppositions about the men as individuals other than that they are psychologically normal. There is no need to look for unusual individual psychological characteristics in the men to explain what happened. Given the situation, obedience is what could be predicted to happen.

By contrast, a *dispositional explanation* might explain the men's participation by appealing to individual psychological characteristics such as strongly held anti-Semitism. In order to present the contrast with the situational explanation in its sharpest form, I shall assume that in this case the men's participation is fully accounted for by their individual trait of anti-Semitism; the situation had nothing to do with it. Let us suppose, for example, that participation was completely voluntary in that men could ask to be excused if they so desired. With these assumptions, the dispositional explanation is a complete explanation of the men's participation, and there is no need to look for any unusual characteristics in the situation. In that case, "the cause" of their participation is their anti-Semitism.

Often the complete explanation of a particular action or set of actions appeals to both situational and dispositional factors. Indeed, one plausible (though not necessarily true) explanation of the participation of men in police battalions in genocidal killing would appeal both to the situational fact that they were coerced and to the dispositional fact that they were anti-Semitic, neither factor being sufficient alone. Furthermore, from a scientific point of view, neither kind of explanation has any logical priority over the other; both are equally respectable. There is, however, a pragmatic dimension to the human inquiry; we are not completely neutral investigators, first, because our values and interests influence our choice of subjects that we deem in need of explanation, and, second, because we often care very much about what the correct explanation turns out to be. It is largely for these pragmatic reasons that the distinction between situational and dispositional explanations takes on significance in the study of the Holocaust.

One fundamental question runs through virtually all historical and psychological studies of the Holocaust: What explains genocidal killing of defenseless men, women, and children, especially on such a massive scale? Because such killing violates a virtual moral taboo the question cries out for an answer. This is an unavoidable pragmatic dimension of inquiry into the Holocaust; we are not neutral in making it a subject of inquiry. Moreover, for a variety of reasons, most people care deeply about what the true explanation turns out to be. The distinction between situational and dispositional explanations is especially relevant to the study of the Holocaust. Everything else being equal, a situational explanation tends to shift the burden of responsibility away from the perpetrators whose actions are being explained; correspondingly, dispositional explanations tend to shift the burden toward them. I am not asserting that situational explanations always excuse and dispositional ones always incriminate. That would be too simple. However, a situational explanation (one that purports to be a complete one, at any rate), in effect, identifies some feature of the situation as "the cause" of immoral behavior, thus tending to absolve the individuals whose behavior is being explained. At the very least, there is an implication that they behaved no better or worse than any other group of men would in the same circumstances, and this has obvious implications for their comparative blameworthiness. In sharp contrast, dispositional explanations for wrongful acts are likely to identify traits of individual perpetrators as "the cause," thus increasing the likelihood that they are blameworthy.

It would be naïve to assume that this difference between the two explanations plays no role in the continuing intellectual debate about the best explanation for why perpetrators participated in genocidal killing; however, we should not become cynical about the motives of investigators who tend to prefer one kind over the other. Potential pitfalls are associated with each kind of explanation.

I cited examples of both kinds of explanation in chapter 5. A main point to keep in mind is the interaction between the individual and the situation. The Bad Political Culture Thesis (BPC) is a good example of a situational explanation, even though the "situation" is an aspect of the society as a whole. According to BPC, a bad political culture plays the role of the situation, which allegedly explains the fact that individuals who are socialized into it suffer from diminished capacity, which in turn explains why these individuals perform certain wrong actions. By contrast, the active learner model of how socialization works assumes that most individuals play an active role in constructing their sense of personal identity and that, as a consequence, socialization does not in fact always have the kind of consistent effects that are postulated by the situational explanation at the heart of BPC. Consequently, if we are to understand the actions of millions of Germans, all of whom were exposed to varying degrees of socialization in the majority's bad political culture but differ greatly from each other as individuals (as any large population in a modern society is bound to do), we have to look for a variety of dispositional explanations to help explain their actions. The discussion of Hitler's active self-construction of his own personal identity in chapter 6 consists, almost entirely, of a series of individual dispositional explanations.

The two main tasks of this chapter are, first, to critically evaluate competing explanations for the actions of the men in police battalions and, second, to assess their blameworthiness for those actions in the light of the best explanation.

The Principal Situational Explanations
for Perpetrators' Wrong Actions

Two situational explanations that have been mentioned already—ideological indoctrination and brutalization in combat—can be excluded because they clearly do not apply to the men in police battalions. The great majority of these men were new draftees, not volunteers; moreover, they had received only perfunctory ideological indoctrination before they were sent on outdoor killing operations;[5] furthermore, they had not been in combat before. Nevertheless, almost all of them participated in the gruesome killing actions, which included shooting individual men, women, and children at close range in the back of the neck as they lay by the edge of burial pits. In the process, the men would become covered with spattered blood, brain matter, and bone splinters.[6] There are, however, several other situational explanations that deserve closer scrutiny.

Bureaucratic Segmentation of the Task

This situational explanation is often used to explain the participation of perpetrators who worked in large and impersonal institutions involved in implementing the Final Solution. For example, railroad planners who scheduled the trains that transported the victims to killing centers performed an essential task without which the mass killings probably could not have been carried out. Because they worked in a central office far removed from the scenes of death, these planners could easily evade acknowledging their essential contribution to the genocide by engaging in tactics of self-deception.[7] They could rationalize that the Jews were really being sent to the "East" to work in labor camps (the cover story put out by the Reich Ministry for Propaganda), or they could convince themselves that they really did not know for sure what was happening to them. By keeping themselves in a (culpable) state of ignorance, they could maintain an attitude of cool professional impersonality and discharge their institutional role responsibilities efficiently and conscientiously. The segmentation of the genocidal task produced a diffusion of responsibility that made it all too easy to avoid explicit awareness of (or inquiry into) the lethal nature of the process. Much the same could be said for a wide range of so-called desk murderers, including judges who decided who was legally a Jew, police who conducted roundups for deportation, and manufacturers of Zyklon B, the gas used for extermination in Auschwitz. Although it took all of these people to perpetrate the Holocaust, no one in particular felt responsible for the killing. It seems very plausible that in fact many German perpetrators used self-deceptive tactics like these to avoid feeling guilty about what they were doing and that these tactics were facilitated psychologically by the bureaucratic structures in which they worked. So this situational explanation correctly describes an important aspect of the process by which the Final Solution was carried out.

The question remains whether this explanation could withstand critical scrutiny as an ethically justified excuse or mitigating circumstance for the blameworthiness of impersonal bureaucrats, but it is seems fairly clear that it is irrelevant to explaining the actions of the men in the police battalions. Outdoor, face-to-face killing operations were not "fragmented tasks." The killers were confronted directly with killing the victims and became immersed in blood and gore; short of psychotic denial, there was no possibility for self-deception about the physical nature of one's deeds. Therefore, we can exclude this particular kind of situational explanation from consideration in our inquiry. (Of course, the men in police battalions performed other duties besides killing Jews. For example, some of them participated in certain tasks assigned to their units, such as rounding up Jews who were to be shot, but refrained from the shooting itself. However, this hardly constitutes the kind of fragmentation of a task that this explanation envisages.)

The Coercive Nature of Military Orders

It is perhaps not surprising that this situational explanation was used by most of the men in police battalions themselves. If they killed only, or primarily, because they were coerced by the threat of severe punishment for refusal to obey an official order, their participation might well be justifiably excused, or at least blame would be greatly mitigated. They could justifiably claim that they "had no choice" in the normative/ethical sense. It would have been unreasonable and unfair to require them to disobey an order under a threat of, say, execution or being sent to a concentration camp. Since many of them faced the possibility of postwar German trials, they had every reason to offer this explanation for their participation when they were interrogated in pretrial investigations.[8] Some of these men may well have convinced themselves through self-deception that they were in fact coerced and had no choice but to participate. However, most historians now agree that the evidence does not support this explanation. Christopher Browning states the consensus among historians:

> Quite simply, in the past forty-five years no defense attorney or defendant in any of the hundreds of postwar trials has been able to document a single case in which refusal to obey an order to kill unarmed civilians resulted in the allegedly dire punishment. The punishment or censure that occasionally did result from such disobedience was never commensurate with the gravity of the crimes the men had been asked to commit.[9]

If they were disciplined at all, the men who refused to participate might be transferred or given alternative onerous duty of some kind. A variation on the coercion explanation, so-called putative duress, is that the men sincerely believed (mistakenly) that they would be severely punished if they refused to participate in the killing, and this false belief is what explains their participation.[10] This explanation is not supported by evidence either; in fact, there is some evidence that Heinrich Himmler, the head of the SS that had police battalions under its control, granted a dispensation to all men who chose not to participate in the killing, and it is likely that this policy was communicated not only to all officers but to most of the men as well. In addition, a study of Police Battalion

101 shows that few men put in for a transfer to other duty and that the few applications that were made were granted.[11]

The official leniency of Himmler and other Nazis in charge of the Final Solution toward men who asked not to take part in the mass killings does not fit the image of authoritarian Germans expecting unquestioning and disciplined obedience to all orders. Indeed, the regular German army executed some 15,000 men for infractions of discipline during World War II.[12] Why did Nazi leaders like Himmler have a lenient attitude toward men who asked to be excused from killing? We can gain some insight into the reasons for this by studying the perverted moral psychology and distorted conception of moral virtues that they used when thinking about the nature of what they were doing. Even though Nazi leaders were utterly convinced by their ideology that killing the Jews was completely justified, they believed that most Germans still suffered from the "weaknesses" of "Christian morality" (as Himmler put it),[13] that is, moral scruples that were the "lingering effect of two thousand years of Western morality and ethics" that would have to be overcome.[14] Moreover, some of the Nazi leaders recognized that many ordinary Germans participating in the slaughter were in danger of being turned into either "neurotics" or "monsters," so precautions would have to be taken to prevent these psychological problems. No doubt the policy of leniency toward men who asked not to participate in the killing was, at least in part, the result of the official view that this was "weakness," not insubordination. A similar distinction was drawn between killing pursuant to an order (in which case a soldier was deemed to have overcome the "weakness" of "Christian morality" in order to do his duty) and killing that was induced by desire (which, by contrast, was seen as a lapse caused by one's own baseness). The distinction can be seen at work in the advisory opinion of a judge on Himmler's staff regarding the procedure to be followed in the case of unauthorized killing of Jews by SS personnel.

> He concluded that if purely political motives prompted the killing, if the act was an expression of idealism, no punishment was necessary unless the maintenance of order required disciplinary action or prosecution. However, if selfish, sadistic, or sexual motives were found, punishment was to be imposed for murder or manslaughter, in accordance with the facts.[15]

According to this Nazi psychology of morals, a conscientious soldier should kill unarmed Jews when ordered to do so, but if he asked to be relieved because of a "weakness" due to outdated Christian morality, he would be excused! By contrast, a soldier who perpetrated an unauthorized killing from base desires or motives should be punished for murder or manslaughter, but if he killed from a motive of political idealism, he, too, could be excused.[16]

In conclusion, most of the men who served in police battalions were not coerced into killing Jews by the threat of dire punishment for refusal to obey military orders. If they had any excuse or mitigating circumstance for their actions, it must be based on other considerations.

Obedience Out of Respect for Authority

The explanation that the men in police battalions participated in killing Jews out of respect for authority, not out of fear of punishment, seems plausible because authoritarianism was a salient feature of the political culture in Germany at the time. Indeed, authoritarianism by definition is a trait consisting of deference to authorities perceived to be established and legitimate, together with aggressiveness directed against targets sanctioned by these authorities and a high degree of adherence to social conventions. It seems quite probable that most of the men in police battalions would perceive their military superiors to be established and legitimate, would be aggressive toward Jews, Gypsies, and other targets of official hostility, and would have some degree of conventional German anti-Semitism. This explanation is primarily situational in nature because it assumes that all individuals (in this case men in police battalions) bring their authoritarian trait of obedience to the situation. It is the situation (defined by a military institution, with hierarchical rankings, official orders, military discipline, and a publicly shared sense of legitimacy) that triggers the obedient behavior. Had they not been in that particular kind of situation, they would not have killed. This way of explaining the obedience of the men is grounded in the particulars of German history and culture, and this gives it an advantage over ahistorical universal explanations drawn from experimental psychology.

As an example of the latter, we can consider the well-known obedience experiments conducted by psychologist Stanley Milgram. They are often cited in discussions of German participation in genocidal killing because some of Milgram's findings seem to confirm the conclusion that virtually all humans have a propensity to obey those whom they perceive to be legitimate authorities, even if this requires them to violate moral norms.[17] The initial experiment used naïve subjects who were told they were taking part in a scientific experiment to study the effects of punishment on learning. In actuality, the "learning experiment" was bogus; the real experiment was to see how long the naïve subjects would continue to administer what they believed to be increasingly stronger electric shocks after each error made by the "learner" (a confederate of the experimenter who provided convincing feedback in the form of ever more vehement crying out in "pain," calls for help, demands that the experiment be stopped, and, finally, just silence). The naïve subjects were under no coercive threats; they were only instructed as to their proper role in the "experiment." The surprising result was that two-thirds of the subjects continued to obey by administering shocks up to the maximum level (ostensibly 450 volts), despite the horrendous protests of the "learner" and their own belief that they were in fact administering painful and potentially dangerous shocks. That the naïve subjects were convinced they were really inflicting severe pain is shown by the fact that most of them exhibited obvious emotional stress and many begged the "experimenter" to stop. Yet two-thirds of them continued to give the shocks. This result is deeply disturbing, and Milgram himself offered several explanations for so many people's willingness to obey to the end.

The explanations he offered include the following: that (1) there is an evolutionary bias that favors adaptability to social hierarchies and organized activity, (2) people tend to continue to administer shocks because they have volunteered for the experiment, (3) people accept the legitimacy of science in general because its purpose is good, (4) people accept the purpose of the "psychological experiment" in particular for the same reason, (5) people are reluctant to disobey or question the instructions to continue because they have been socialized to defer to superior authority, and they would be embarrassed to object, and (6) people tend to see themselves as agents of the scientific experimenter who has the responsibility for the safety and well-being of the learner.[18]

Milgram also devised a number of ingenious variations in the design of his obedience experiments that used actor/collaborators together with naïve subjects to ascertain the effect of peer pressure on conformity. He discovered that peer pressure could either reinforce obedience or bolster an individual's capacity to resist authority, depending on the opinions expressed by the actor/collaborators.[19] I shall return to the question of the role played by peer pressure later.

There can be little doubt that the disturbing results of Milgram's obedience experiments are relevant for gaining some understanding of how people in general are capable of following orders to harm, and even kill, others. However, there are good reasons for being skeptical about drawing direct parallels with the participation in genocidal killing by men in the police battalions. Although Milgram sometimes compared the behavior of the subjects in his experiments to the behavior of Germans in the Final Solution, he himself explicitly noted some of the important differences between them. His subjects were all volunteers, they were explicitly assured that they would not cause the "learner" any permanent physical injury, and they were not indoctrinated into an ideology that devalued the "learner."[20] Additionally, both the "learner" and the "teacher" were assigned their roles by a (rigged) drawing at the beginning of the experiment; thus, there was no reason for the subject who was assigned the role of teacher to assume anything whatever about the other person who (it appeared) had been assigned the role of learner by chance.

Moreover, the peacetime social context of an American university in which the experiments were conducted differed enormously from that in which the men in the police battalions had to choose whether or not to participate in genocidal killing. They were serving in the military in wartime, operating out of doors, rounding up hundreds of unarmed Jews either in occupied Poland or in the Soviet Union, whom they were then ordered to kill, often one-on-one, including women and children. Milgram's findings are relevant to explanations for the actions of these men, but only in an indirect way. They provide empirical confirmation of the general conclusion that people can more easily be induced to obey orders to harm, and even kill, their fellow human beings than common sense is likely to admit. However, that general conclusion sheds no light on the particular reasons why these men came to participate in mass genocidal killing.[21]

There is one good, historically grounded clue that at least helps explain the participation in genocidal killing by the men in police battalions, namely, that they were all subjected to varying levels of socialization into German political culture, the salient features of which included not only authoritarianism (already noted) but also anti-Semitism and an especially virulent version of nationalism. I shall argue that these features lead us to an explanation that is not only historically grounded and plausible but seems very likely to be correct, all things considered. Or so I shall argue.

Peer Pressure

An appeal to peer pressure functions as a situational explanation; it purports to explain the fact that particular individuals acted in a certain way by showing that they were situated in a peer group that exerted psychological pressure on them. Milgram found that peer pressure or conformity can influence the choice to obey an order or not, even when the "peers" were only randomly selected temporary collaborators in an experiment. Peer pressure from a relatively anonymous group of people in a crowd can have the same kind of effect on an individual's behavior. What this shows is that people are very sensitive to the presence of bystanders and to how others view their behavior. However, peer pressure can affect individuals only if (1) they get information about the attitudes of their peers (from their behavior, from what they say, or from some independent source) and (2) they care about what those peers will think or do as a consequence of the choice they make. We need to look more closely at the different ways in which people "care" about what others will think or do. There is a relatively shallow kind of "care" that people have to keep up appearances in public places in front of anonymous audiences; the main purpose of this kind of concern is to avoid embarrassment. Most people usually want to remain anonymous and free from the close scrutiny of others, not to preserve their self-respect but just to avoid momentary discomfiture. This kind of care is usually quite impersonal, since there are no ongoing relationships that need to be sustained with such "peers." Moreover, it need not be altruistic and, in fact, it is usually quite innocently self-centered. Presumably it was this kind of care that was at work in Milgram's experiments to ascertain the effect of peer pressure; the naïve subjects did not want to "make waves" or "stand out" even in the relatively small group of collaborators who function as the peer group in such a setting.

Peer pressure or conformity that involves this shallow kind of care about what others will think or do must be distinguished from peer pressure that involves other, deeper kinds of care that include mutual feelings of benevolence between individuals such as love, affection, friendship, and communal solidarity. Being forms of benevolence, they involve some degree of care for the well-being of other persons for their own sake. The deeper kind of peer pressure typically occurs among people who are engaged in a cooperative activity for mutual benefit who have learned to trust each other and begin to reap the rewards of reciprocity. The psychology of this deeper kind of peer pressure is correspondingly more complex, since individuals respond to this kind of "pressure" for reasons other than merely wanting to avoid momentary discomfiture or embarrassment for themselves. There is, first of all, their ongoing, mutual relationship with their "peers," for whom they feel respect, love, or friendship, and from whom they receive a corresponding kind of care and respect in return. Consequently, individuals responding to this deeper kind of peer pressure are concerned to keep the care and respect of their peers by acting in a way that they believe the peers deserve to be treated, given their ongoing relationship with them; this is quite different from merely wanting to avoid momentary discomfiture or embarrassment in front of an anonymous audience. Moreover, the individuals want to keep the respect of their peers because they know and generally share the standards of conduct that their peers hold. Correspondingly, a performance that responds to this deeper kind of peer pressure is motivated by a desire to earn the respect of one's peers because it is deemed worth having for its own sake. Finally, individuals who respond to this kind of peer pressure desire to keep their own self-respect; they want to be able to think well of themselves, which is clearly different from wanting to avoid public embarrassment.

Both the shallow and deeper kinds of peer pressure may have been at work in the actions of the men in police battalions, but there are good reasons for thinking that it was most likely a form of the deeper kind, involving strong feelings of comradeship, that played the greater role. Throughout history, armies have relied heavily on the bonds of friendship and loyalty among individual soldiers in order to maintain discipline, and great care is taken to foster this familiar kind of social bonding within small units during basic training. The official ideology or political theory that provides the justification for going to war differs from country to country, but in any army, what most often provides the strongest motivation for ordinary soldiers to risk their lives and obey orders to kill is their feeling of loyalty to their buddies:

> What really enables men to fight is their own self-respect, and a special kind of love that has nothing to do with sex or idealism. Very few men have died in battle, when the moment actually arrived, for the United States of America or for the sacred cause of Communism, or even for their homes and families; if they had any choice in the matter at all, they chose to die for each other and for their own vision of themselves.[22]

In the German army during World War II, recruits were socialized to regard their unit (the "primary group") as a "family" or "home" that took care of them and toward which they developed a sense of belonging. Junior officers in the Wehrmacht even addressed their men as *Kinder* (children). As it so happened, this very powerful force for cohesion was drastically reduced on the eastern front because of the extremely high attrition rates, and intensive ideological indoctrination was used to compensate for it.[23] Since there was no such problem for the men in the police battalions, it seems reasonable to assume that they, like soldiers nearly everywhere, developed strong bonds of comradeship and loyalty among themselves, especially at the platoon or squad level. Comradeship of this kind could easily give rise to a deep form of peer pressure.

Were the feelings of comradeship among the men in police battalions sufficient to cause them to obey orders to kill unarmed and defenseless Jews one-on-one? If nothing else were known about the beliefs and values of the men except that a strong sense of comradeship existed among them, the answer would probably be no. After all, it could be assumed that these men would realize that it is immoral to kill unarmed men, women, and children and that most men, in whatever culture, would have a strong aversion to committing the horrendous acts that the men in police battalions routinely performed. However, in fact, the great majority of these men, because they were socialized into German political culture, were rather strongly authoritarian, anti-Semitic, and nationalistic (indeed, some of them would surely have been quite strongly so). Since most of these men shared these beliefs and values in a fairly strong or quite strong form, there would have been a strong sense of comradeship among them. Thus it seems quite reasonable to conclude that they mutually motivated each other to obey the orders to kill unarmed Jews. In short, most of the men were to some degree motivated by a deep form of peer pressure that, in varying degrees, counteracted any conflicting motives and hesitation they might have had. Many perpetrators who had no moral qualms about participating in the killing were nevertheless revolted by the gruesomeness of the direct, one-on-one method of killing that was carried out.[24] Other men might have suffered from the lingering "weakness" of their Christian morality. These potential dropouts very probably did not want to be seen as slackers who left the "dirty work" to their comrades. Although it cannot be said with certainty that this peer pressure was by itself sufficient to cause them to kill, it was almost certainly a major factor in their motivation.

Often individuals use peer pressure to excuse or mitigate their wrong acts; the reasoning underlying such an excuse is that "others made me do it; it was not my idea and I really did not want to do it." But this lame excuse cannot be used by all members of a group accused of wrongdoing; some sizable percentage of the individuals who make up the group have to serve as the peers who apply pressure on a minority of reluctant individuals. Daniel Goldhagen, in particular, uses this objection to great effect in his critical analysis of peer pressure as an explanation for the motivation to obey orders to kill.[25] Nevertheless, there may have been a minority of men who opposed the killing but obeyed orders to kill Jews anyway because of peer pressure; however, if they were truly opposed for reasons of moral principle, then the peer pressure would have to have been the shallow kind.

Principal Dispositional Explanations of Perpetrators' Wrong Actions

Anti-Semitism

An explanation that appeals directly to anti-Semitism as a trait of individuals is a dispositional explanation. This can be most easily seen when the claim is interpreted in a strong sense, namely, that anti-Semitism was a sufficient condition for the men to participate in genocide. Interpreted this way, the claim would be that the men in police battalions obeyed orders to kill unarmed Jews because of their individual psychological trait of anti-Semitism, and *they would have done so even if there had been no situational factors such as peer pressure present*. In this formulation the individual trait of anti-Semitism is not only distinct from peer pressure, but it also differs from it in kind. Peer pressure is not an individual psychological trait at all; it is a characteristic of the social situation, which is composed of the group, and it is manifested in the way that individuals are related to each other. Of course, individual traits like anti-Semitism (among others) play an indirect role in the situational explanation that appeals to peer pressure; they help explain the fact that there is a shared sense of comradeship (a characteristic of the group), which, in turn, partly explains the peer pressure to participate in the killing.

Those who argue that German anti-Semitism was the principal motive for participation in the Final Solution also tend to argue that it was a sufficient motive, with other motives playing a relatively insignificant role. Daniel Goldhagen is the best known recent defender of this position, perhaps because he defends it in such an insistent and uncompromising form.[26] Other defenders of it have received less attention.[27] I have argued that most of the men in police battalions probably had the individual trait of anti-Semitism in a form that was fairly strong to strong and that this trait (along with authoritarianism and nationalism) helps to explain the comradeship, and its attendant peer pressure, within their units. I stopped short of asserting that the situational peer pressure was sufficient to cause the men to kill. However, there is also the possibility that the individual trait of anti-Semitism was sufficient to motivate individual men to kill independently of peer pressure. According to Goldhagen, this is exactly what happened. Consequently, Goldhagen's thesis needs careful scrutiny.

Goldhagen's Strong Thesis

Goldhagen's claim about the role of German anti-Semitism in the perpetration of the Holocaust is embedded in a sustained argument that has a fairly complex logical structure that many critics fail to grasp. As a result they often end up attacking a straw man instead of the thesis that Goldhagen actually defends. For example, Goldhagen is often criticized for defending a "monocausal" explanation for the occurrence of the Holocaust.[28] This is clearly a mistaken reading. Early in his book Goldhagen lists "four principal things [that] were necessary" for the extermination of the Jews to occur: (1) Hitler had to decide to exterminate the Jews, (2) the Nazis had to gain control of the Jews, (3) organize and implement the extermination, and (4) induce a large number of people to carry out the killings.[29] His main thesis about German anti-Semitism concerns only the fourth necessary condition; he argues that the especially virulent form of German anti-Semitism was necessary to provide the motivation for the tens of thousands (perhaps 100,000 or more) perpetrators who in fact carried out the millions of killings.[30] However, without the other three necessary conditions, Goldhagen admits, the Holocaust would not have happened.[31]

In defending his main thesis, Goldhagen is particularly keen to establish that German anti-Semitism was especially strong and that it contained what he calls an "eliminationist" element, namely, the conviction that there was a "Jewish problem" that threatened the well-being and existence of the German people so seriously that the only way to solve it was to "eliminate" the Jews from national life, one way or the other.[32] According to Goldhagen, this eliminationist anti-Semitism evolved and became the "common sense" of German culture before the advent of Hitler and the Nazis. Thus they could take for granted that they had the great majority of Germans with them when they called for a war against the Jews. Goldhagen grants that for Germans, "eliminate" did not necessarily mean "exterminate." However, when they were called upon to take part in the Final Solution, most of them did so willingly, a fact that he thinks can only be explained by their already existing eliminationist convictions. He also admits that the Nazi regime radicalized the German people incrementally throughout the years leading up to the Final Solution by increasingly harsh anti-Semitic policies and laws, propaganda, and violence, but Goldhagen argues that these measures would not have been sufficient to produce "willing killers" if the great majority had not already been convinced that the Jews had to be eliminated.[33]

Goldhagen defends his very strong thesis, that virtually all Germans were eliminationist anti-Semites, by culling confirmatory evidence from the history of German culture during the nineteenth and early twentieth centuries (he also includes three case studies of German genocidal institutions: police battalions, work camps, and death marches). One obvious flaw in this culling procedure is that he ignores most of the evidence that disagrees with his thesis. In addition, as I point out in chapter 5, we should be careful about drawing general conclusions regarding the alleged lack of capacity responsibility from which all Germans were supposed to suffer as the result of having been brought up in a bad political culture. Thus there is good reason to be similarly skeptical about Goldhagen's thesis. No one doubts that most Germans were to some degree anti-Semitic. But it is not plausible that nearly all Germans were eliminationist anti-Semites who willingly accepted the necessity of genocide. Indeed, Goldhagen has failed to convince most professional historians on this key point.[34]

Goldhagen also tries to support his strong dispositional explanation by marshaling evidence against competing situational explanations. He does this by providing detailed accounts of the cruel manner in which perpetrators in the police battalions treated their victims before they killed them, as well as by documenting the voluntariness, zeal, and excesses with which they did the actual killing. The mass of evidence he adduces–that many of the men routinely engaged in cruelty, torture, and humiliation of the victims–is devastating and compelling. It is not possible to survey all of the evidence he presents, much less present it in detail, but there are a few representative passages that convey the cruelty and humiliation that occurred. Goldhagen describes an operation at Bialystok in Poland in 1942:

> Another scene saw some Germans in this battalion compel old Jewish men to dance before them. In addition to the amusement that they evidently derived from their choreography, the Germans were mocking, denigrating, and asserting their mastery over these Jews, particularly since the selected Jews were their elders, people of an age to whom normally regard and respect are due. Apparently, and to their great misfortune, the Jews failed to dance to a sufficiently brisk and pleasing tempo, so the Germans set the Jews' beards on fire.[35]

His account of a roundup operation at Miedzyrzec in Poland in 1942 includes the following description:

> The survivors are adamant that the Germans were incredibly brutal, that their cruelty that day was wanton, at times turning into sadistic sport. At the marketplace, the Jews, who had been forced to squat for hours, were "mocked" (*khoyzek gemacht*) and "kicked," and some of the Germans organized "a game" (*shpil*) of "tossing apples and whoever was struck by the apple was then killed."
>
> This sport was continued at the railway station, this time with empty liquor bottles. "Bottles were tossed over Jewish heads and whoever was struck by a bottle was dragged out of the crowd and beaten murderously amid roaring laughter. Then some of those who were thus mangled (*tseharget*) were shot." Afterwards, they loaded the dead together with the living onto freight cars bound for Treblinka [the killing center].[36]

Goldhagen also presents evidence that the men generally killed voluntarily, not merely in the sense that they were under no coercion of dire punishment for refusing to kill (a fact that we have already noted) but because they volunteered to serve on the killing squads instead of asking for other duties such as serving as guards. For example, most of the killing squads in operations by Police Battalion 101 were made up of men who volunteered for them; in fact, most of the time there were more volunteers for the squads than were needed.[37] Moreover, Goldhagen provides evidence that many of the men killed with zeal and in excess of what their orders called for. Here is another passage that describes the roundup at Bialystok in which the men were ordered to take the Jews to a collection point from which they would be taken to a waiting train:

> One Jew recalls that "the unit had barely driven into the city when the soldiers swarmed out and, without any sensible cause, shot up the entire city, apparently also in order to frighten the people. The incessant shooting was utterly horrible. They shot blindly, in fact, into houses and windows, without regard for whether they hit anyone. The shooting (*Schiesserei*) lasted the entire day." The Germans of this battalion broke into people's homes who had not lifted a finger in hostility, dragged them out, kicked them, beat them with their rifle butts, and shot them. The streets were strewn with corpses.[38]

In summary, the detailed evidence Goldhagen presents makes a convincing case: Many men acted cruelly and brutally toward their Jewish victims; there were always more than enough volunteers for killing squads; many men acted with zeal and in excess of what their orders demanded. These facts would be difficult (though not completely impossible) to explain by purely situational factors, that is, without any individual psychological traits playing a part. It certainly seems plausible to conclude that many of the men in police battalions were motivated by strong anti-Semitic beliefs and attitudes and not just by a fear of disobeying orders.

However, Goldhagen is mistaken in thinking that this evidence necessarily helps to confirm his main thesis that most Germans were imbued with eliminationist anti-Semitism. Because there is hardly any information on the identity of the individual men who volunteered for killing squads, the possibility cannot be dismissed, for example, that there was a minority of the men who repeatedly did all or most of the shooting in the killing squads. Neither are there exact figures on the number of men who were strongly anti-Semitic compared to those who were not. Consequently, there is no clear indication how large a percentage of the men were strongly anti-Semitic. So even if the men in police battalions were, as a group, roughly representative of the rest of German society regarding membership in the Nazi Party and the SS, as well as distribution of educational level and occupations (as Goldhagen argues),[39] this evidence is insufficient to warrant any inference about the percentage of the German population that was strongly anti-Semitic. Neither does the evidence disconfirm (much less refute) all situational explanations of the men's actions, if only because (as I have argued) the individual trait of anti-Semitism can play a role in one important kind of situational explanation, namely, the form of peer pressure that involves a shared sense of comradeship. Finally, Goldhagen himself makes an admission (late in the book) that competing explanations might well account for the motives of *individuals* among the men in police battalions, but he insists that these could not possibly explain the motives of the great majority who participated in the killing.[40] This is a telling admission, given the fact, already noted, that there are no exact figures on the numbers of men who were strongly anti-Semitic or killed regularly. How can Goldhagen be so sure that the other explanations do not apply to a fairly sizable minority of the men?

Even though Goldhagen fails to prove his strong main thesis about the extent of eliminationist anti-Semitism, his presentation of detailed evidence is nevertheless tremendously valuable in soundly refuting the popular rationalization that most German perpetrators were reluctant participants acting under coercion against their moral scruples. He may well have made it impossible for any serious historian to revive those comforting myths; he may also have succeeded in nudging more historical researchers to finally adopt conclusions about the cruelty and wantonness of most German perpetrators that are consistent with the nearly universal reports of thousands of survivors. Primo Levi, for example (among many, many others), has stressed their cruelty and inhumanity.[41]

In summary, it is apparent that most of the men in police battalions were fairly strongly or quite strongly anti-Semitic, particularly in light of Goldhagen's evidence that many of them volunteered for killing duty and treated the Jewish victims with cruelty, brutality, and humiliation. This supports the conclusion that anti-Semitism as an individual trait directly motivated many men to participate in the killing independent of the deep kind of peer pressure stemming from the shared sense of comradeship that I have already noted. Although this deep kind of peer pressure was not necessary to get the strongly anti-Semitic men to kill, it most likely intensified their motivation. In addition, the peer pressure would encourage those men whose anti-Semitism was weak or nonexistent, as well as men who were reluctant for a variety of reasons, such as moral qualms, the repulsiveness of the killing, or cowardice. Taken together, these two explanations go a long way toward showing why so many of the men in the police battalions participated in the killing at least once and why so few took advantage of the opportunity to excuse themselves. (Browning estimates that 10–20 percent of the approximately five hundred men in Police Battalion 101 did not participate in the killing; Goldhagen accepts accounts of particular killing operations, such as that at Josefow, Poland, in 1942, according to which about twelve men accepted the offer not to participate.)[42] It seems plausible that the combination of individual anti-Semitism and peer pressure provided sufficient motivation for many of the men to participate in killing. However, it cannot be concluded that this combination explains why the level of participation was so high and why so few asked to be excused from the killing.

The Role of Triumphant Nationalism

What is missing from this discussion (as well as from most of the debates about the motives of the men in police battalions) is the larger historical context in which Hitler and the Nazi regime initiated the Final Solution. Some historical imagination will help recreate the way in which Hitler and his regime were viewed by the great majority of Germans in 1941, when the policy of genocide was set in motion, and to see clearly why the great majority of men in police battalions were so highly motivated to carry out their grisly tasks. In 1941 Hitler and his regime were at the height of their popularity and power owing to eight years of unbroken and spectacular successes in both domestic and foreign affairs, including military victories that made them the masters of most of Europe. This context supplies a historically grounded situational explanation for the emergence of an additional dimension of motivation—the admiration, not to say adulation, that most Germans felt toward Hitler and, to a lesser extent, the Nazi regime. This additional motivation complemented and greatly reinforced the authoritarianism and nationalism that most Germans felt; of course, the prestige and power of Hitler and the regime also strengthened the men's anti-Semitism. But above all, the literature on the development of German attitudes toward the regime between 1933 and 1941 and on Hitler's becoming a charismatic leader, the beloved "Führer," clearly shows the emergence of what I call "triumphant nationalism" among most Germans.

Since most of the men in police battalions were carried along with this pervasive triumphant nationalism of the time, they saw the genocide against the Jews as an important campaign in a general war to establish themselves, the Germans, as the masters of Europe (thus exhibiting their intensified nationalism). They did not see their killing operations as atrocities but as necessarily brutal tactics against a people who had been officially identified as a dangerous racial enemy (thus exhibiting a salient feature of their authoritarianism, now intensified by the success and prestige of Hitler and his regime). These beliefs and attitudes of triumphant nationalism, together with whatever level of anti-Semitism they individually happened to have, very likely increased the shared sense of comradeship they felt, thus strengthening the peer pressure to participate in the killing operations. This explanation for the killing includes the important effects of triumphant nationalism: a general strengthening of individual authoritarianism, nationalism, and anti-Semitism, which in turn enhanced the sense of comradeship with its consequent peer pressure. This explanation accounts more adequately than the simpler one does for the high level of participation in the killing and for the fact that relatively few men asked to be excused.[43]

Purely self-interested motives also played a role that needs to be recognized. Although self-interest and selfishness were pervasive in the implementation of the Final Solution, it played only a secondary role in the activities of the men in the police battalions. However, these motives are relevant for assessing the blameworthiness of individual men.

A Variety of Self-Interested Motives

Psychopathology and Sadism

Psychopathology and sadism were often invoked in the immediate postwar years when people were still stunned by the discovery that millions of Jews had been killed in an all-out attempt at genocide. It seemed to many that only mental illness or psychopathology could explain such barbaric behavior. Indeed, there was a concerted effort in psychology and psychiatry to define and explain what came to be called "the Nazi personality," a hypothesized pathological personality shared by the leaders of the Nazi regime that would explain their criminal actions. The twenty-one principal defendants in the first major war crimes trial in Nuremberg were given Rorschach tests, IQ tests, and intensive psychological interviews in order to ascertain whether they suffered from any psychopathology. Moreover, many rank-and-file defendants who had "participated in atrocities" were also tested and interviewed. No "diagnosable impairments that would account for their actions were found" among either the leaders or the rank-and-file.[44] With the passage of time and increasing understanding of the historical processes that led to the Holocaust, the appeal to psychiatric explanations for sadism has been restricted to those relatively few individuals who clearly fit into these categories. Just as in the case of Hitler himself, explanations drawn from normal psychology, social theory, and history need to be marshaled in an attempt to explain the character and actions of most of the men in police battalions.

Careerism

Only a few dedicated SS leaders and Nazi bureaucrats directly involved in the killing process seem to have been motivated primarily by a desire to advance themselves by doing a "good job." An example is Rudolph Hoess, who served as the commandant of Auschwitz. By his own account, he was concerned solely with being an efficient administrator. Although he claimed to be a staunch Nazi, he thought the killing of the Jews was a mistake in the sense of being a tactical error; however, he seems not to have given any thought to the morality of the genocide, since he regarded that as a matter of Reich policy that fell outside his area of responsibility.[45] Careerism is a much more likely explanation for the participation in the Final Solution by the many different kinds of impersonal bureaucrats who were far removed from the grisly business of direct killing. Beyond these two categories, however, careerism would seem to have played a relatively minor role in the motivation of perpetrators. It does not seem plausible as an explanation of the motivation of most men in police battalions.

Greed

Historians have given detailed accounts of the various ways in which Germans enriched themselves at the expense of the Jews during the years of anti-Semitic policies such as Aryanization of Jewish-owned businesses,[46] as well as the deportations, ghettoization, and the final steps of the killing process itself, which included taking gold fillings from victims' teeth. For example, the entry "confiscations" in the index of Raul Hilberg's *The Destruction of the European Jews* contains the following subheadings: abandoned property, bank deposits, claims and credits, in death camps, distribution of seized property, furniture, furs, and gold and jewelry.[47] SS personnel, bureaucrats, and ordinary workers by the thousands had ample opportunities to help themselves to a part of the loot, and they did. So there is no denying that greed was a major motive among perpetrators. Still there is little evidence that the men in the police battalions were motivated by greed or that they in fact got anything of monetary value from their killing activities. At most only a few men robbed victims before they were killed.

Assessment of the Men's Blameworthiness for Their Wrong Actions

In contrast to the principal perpetrator, Hitler, little biographical information is available about individual men in police battalions; consequently, it is seldom possible to make justified judgments about the blameworthiness of particular men for having taken part in killing unarmed Jewish men, women, and children. However, it is possible to construct realistic moral profiles of several types of men that we can be reasonably certain were found among the men in the police battalions, based on the evidence about the nature of their actions that has been surveyed, as well as the explanation that I have constructed for those actions. I shall then assess the comparative blameworthiness of each type of perpetrator using several relevant variables that should be familiar by now: (1) the nature of their acts, (2) the moral seriousness of their acts (wrongness, badness), (3) their knowledge or ignorance of variables 1 and 2, (4) whether they acted intentionally, (5) whether they acted freely and voluntarily and, if not, whether they had a justified excuse or mitigating circumstance, and (6) whether they were culpable for their own ignorance, negligence, lack of capacity, bad character, or flawed personal identity (if any) through active construction of their self and tactics of self-deception.

The most blameworthy type of perpetrator among the men in the police battalions would have had the following moral profile: He was aware of and approved of the official policy of genocide against the Jews. He repeatedly brutalized, tormented, and humiliated defenseless Jewish men, women, and children before killing them in one-on-one fashion (objectively immoral and very seriously wrong). He was aware that he could be excused from killing if he requested it, but he regularly volunteered to serve on the killing squads because he enjoyed tormenting and killing Jews; he killed them knowingly and intentionally, believing that he was justified in killing them (for authoritarian, nationalistic, and anti-Semitic reasons). His ignorance of the immorality of his acts was largely his own fault, since he was not subjected to socialization that left him with diminished capacities; rather, it was the result of his own active construction (from selfish motives to ingratiate himself with others and be successful) of a conformist and conventional self with strong traits of authoritarianism, nationalism, and anti-Semitism. He also developed a self-deceptive cognitive style that made him virtually immune to doubts about his beliefs and attitudes. He was contemptuous of the men who asked to be excused from the killing and often criticized them to their face, and he always attempted to stop anyone contemplating asking to be relieved. Finally, he was very ambitious and believed that his conscientious performance would advance his career in the police battalions; and he took every opportunity to steal money, gold, and jewelry from his victims before killing them.

This description is a moral profile in the sense that it can be used to infer the kind of moral character that a man of this type would have. Obviously he would lack certain virtues: benevolence (since he would not have a direct care for the well-being of Jews for their sake), self-control (since he would routinely steal valuables from them), self-knowledge (since he would evade recognizing his selfish motives), practical wisdom and autonomy (since he would rely on authority and convention to form his moral opinions). Although he would have a trait of conscientiousness (he would do his duty as he saw it and more), it would be perverted (by his mistaken belief that he had no moral duty to refrain from harming Jews) and thus would not truly be a virtue; on the other hand, he would have the vices of cruelty (because he enjoyed humiliating and killing Jews) and greed (because he stole from them), as well as dogmatism, self-righteousness, and self-deception.

This profile may seem overdrawn and exaggerated, but, given the evidence of the behavior of the police battalions, there is every reason to think that many men fit it very closely. There is no way of knowing exactly how many there were, of course, but we can be fairly sure that they constituted a significant percentage of the personnel.

There are some factors that, everything else being equal, would decrease the blameworthiness of a person and could be used to construct a few additional moral profiles of other types of men that very likely were found in police battalions but were in varying degrees less blameworthy than the type in the first moral profile. Thus there were some men who were not blameworthy at all because they refrained from wrong actions. They did not take part in killing, inflicting cruelty and humiliation, stealing, or pressuring their comrades to participate in the killing. And there were men (perhaps the same men) who lacked one or more of the following vices: authoritarianism, triumphant nationalism, anti-Semitism, cruelty, greed, or self-deception. And, finally, some men possessed one or more of the following virtues: benevolence, conscientiousness, self-control, self-knowledge, practical wisdom, and autonomy. Some men who were anti-Semitic and killed probably lacked the capacity to realize that their acts were morally wrong because they had been largely passive victims of socialization into the majority's bad political culture. Some men killed, even though they knew that they could be excused, because they were cowards who could not stand up to peer pressure. The open-endedness of the possibilities should be clear from this partial list.

Judging the blameworthiness of particular men in the police battalions requires being very well informed about those men's deeds, thoughts, beliefs, intentions, character, and the circumstances in which they acted. We do not have that information. In 1947, German philosopher Karl Jaspers warned his fellow citizens not to try to judge each other morally because he realized that few of them were in a position to do so. In his short but profound book, *The Question of German Guilt,* Jaspers sharply distinguished moral guilt (blameworthiness) from political and legal guilt because, unlike the latter two forms of guilt, with moral guilt "jurisdiction rests with my conscience, *and in communication with my friends and intimates who are lovingly concerned with my soul*"[48] (emphasis added). We should heed Jaspers's advice. This does not mean that the discussion in this chapter of the blameworthiness of the men in police battalions is useless. My purpose was not to enable us to assess the blameworthiness of individual men, but rather to arrive at an overall assessment of the range of possible blameworthiness among them, and to gain an understanding of the way in which men who by and large had adequate powers of agency and were responsible and competent human beings in control of their actions nonetheless came to perpetrate some of the most horrendously evil acts that humans have ever inflicted on each other. We have the right to say to ourselves at least, "We do not know for sure which ones among you are most to blame, or which of you are not to blame at all, or how many of you fall somewhere in between; but given what we know about the various ways in which all of you acted, we are justified in thinking that you have brought great discredit and shame on the human race, and, to a degree that each of you knows in your own case (or ought to know), discredit and shame on yourselves."

Notes

1. Christopher Browning, *Ordinary Men: Reserve Police Battalion 101 and the Final Solution in Poland* (New York: HarperCollins, 1992), 176–184; Daniel Jonah Goldhagen, *Hitler's Willing Executioners: Ordinary Germans and the Holocaust* (New York: Knopf, 1996), chap. 6.

2. Ernst Klee, Willi Dressen, and Volker Riess, *"The Good Old Days"*: *The Holocaust as Seen by Its Perpetrators and Bystanders* (New York: Free Press, 1988); Browning, *Ordinary Men;* Goldhagen, *Hitler's Willing Executioners.*

3. Jackson J. Spielvogel, *Hitler and Nazi Germany: A History* (Englewood Cliffs, N.J.: Prentice-Hall, 1992), 103–108, 276.

4. Goldhagen, *Hitler's Willing Executioners,* 182–185.

5. Browning, *Ordinary Men,* 178–184.

6. Browning, *Ordinary Men,* chap. 7; Goldhagen, *Hitler's Willing Executioners,* chap. 7.

7. Raul Hilberg, *The Destruction of the European Jews* (New York: Holmes & Meier, 1985), 3:993–1002, 3:1007–1017.

8. Goldhagen, *Hitler's Willing Executioners,* 471.

9. Browning, *Ordinary Men,* 170.

10. Browning, *Ordinary Men,* 171.

11. Goldhagen, *Hitler's Willing Executioners,* 253–254, 278.

12. Omer Bartov, *Hitler's Army: Soldiers, Nazis, and War in the Third Reich* (New York: Oxford University Press, 1991), 6.

13. Hilberg, *Destruction of the European Jews,* 3:1009.

14. Hilberg, *Destruction of the European Jews,* 3:1007–1112.

15. Hilberg, *Destruction of the European Jews,* 3:1010.

16. Hilberg, *Destruction of the European Jews,* 1:326.

17. Stanley Milgram, *Obedience to Authority: An Experimental View* (New York: Harper & Row 1974), 1.

18. Milgram, *Obedience,* 135–147.

19. Stanley Milgram, "Group Pressure and Action against a Person," *Journal of Abnormal and Social Psychology* 9 (1964): 137–143.

20. Milgram, *Obedience,* 176–177.

21. Goldhagen, *Hitler's Willing Executioners,* 592n19.

22. Gwynne Dwyer, *War* (New York: Crown, 1985), 104.

23. Bartov, *Hitler's Army,* chap. 2.

24. Hilberg, *Destruction of the European Jews,* 1:327–328.

25. Goldhagen, *Hitler's Willing Executioners,* 384.

26. Goldhagen, *Hitler's Willing Executioners.*

27. John Weiss, *Ideology of Death: Why the Holocaust Happened in Germany* (Chicago: Ivan R. Dee, 1996).

28. Norman G. Finkelstein and Ruth Bettina Birn, *A Nation on Trial: The Goldhagen Thesis and Historical Truth* (New York: Holt, 1998), 8.

29. Goldhagen, *Hitler's Willing Executioners,* 9.

30. Goldhagen, *Hitler's Willing Executioners,* 167.

31. Goldhagen, *Hitler's Willing Executioners,* 416.

32. Goldhagen, *Hitler's Willing Executioners,* chap. 2.

33. Goldhagen, *Hitler's Willing Executioners,* chap. 3.

34. *Unwilling Germans: The Goldhagen Debate,* ed. Robert R. Shandley, trans. Jeremiah Reimer (Minneapolis: University of Minnesota Press, 1998).

35. Goldhagen, *Hitler's Willing Executioners,* 188–189.

36. Goldhagen, *Hitler's Willing Executioners,* 256–257.

37. Goldhagen, *Hitler's Willing Executioners,* 179, 191–192, 452.

38. Goldhagen, *Hitler's Willing Executioners,* 188.
39. Goldhagen, *Hitler's Willing Executioners,* 205–211.
40. Goldhagen, *Hitler's Willing Executioners,* 417.
41. Primo Levi, *The Drowned and the Saved* (New York: Summit, 1986), chap. 5, "Useless Violence."
42. Browning, *Ordinary Men,* 159; Goldhagen, *Hitler's Willing Executioners,* 212–215.
43. Notice that this historical explanation is quite different from the one that we considered (and rejected) in chapter 5, namely, that being socialized in the bad political culture of Germany left perpetrators with a cognitive capacity too diminished to realize that killing Jews was immoral. My view is that triumphant nationalism is an excellent example of how people fail to use or misuse their cognitive capacities.
44. Eric A. Zillmer et al., *The Quest for the Nazi Personality: A Psychological Investigation of Nazi War Criminals* (Hillsdale, N.J.: Erlbaum, 1995), 96–100, 144.
45. Steven Paskuly, *The Memoirs of the SS Kommandant in Auschwitz Rudolph Hoess,* trans. Andrew Pollinger (Buffalo, N.Y.: Prometheus, 1992), 196–205.
46. Marion Kaplan, *Between Dignity and Despair: Jewish Life in Nazi Germany* (New York: Oxford University Press, 1998), 23–24, 145–146.
47. Hilberg, *Destruction of the European Jews,* 3:1240.
48. Karl Jaspers, *The Question of German Guilt* (New York: Capricorn, 1947), 32.

Suggestions for Further Reading

Bartov, Omer. *The Eastern Front, 1941–45: German Troops and the Barbarisation of War.* New York: St. Martin's, 1986. A study of regular German army troops and the role of ideological indoctrination in the perpetration of war crimes and atrocities.

———. *Hitler's Army: Soldiers, Nazis, and War in the Third Reich.* New York: Oxford University Press, 1991. A study that follows up on the topics treated in his book *The Eastern Front* (1986); his main thesis is that the German army in World War II became a largely Nazified people's army.

Browning, Christopher R. *Ordinary Men: Reserve Police Battalion 101 and the Final Solution in Poland.* New York: HarperCollins, 1991. A pioneering work and a principal source of information about the actions and motives of men in police battalions.

Goldhagen, Daniel J. *Hitler's Willing Executioners: Ordinary Germans and the Holocaust.* New York: Vintage, 1996. Defends the controversial view that German anti-Semitism explains why most Germans who participated in the Holocaust did so willingly.

Hilberg, Raul. *The Destruction of the European Jews.* Rev. and definitive ed. New York: Holmes & Meier, 1985, Chap. 7, "Mobile Killing Operations."

———. *Perpetrators Victims Bystanders: The Jewish Catastrophe, 1933–1945.* New York: HarperCollins, 1992, Pt. 1, "Perpetrators."

Klee, Ernst, et al. *"The Good Old Days": The Holocaust as Seen by Its Perpetrators and Bystanders.* New York: Free Press, 1988. Another pioneering work by German historians that studies the killing actions and daily life of men in the SS Einsatzgruppen and police battalions, among others; includes letters and photographs.

Chapter 8

Victims

It is extremely important to address two questions that are very likely to arise in the minds of readers as they begin this chapter. First, they are likely to wonder why there is any need for a chapter on moral responsibility of *victims,* especially since I have been occupied almost exclusively with blameworthiness for wrongdoing. Surely, it will be thought, the victims were blameless; they did no wrong. They were the ones killed and tormented by the German perpetrators. And, second, why is it that only Jewish victims of German atrocities and exploitation are discussed, since there were millions of non-Jewish victims in what has been called "the other Holocaust" perpetrated by Germany.[1]

How Can Victims Be Morally Responsible?

One of the most reprehensible tactics used to evade responsibility for wrongdoing is "blaming the victim." It is almost a cliché in feminist thought that both traditional law and conventional morality tended to excuse men's permissive attitudes toward rape by accepting the relevance of the plea that "she asked for it." My reasons for devoting a chapter to the victims of the Holocaust have nothing to do with blaming them for the fact that the genocide occurred. Raul Hilberg is quite correct to insist that there can be no question about the primary moral responsibility of the Germans who planned, initiated, and provided the driving force for implementation and perpetration of the Final Solution.

Nevertheless, being a victim does not automatically make one completely innocent, even though references are often made to the "innocent victims" of genocide and other atrocities. Otherwise sophisticated writers on the Holocaust can be found using titles such as *Lest Innocent Blood Be Shed*[2] and *On Destroying the Innocent with a Clear Conscience.*[3] The word "innocent" can be very misleading in this context. For example, references to people as "innocent victims" of an attack deny that they did anything to provoke it; it does not follow that the victims have never done anything wrong or that their moral

171

characters are beyond reproach. The term "innocent victims" is also used to convey the fact that the people who have been harmed or killed were defenseless or unarmed, not that they have never done wrong or that they are utterly without any faults or vices. In short, the term "innocent" should not be used to describe unarmed and defenseless people who are the victims of unprovoked attacks or killings. Referring to victims as unarmed or defenseless rather than "innocent" is factually accurate and captures all of the morally relevant aspects of the actions performed. Having deep concern for the plight of victims is perfectly consistent with acknowledging that most victims, like other ordinary fallible human beings, are capable of making moral mistakes and are likely to have some character flaws. Thus the question whether Jewish victims were to some extent blameworthy for some of the ways in which they acted during the Holocaust must be kept open.

I am particularly interested in whether Jewish victims failed to live up to the three prima facie duties that constitute the core content of morality: not to harm others, to do good in accordance with one's justified role responsibilities, and to give aid in emergency situations. These duties were still binding on them as victims; being a victim of wrongdoing does not automatically exempt anyone from moral obligations. The great majority of Jewish victims fully appreciated their basic kinds of moral obligations to each other, and most of them made strenuous efforts to live up to their obligations under conditions that were often harrowing. When they sometimes failed in these efforts, it was not usually the victims' fault. Often enough they not only succeeded in fulfilling their duties but went far beyond them, displaying great courage and heroism in the face of the German onslaught. Thus there is a very positive reason for considering the moral responsibility of victims, namely, to recognize the great extent to which they acted in ways that were praiseworthy and admirable.

Criticism has been directed at the behavior of some of the Jewish victims. A number of these criticisms have been raised by people who are ill informed about the very serious constraints under which German Jews lived during the eight years of anti-Semitic policies that preceded the Holocaust and are also ignorant about the dire straits in which most European Jews found themselves when the deportations to killing centers began. However, not all of the criticisms can be ascribed to ignorance. Some eminent historians, including Raul Hilberg, have described and explained the behavior of Jewish victims in ways that clearly imply (without explicitly stating) that they were complicit in their own deaths in ways that seem to make them blameworthy.[4] In this chapter, I discuss three main criticisms that have been made either in popular writing about the Holocaust or in scholarly works or both. The first criticism is that the Jews should have realized the truth about German genocidal intentions before it was too late. The second is that the Jews should not have collaborated with the Germans in implementing the Final Solution, thereby sealing their own fate.

And, finally, there is the criticism that they should have resisted the Germans instead of "going like lambs to the slaughter."[5]

Is It Fair to Ignore Non-Jewish Victims of the "Other Holocaust"?

It would be very unfair to disregard what happened to the millions of non-Jewish victims of German military aggression, their racial policies aimed at "reducing" allegedly "subhuman species," and their exploitation of slave labor. Consequently, we have an obligation to summarize the nature and extent of the "other Holocaust" in order to acknowledge the fact that even if there had been no Jewish Holocaust, Nazi Germany would still go down in history as one of the most brutal and inhuman regimes that has ever existed:

> In addition to the 5 to 6 million Jews, the Nazis were also directly responsible for the death by starvation, shooting, and overwork of probably another 9 to 10 million human beings. Nazi racial ideology encouraged German mistreatment of peoples other than just the Jews. The Gypsies of Europe were placed in the same category as the Jews—a race containing alien blood and consequently fit only for extermination. About 40 percent of Europe's 1 million Gypsies were gassed and burned. Slavic peoples, such as Poles, Ukrainians, and Belorussians, were not in the same category as the Jews and Gypsies but were nevertheless considered inferior by the Germans and suited only for slave labor. The leading elements of these peoples—clergy, aristocracy, intelligentsia, civil and political leaders, judges and lawyers—were arrested and exterminated. The remaining population was to be treated as slave labor, permanently reduced to a lower-class status. It has been estimated that almost 4 million Poles, Ukrainians, and Belorussians lost their lives as slave labor for the Third Reich. Finally, the Germans deliberately allowed between 2 and 3 million Soviet prisoners of war to die in captivity.[6]

Another way to appreciate the magnitude of the toll in human lives lost in the "other Holocaust" is to note that the total of non-Jewish victims killed was greater than the total number of civilians killed on both sides in World War I. It is painfully clear that what I have called German "triumphant nationalism" reached far beyond the Jewish community for its victims.

However, since this is a study of moral responsibility in the Jewish Holocaust, I do not devote the attention to the crimes against non-Jewish victims that the subject deserves. The focus on Jewish victims also reflects the historical fact that they were ideologically defined by the Nazis as the principal target; consequently, the genocidal assault against the Jews was proportionally the most destructive. For example, the percentage of Jews living in Greater Germany, Poland, and the Ukraine in 1941 who were killed approached 100 percent.[7] This should not be taken to mean that the crimes against non-Jews were less serious (for one thing, the total number of victims was greater) or that the individual deaths of these victims were not as great a loss as the deaths of individual Jews. It must be admitted that there has been a comparative lack of scholarly interest in the victims of the "other Holocaust" in the literature. Some recent work, however, indicates that a welcome change is beginning to develop.[8] I turn now to three criticisms raised against the ways in which Jewish victims reacted to German anti-Semitic policies and the Final Solution.

The Jews Should Have Realized the Truth about German Intentions before It Was Too Late

Arriving at justified judgments requires the use of relevant ethical principles. The core content of morality includes the prima facie duties not to harm others, to do good for others in accordance with one's justified role responsibilities, and to render aid in Good Samaritan situations. Each of the three criticisms I consider in this chapter identifies one or more ways in which Jewish victims allegedly failed to live up to these basic moral duties is some manner that made them blameworthy. The first criticism consists largely of the accusation that many Jews (especially Jewish leaders) suffered from culpable ignorance of relevant facts. Recall that a person of good character should have the virtue of practical wisdom, which, among other things, is a strong inclination to be well informed in any situation in which a moral decision is to be made, as well as a capacity to weigh competing factors such as conflicting duties in particular situations. Persons with these characteristics are most likely to be able to come to a justified judgment about what ought to be done, all things considered. The most highly relevant fact about which Jews should have taken the most pains to be accurately informed was the exact nature of German intentions toward them: What were the Germans going to do with (or to) them? In particular, individual Jews who served on Jewish councils charged with carrying out German orders had a clear role responsibility to be well informed about German intentions in order to make sure that they did not harm the community. But many Jewish leaders lacked this kind of practical wisdom. It must not be assumed, however, that all instances of ignorance on the part of Jewish leaders was due to a lack of practical wisdom; often there was no reliable information on which to act, not least because the Germans systematically gave false assurances or lied about their genocidal plans, as one would expect. In addition to practical wisdom, Jewish leaders should have had courage and self-control to act in accordance with their basic duties to take care of the community in the light of whatever information they were able to get about German intentions.

It is important to note that European Jews were very far from being a homogeneous group. The most important differences for the purpose of this discussion are:

1. Jews who lived in what was designated as Greater Germany during the Third Reich, that is, prewar Germany and Austria; almost all of these Jews were highly assimilated, spoke German, and lived dispersed throughout society, without distinctive dress or customs; many were not observant;
2. Jews who lived in Italy and in western European countries under German control (Norway, Denmark, the Netherlands, Belgium, Luxembourg, and France) who were also highly assimilated; and
3. Jews who lived in eastern European countries that were variously occupied by, invaded by, or allied with Germany (the former Czechoslovakia, the Baltic states, Poland, Hungary, Bulgaria, Romania, and large areas in the Soviet Union); the great majority of these Jews were not assimilated into the societies in which they lived; they were practicing Jews who lived in distinct religious communities or ghettos, spoke Yiddish or Hebrew; and had distinctive dress and customs.

For the most part, this discussion focuses on Jews who lived in what had been prewar Germany and Jews who lived in occupied Poland and in the areas of the Soviet Union invaded by Germany.

Jews Who Lived in What Had Been Prewar Germany

German Jews were highly assimilated, thought of themselves as Germans (most of them were citizens born in Germany), and, like most Germans, they tended to be strongly nationalistic and patriotic. For example, Jews served in the armed forces during World War I and many lost their lives or were wounded. In short, most Jews constructed their sense of personal identity on the basis of membership in German society. Unlike the Jews of eastern Europe, German Jews did not live in ghettos isolated from the rest of society, and their first language was German. Moreover, they generally attended school with other Germans and were represented in all occupations and professions. Most German Jews also had a strong sense of their Jewish identity and practiced their religion. A significant minority, however, converted to Christianity or adopted a secular lifestyle in order to become more fully assimilated into the majority culture. Moreover, intermarriage with Christians was increasing during World War I and the years of the Weimar Republic.[9]

The German Jews' sense of German identity points up the great psychological difficulty that most of them had in digesting the mounting evidence of the enormity of their fate under the Nazi regime. In addition, the anti-Semitic policies of the regime were introduced gradually, and their severity increased incrementally during the years 1933–1941 before the implementation of the Final Solution. For example, it was not until 1935 that the Nuremberg Laws deprived Jews of citizenship.[10] This gradualism kept German Jews off guard and facilitated wishful thinking that prevented many from undertaking drastic actions like emigrating. Jews kept hoping that the Hitler regime would not last, or, at the very least, that it would moderate its anti-Semitic policies. This wishful thinking was reflected in fluctuations in the rate of emigration, which dropped whenever there was an apparent halt or moderation in the regime's anti-Semitic activity. For example, 37,000 Jews left in the initial rush of emigration in 1933, but only 23,000 emigrated in 1936, when the Olympic Games were being held in Berlin and the Nazis put on a benevolent face for foreign visitors. By contrast, another 150,000 emigrated after the November 1938 pogrom (the so-called *Kristallnacht*).[11]

By the fall of 1941, when the first steps for implementing the Final Solution were being taken, over 300,000 German Jews (out of the 525,000 in 1933) had emigrated. The great majority of Jews who remained did so not because they were unaware of the danger posed by the Nazi regime but because emigration, which the German government deliberately made difficult, was especially difficult for them, for example, the poor, the elderly, women without a vocation or profession. Others stayed behind in order to care for an elderly family member who was unable to emigrate.[12] Additionally, most foreign countries had severe restrictions that hampered German Jews trying to immigrate.[13]

By 1938 most German Jews realized that they had no viable political or social future in Nazi Germany and, in fact, a large majority who were able to do so eventually emigrated. Thus there is little justification for the criticism that Jews were in a state of self-deception that left them vulnerable to the Nazis. Very few Jews remained in Germany solely because they were self-deceived about their political and social future if they remained. This does not mean, of course, that they were also aware that they would face death later as the Final Solution was implemented. Such knowledge would have been impossible in the years prior to 1941. Historians are in general agreement that the decision to kill all European Jews, including German Jews, was not made until sometime in 1941 and that the first steps to implement that decision were not taken until the fall of that year at the earliest.[14] Deportations of German Jews did not begin until October 1941.[15] For all of the foregoing reasons, our assessment of what Jews knew of the Final Solution must focus on the period after late 1941.

Prior to the implementation of the Final Solution German Jews had been reduced to a condition of "social death." They were virtually excluded from all gainful work and professional employment and were subject to slave labor, restricted to so-called *Judenhäuser* (Jewish living quarters) wherever possible, subjected to stringent curfews, and forbidden to shop in public except for a few hours in each day. One of the most devastating aspects of this legally imposed social death was the requirement that all Jews over the age of six wear a yellow Star of David with the word "Jew" on it whenever they were in public.[16]

This subjected Jews to hostile scrutiny and verbal abuse wherever they went. Jews were also forbidden to have telephones or radios.

This extreme isolation meant that Jews could learn very little about what was going on in Germany or the world. Consequently, when the deportations to the killing centers began, they had no way of knowing whether the official story was correct or not. At first many believed that the deported Jews really were being sent to work camps in the "East," but rumors of killings and gassing gradually filtered back into Germany. Of course, in 1941 and 1942 most people, Jews and non-Jews alike, initially found the idea that Jewish genocide was actually being carried out literally incredible. Enough information was available to most Germans that they could have confirmed the Jews' fate if they had taken the trouble to find out. Jews, however, had only rumors and very little information, so some clung to the hope that the rumors were false. Nevertheless, there is plenty of evidence (including the soaring Jewish suicide rate) that probably the majority of Jews came to realize the truth by late 1942 and 1943. Of course, by that time most Jews had already been killed. Even many of those who believed that they were deported for forced labor expected to die because they would not be able to survive the conditions imposed on them. There was a realistic basis for this fear, since two-thirds of the deportees were over forty-five years of age.[17]

In summary, it seems clear that the Jews who lived in what had been prewar Germany were not lacking in practical wisdom or especially prone to culpable self-deception. In general, they were as well informed about the true intentions of the Nazi regime as it was possible to be, given official secrecy and dissimulation. Most German Jews came to recognize that they had no political or social future under the Nazi regime, and by 1938 and 1939, a large majority had in fact emigrated; many of those who remained would also have emigrated given the opportunity. As for their knowledge of the Final Solution, there is no way that they could have known the truth "before it was too late." By the time they were able to realize the truth, they were utterly helpless in the face of the legally imposed social death.

Jews Who Lived in Ghettos in Occupied Poland

Eastern Jews differed greatly from German Jews, hardly any of them assimilating into the societies in which they lived. Polish Jews tended not to speak Polish as their first language. Most of them retained their traditional distinctive dress, were very devout and religiously observant, and lived separately in tightly knit communities. By contrast, most non-Jewish Poles were devoutly Catholic and strongly anti-Semitic and had a long history of engaging in sporadic pogroms against Jewish communities. When the Germans conquered and occupied Poland in 1939, they killed large numbers of both Poles and Jews, but the Final Solution was not officially begun until 1941. Beginning in late 1939 and into 1940, the Germans established Jewish ghettos throughout Poland. Except for a relative few who lived in isolated rural areas, all Jews were required to live in a ghetto that was sealed off from the rest of the town or city and was completely dependent on the Germans for food, clothing, fuel, and other necessities of life. The death rate among ghetto Jews soared as disease and starvation took their toll; many ghetto inhabitants became listless and apathetic, a factor that helps explain why there was little Jewish resistance. Polish Jews had virtually no sources of reliable information about the outside world, and their German masters used secrecy and disinformation to systematically mislead them about their intentions. The largest Jewish ghetto in Warsaw had a population over 400,000, with other large ghettos in cities like Lublin, Lodz, and Cracow.

The Hilberg Thesis

Raul Hilberg has defended the controversial thesis that eastern Jews were complicit in their own destruction because they were trapped in a debilitating way of thinking and acting dictated by their own historically developed Jewish ghetto culture.[18] According to Hilberg, the salient feature of ghetto culture was that resistance was not among the reactions it used to meet force:

> The Jewish posture in the face of destruction was not shaped on the spur of the moment. The Jews of Europe had been confronted by force many times in their history, and during these encounters they had evolved a set of reactions that were to remain remarkably constant over the centuries. . . . Preventive attack, armed resistance, and revenge were almost completely absent in Jewish exilic history. The last, and only, major revolt took place in the Roman Empire at the beginning of the second century, when the Jews were still living in compact settlements in the eastern Mediterranean region and when they were still envisaging an independent Judea.[19]

Instead of resistance, Jews relied legally, physically, and psychologically on the protection of constituted authority in the country or place of their residence. Thus they would engage in tactics like petitioning and offering bribes in order to evade danger. They resorted to relief, salvage, and rescue activities to alleviate any harm or damage that they had not been able to avert. Evasive reactions also included flight, concealment, or hiding. Hilberg emphasizes that the term "Jewish reactions" applies only to ghetto Jews. When all else failed, the reaction of paralysis would usually set in. "This reaction pattern was born in the ghetto and it will die there."[20]

One thing that Hilberg does not emphasize, though he does devote two paragraphs to it toward the end of his book, is that these culturally transmitted reaction patterns persisted because they worked; they had proven to be the best way for the Jewish community to survive.[21] European Jews were always a small minority in a generally hostile or barely tolerant Christian society prone to engaging in pogroms, many of which were extremely violent and destructive. Although Jews sometimes had political rights (albeit as second-class citizens) and community autonomy, they did not achieve emancipation with full political rights in most countries until well into the nineteenth century.[22] Since the Jews had no political state of their own, they had no independent political power; they were necessarily dependent on the goodwill of the political leaders of the community in which they resided. Consequently, Jewish communities learned by empirical trial and error which tactics enabled them to survive; the result was the set of objectively grounded adaptive reactions outlined in Hilberg's thesis. Moreover, it is difficult to see how radically different tactics would have had a more desirable result; certainly, direct confrontation and resistance would only have provoked even greater hostility and violence toward the Jews by the majority Christian community. In addition, Jewish ghetto culture was also well suited to respond to sometimes radical changes in the Christian political power structure brought about by war and conquest. The Jews of Poland, for example, had been adjusting to new political masters for centuries as Poland was conquered or partitioned in an almost continuous rivalry between Russia, Germany, and the Baltic states. When Germany conquered Poland in 1939, it was only the latest in a long series of conquerors.

Since Jewish ghetto culture represented a rational adaptation to objective conditions that had prevailed in the past, there was no reason for Polish Jews living in 1939–1940 to conclude that the German conquest would have the radically different genocidal character that in fact it turned out to have, a conclusion that would have required a correspondingly radical change in their traditional reactions and tactics, especially a willingness to consider forceful resistance at an early stage. To hold otherwise is to indulge in the luxury of hindsight; we know what was coming, and therefore the Jews should also have known. Some Polish Jews did engage in self-deception, especially as evidence of the horrendous nature of the Final Solution began to mount, but it is not fair to label their initial confidence in their culturally inherited tactics of survival as self-deception. They were rationally justified in their confidence, given their historical experience and their understandable ignorance at the time about the genocidal plans of the Germans. This leads to the conclusion that although Polish Jews were ignorant of German intentions when the Final Solution began to be implemented in late 1941, their ignorance was not culpable; they brought no moral discredit on themselves through the way in which they reached their conclusions.

Nevertheless much popular opinion and the writings of some historians tend to be critical of the Jews. Hilberg does not explicitly express moral disapproval of the ghetto Jews, but his disapproving attitude is often implied in his descriptions. A good example lies in his description of Jewish passivity in the face of mounting evidence in 1942 that deportees were all being killed: "Without a doubt, the Jews were not preparing for armed resistance. They were preparing for automatic compliance with German orders."[23] Sometimes Hilberg conveys his disapproval through the use of sarcasm. For example, after recounting how Jewish self-deception supposedly kept them from seeing through "the very crude deceptions and ruses" used by the Germans to lull them into complacency about their ultimate intentions, Hilberg comments, "At each stage of the destruction process the victims thought they were going through the last stage. And so it appears that one of the most gigantic hoaxes in world history was perpetrated on five million people noted for their intellect. But were these people really fooled? Or did they deliberately fool themselves?"[24]

On the other hand, Hannah Arendt was not reluctant to explicitly express her disapproval of ghetto Jews' behavior during the Holocaust. "To a Jew this role of the Jewish leaders in the destruction of their own people is undoubtedly the darkest chapter of the whole dark story. It had not been known about before, but it has now been exposed in all its pathetic and sordid detail by Raul Hilberg, whose standard work *The Destruction of the European Jews* I mentioned before."[25]

Judgments of blameworthiness, whether implied ("automatic compliance," "gigantic hoax") or explicit ("pathetic," "sordid"), are justified only if Jewish ignorance was culpable. There is no good reason to blame Polish Jews for their initial confidence in their culturally inherited ways of reacting to political power that threatened harm. It is not altogether clear whether either Hilberg or Arendt believe that Polish Jews could have known, and (morally) should have known, the true nature of German genocidal intentions in the period from 1939 to 1941. However, if they do assume this, they are almost certainly mistaken. Just as in the case of German Jews, it would have been impossible to have such knowledge before the decision to implement the Final Solution had even been made.

It might be thought that Hilberg and Arendt only blame ghetto Jews for having failed to realize soon enough the true nature of German intentions *after* 1941, when deportations to the killing centers commenced. Once the wholesale deportations from the ghettos were well under way, perhaps there was enough evidence available to conclude that genocide was occurring; if so, it would seem reasonable to hold ghetto Jews blameworthy if by that time they did not realize the true nature of German intentions. Did ghetto Jews have available sufficient evidence to allow them to draw the correct conclusion that deportees were in fact being killed? If so, when did they get it?

Hilberg's own account of what the ghetto Jews knew or suspected about the genocidal program and the reason for the deportations does not support a conclusion that they should have been able to see the truth right away. Even though the deportations from some of the Polish ghettos began in the early spring of 1942, Hilberg makes clear that it was it only *after* the great majority of Jews had been deported and killed, in late summer of 1942, that "almost every inhabitant of Poland, whether outside or inside a ghetto, had some inkling of what was going on."[26] However, having an "inkling" is far from having knowledge; it does not even rise to the level of a justified suspicion that it was more likely than not that the Germans were killing all Jews. And that fact has great ethical significance. Since the ghetto Jews did not know and did not even have a justified suspicion that the Germans did indeed intend to kill all Jews, and since for most of them there was no way to get the relevant information, they are blameless for not taking actions that might possibly have averted some of their deaths. Whether such actions would in fact have made any difference in the overall result is a separate question that I shall discuss shortly.

If Hilberg and Arendt are justified in blaming ghetto Jews, it cannot be based on their having failed to know in time what they should have known, or on their having engaged in blameworthy self-deception. Instead, these historians must base their blame on the assumption that ghetto Jews had a duty to act on an "inkling" or mere suspicion that all Jews were going to be killed and not wait until they had enough evidence to make it probable, much less certain, that the Germans were going to kill all Jews regardless. If their blame is based on such a principle (or one similar to it), it raises other questions about the character of ghetto Jews in general and about Jewish leaders in particular, for example, questions about their courage and self-control, that go beyond their alleged culpability for being ignorant.

Jews Should Not Have Collaborated with the Germans in Their Own Destruction

The picture of the Jewish ghetto is further complicated by the manner in which the Germans used Jewish leaders to do their bidding and implicate them in the destruction process. Although the Germans also used Jewish organizations for this purpose in Greater Germany, I shall concentrate on the role of Jewish councils (*Judenräte*) that were appointed by the Germans to govern the ghettos in Poland. It was largely the behavior of some of these councils, as well as the behavior of some of their individual members, that have given rise to the charges of collaboration that we are considering. Hilberg very acutely identifies a structural weakness in the kind of governance that Jewish councils were made to exert that proved to be the main source of their moral dilemma. Whereas before the German occupation, "these Jewish leaders had been concerned with synagogues, religious schools, cemeteries, orphanages, and hospitals" now they had a new function,

> the transmission of German directives and orders to the Jewish population, the use of Jewish police to enforce German will, the deliverance of Jewish property, Jewish labor, and Jewish lives to the German enemy. The Jewish councils, in the

exercise of their historic function, continued to the end to make desperate attempts to alleviate the suffering and to stop the masses dying in the ghettos. But, at the same time, the councils responded to German demands with automatic compliance and invoked German authority to compel the community's obedience. Thus the Jewish leadership both saved and destroyed its people, saving some Jews and destroying others, saving the Jews at one moment and destroying them at the next. Some leaders refused to keep this power, others became intoxicated with it.[27]

Although Hilberg makes some attempt in this passage to suggest the good things that the councils did, as well as the ambivalence and conflict felt by the Jewish leaders caught in a very real dilemma, he goes on to draw a devastating picture that some historians criticize as being too one-sided in emphasizing Jewish collaboration and venality. For example, Yehuda Bauer warns against making generalizations about the behavior of Jewish councils or their individual members because they exhibited a wide variety of reactions to German pressure, including defiance ("some councils tried to stand up to the Germans and were murdered as a result"), compliance mixed with attempts to help their communities, subterfuge, and delay.[28] However, he acknowledges that there were Jewish councils

who saw no alternative but complete submission to the Germans, including handing over of Jews for deportation, even after there were no illusions about the consequences. Such were the Judenraete of Lodz or Vilna or Lublin. But in the case of Lodz and Vilna submission resulted from the conviction that the only way for a *part* of a community to survive was by doing the Germans' bidding and performing slave labor for them. In the case of Lublin, no policy at all was followed — only terror and frightened submission.[29]

Nonetheless, Bauer thinks it is wrong to focus only on councils that exhibited complete submission, since "we find resisters among Judenraete as groups and among Judenrat members as individuals in a fairly wide variety of cases."[30] It is fairly easy to find a variety of examples that confirm the essential correctness of Bauer's view. First, one of the most troubling kinds of action engaged in by Jewish councils during the deportations to the killing centers was the deliberate sacrifice of some Jews in order to save the rest. A typical example of this was the Central Council of Elders in Eastern Upper Silesia.

On the eve of the first deportations, Merin [the president of the council] made his first decision. "I will not be afraid," he said, to "sacrifice 50,000 of our community in order to save the other 50,000." During the summer of 1942 the other 50,000 Jews were lined up in a mass review, from which half were sent to Auschwitz. Merin commented after that deportation: "I feel like a captain whose ship was about to sink and who succeeded in bringing it safe to port by casting overboard a great part of his precious cargo."[31]

In the end, nearly all of the ghetto inhabitants were deported anyway, and the Germans made sure that the compliant council members were deported as well. It is very likely that many Jewish leaders like Merin were at first simply self-deceived (perhaps culpably so) about the possibility of being able to save half of their community by sacrificing the other; however, there is no excuse for their having continued such a disastrous policy after it had been proven to be based on a delusion. All too often individual Jewish leaders were self-deceived and cowardly, and they behaved irresponsibly.

Quite a few Jewish councils used another rationalization for cooperating with the Germans, one alluded to by Bauer, namely, that the only way to save the lives of most Jews was to make them too valuable to lose. If the Jews in the ghetto could perform valuable labor that was essential to the German war effort or to the German economy, their reasoning went, then the specter of death could be put off indefinitely into the future. This rationalization at least had some basis in empirical reality, since tens of thousands of ghetto Jews were in fact employed by the Germans to produce all kinds of military and commercial goods. The prime example of a Jewish leader who thought this way was Chaim Rumkowski, the so-called dictator of the Lodz ghetto, who became an autocrat "intoxicated" (to use Hilberg's term) with the power of his position. Rumkowski governed the Lodz ghetto for almost five years, driving "his Jews" (as he referred to them) to meet German work quotas, printing ghetto currency with his portrait on it, rewarding his friends, and intimidating his adversaries.[32]

Even though the Lodz ghetto existed four years and four months (the longest of any ghetto), its 80,000 Jewish workers were removed by one "liquidation" after another, until the final deportation to Auschwitz and closure in August 1944.[33] In effect, the Germans were able to wring the last bit of life and effort out of the Jews in the Lodz ghetto and use it for the benefit of the Reich, all the while maintaining their insane commitment to kill all the Jews they could get their hands on. And Chaim Rumkowski helped them every step of the way, repeatedly giving speeches in which he implored ghetto Jews to cooperate with German orders, including giving up their children for "resettlement."[34] At the very end, he even introduced the SS officer who gave a speech to striking ghetto workers, promising them that they were going to be sent to work in Germany where their labor was badly needed but also warning them that they would be removed forcibly if necessary. The workers relented and agreed to board the train; they were sent to Auschwitz.[35]

Jewish leaders like Rumkowski were not only self-deceived and cowardly, but they were also seduced by the power and privileges the Germans conferred on them:

> With the growth of the destructive function of the Judenräte, many Jewish leaders felt an almost irresistible urge to look like their German masters. In March 1940 a Nazi observer in Krakow was struck by the contrast between the poverty and filth

in the Jewish quarter and the businesslike luxury of the Jewish community head-quarters, which was filled with beautiful charts, comfortable leather chairs, and heavy carpets. In Warsaw, the Jewish oligarchy took to wearing boots.[36]

Such self-indulgence in the midst of general poverty and the horror of roundups and deportations was doubly reprehensible.

In sharp contrast, many Jewish leaders sacrificed themselves to perform their duties of caring for the well-being of the community as well as they could. Many of them were able to score small successes within the severe limits set by the Germans. It was obviously not possible to confront German power directly, and we have already noted that some councils were even put to death for defying the Germans. Another especially noteworthy exemplar was Adam Czerniakow, the chairman of the Warsaw Jewish Council. When he learned from the Germans that all Warsaw Jews would be "evacuated to the East," he understood what that really meant and decided that he would not take part in the deportations. He committed suicide by taking a cyanide pill.[37] Thus Bauer is right when he warns against making generalizations about the behavior of Jewish councils and individual Jewish leaders. The variability in the behavior of Jewish leaders serves as a reminder that moral blameworthiness is first and foremost a matter of individual conduct and character.

Another major form of collaboration that has drawn a great deal of criticism is the role of Jewish ghetto police in enforcing German regulations and conducting roundups for deportations. All of the large ghettos had uniformed Jewish police forces; they were "order service" (German *Ordnungsdienst*), not police. They were not issued firearms (for obvious reasons), but they were usually equipped with truncheons or whips. Altogether, there was a large number of Jewish policemen in occupied Poland; for example, the Warsaw Jewish police numbered two thousand, Lodz had six hundred, and Lvov, five hundred. Serving in the police conferred a number of benefits, so there were lots of volunteers.[38] One especially important advantage of serving in the ghetto police was immunity from deportation for oneself and (sometimes) for members of one's family. This alone generated a great deal of resentment in the rest of the community. But like all privileges allowed by the Germans, this one too was only temporary. Because the Jewish police had to enforce extremely unpopular German regulations such as the prohibition of smuggling food into the ghetto and because they did so with considerable brutality while also taking advantage of opportunities for profit, they were widely hated and resented. One anecdote tells of the order service men tossing their official caps out of the deportation train as it moved from the Treblinka station into the killing center, fearful of how they might be treated by other Jews once they were inside.[39]

Why Jewish men would want the great advantage of (even temporary) immunity from deportation for themselves and their families is understandable; the fear they felt for their own lives and their love for their families are mitigating circumstances that reduce the degree of blame that would otherwise be their due. However, there is no excuse for using brutality against fellow Jews or for making a profit out of their misery; quite the contrary, since harming others from motives of cruelty and greed makes one especially blameworthy. There is ample evidence that many Jews took unfair and cruel advantage of their official position as police in the ghettos. However, there were also many courageous and benevolent Jewish police. For example, in Kovno, Lithuania, the Jewish police were at the heart of an organized resistance movement that, among other things, illegally smuggled food into the ghetto to avert the mass starvation that would have resulted from the meager daily rations allotted by the Germans.[40] Although such exemplary police behavior was somewhat unusual, many Jewish police at least refrained from doing harm, merely going through the motions whenever it was possible to do so. Again, it is unwise to make generalizations, in this case about the behavior of individual members of the Jewish police. These men faced terrible moral dilemmas as they tried to serve both their German masters and the often demanding and autocratic Jewish councils under whom they worked; all the while they were fearful for their own lives and the lives of their families.

A stark example of the fate that awaited many of these Jewish police is presented by the story of Calel Perechodnik. In February 1941 he joined the Warsaw ghetto police, primarily to keep himself, his wife, and his daughter safe from whatever the Germans had in store for them. Later he became convinced that his being in the police was very likely the only way that he and his family could avoid deportation. His account of the next two years is harrowing and includes vivid descriptions of how life in the ghetto gradually became a war of all against all, with the rich bribing their way out of being deported by having a substitute sent in their place. In the end, Perechodnik himself evaded deportation only to see his wife and daughter caught by a German ruse designed to persuade them to report to the infamous Umschlagplatz, the railway platform from which deportation trains departed for Treblinka.[41]

I have already rejected Hilberg's thesis that the alleged deleterious effects of ghetto culture explain Jewish ignorance of German intentions. I must also reject his claim that ghetto culture is sufficient to explain Jewish collaboration with the Germans. First, it is not factually accurate to hold that all or even most Jews collaborated with the Germans; there were many defiant and noncooperative Jews, as well as many who are best described not as collaborators but as passive bystanders who endured the German oppression as well as they could. There was also a wide variation in the behavior of Jewish councils. Second, the ghetto culture explanation misses important differences in the motives and character of individuals who collaborated. Their motives included fear, benevolence, greed, love of power, and cruelty, among others, and their characters ranged widely from being decent to pitiful, to reprehensible in the extreme. Obviously, the degree of moral blameworthiness of individual collaborators varied greatly.

The Jews Should Have Resisted: They Should Not Have "Gone Like Lambs to the Slaughter"

The third main criticism of Jewish behavior during the Holocaust is perhaps the one most frequently encountered, especially in everyday discussions. The accusation that ghetto Jews went like lambs to the slaughter is not just a retrospective judgment made years later with the benefit of hindsight; it can be found in a proclamation written by the young leader of the first Jewish resistance group formed in Vilna, Lithuania, in January 1942, after several months of outdoor shootings in a nearby village, Ponary, had decimated the ghetto.

> Let us not be led like sheep to the slaughter!
>
> Let us defend ourselves during a deportation!
>
> For several months now, day and night, thousands and tens of thousands have been torn away from our midst, men, the aged, the women, and children, led away like cattle—and we, the remainder, are numbered. The illusion still lives within us that they are still alive somewhere, in an undisclosed concentration camp, in a ghetto.
>
> You believe and hope to see your mother, your father, your brother who was seized and disappeared.
>
> In the face of the next day which arrives with the horror of deportation and murder, the hour has struck to dispel the illusion: There is no way out of the ghetto, except the way of death![42]

This proclamation appeared after some 60,000 Jews of the Vilna ghetto (mostly the elderly, women, and children) had already been killed. The remaining 12,000 consisted of younger men and women who tended to be more realistic about the intentions of the Germans and also more willing to engage in resistance. The proclamation continues with a note of defiance absent from most Jewish utterances of the time:

> We will not go!
>
> Comrades! Uphold this awareness and impart to your families, to the remnants of the Jerusalem of Lithuania [Vilna].
>
> —Do not surrender into the hands of the kidnappers!
>
> —Do not hand over any other Jews!
>
> —If you are caught, you have nothing to lose!
>
> —Let us defend ourselves, and not go!
>
> Better to fall with honor in the ghetto than to be led like sheep to Ponary![43]

This example of resistance by the remnant of the Vilna ghetto is a good illustration of the nature of virtually all instances of armed resistance by Jews: (1) it occurred late after most of the Jews had already been killed; (2) it was not carried out by the Jewish councils but by a new, generally younger, leadership; (3) its aim was not to stop or even slow down the German genocide (since by that time most Jews realized that that was physically impossible); and (4) although it was hoped that resistance would exact some measure of vengeance against the Germans, it was undertaken primarily as a symbolic act of defiance that would at least preserve Jewish honor.[44]

Any tendency to blame the older established leadership for being too passive during the first deportations must take into account the objective constraints under which ghetto Jews labored that made successful armed resistance so difficult. First and foremost, it was virtually impossible to get arms and ammunition into the ghetto. The non-Jewish Polish resistance had the only available stockpile of arms and did not want to share it with Jews in the ghettos.[45] For example, the Jews of the Warsaw ghetto were consistently refused arms by the Poles until the very end, when they were given a small supply of revolvers, rifles, some machine guns, hand grenades, and explosives to battle the Germans when they came to liquidate the ghetto.[46] Second, most Jews were very reluctant to engage in resistance that would certainly bring swift and terrible collective punishment by the Germans on the rest of the Jewish community. The death penalty was meted out even to Poles interfering with deportations or giving shelter to Jews.[47] Third, even if Jews had gotten arms and used them, they would most likely have been unsuccessful in either stopping or slowing down the German genocidal program. Hilberg himself gives the most telling summary of the overall outcome of the Jewish resistance that did occur:

> It is doubtful that the Germans and their collaborators lost more than a few hundred men, dead and wounded, in the course of the destruction process. The number of men who dropped out because of disease, nervous breakdown, or court martial was probably greater. The Jewish resistance effort could not seriously impede or retard the progress of destructive operations. The Germans brushed that resistance aside as a minor obstacle, and in the totality of the destruction process it was of no consequence.[48]

No one will never know for sure what would have happened if ghetto Jews had gotten sufficient arms and ammunition early in the deportation process, but there is little reason to think that the outcome would have been significantly different if the ghetto Jews had attempted to resist early in the process. All of the evidence indicates that the Germans would have immediately allocated greater military resources to ensure that the destruction process did not break down.

Were most ghetto Jews blameworthy for failing to engage in armed resistance early in the process? Should they have resisted even though they had no real hope of defeating the Germans or averting their own deaths? In other words, is there an ethical case to be made for the view of the youthful resisters of Vilna who declared that it was better to die in the ghetto with honor than to go like sheep to their slaughter? Notice that this question does not ask whether the ghetto Jews had a *duty* to resist. Surely, they had no moral duty to deliberately sacrifice themselves in order to engage in a symbolic act of defiance, however admirable that might have been. This becomes quite clear if we keep in mind that during the initial phase of deportations, the Jewish community was still composed mostly of extended families, including the elderly, women with infants, and children. Who would argue that these Jews had a duty to deliberately sacrifice not just themselves but each other, their own children, and their elders in order to keep their honor? This would be romantic moralism run amok. It anything, it seems just as plausible to argue that, all things considered, ghetto Jews had a duty to protect their children and elderly as long as there was some hope, however slim, of saving them.

If ghetto Jews had no duty to sacrifice themselves, might it not still be the case that armed resistance, however futile, would at least have been admirable in a way that their actual passivity was not? If this way of posing the issue is also based on the idea that the entire community should deliberately bring about the deaths of their own elders and children as a means of preserving Jewish honor, it remains deeply problematical. Like any ethical claim about supererogatory action (i.e., any action going beyond duty), it is morally *optional*. Given that starting point, it is not at all obvious why, on the one hand, it is deemed shameful and blameworthy to stoically hope that what appears to be inevitable (the destruction of one's community) may yet be averted. All the while people can continue to take care of themselves and their families, and help others in the community, as well as they can—which actually happened. Nor is it clear why, on the other hand, it is deemed admirable and praiseworthy to deliberately sacrifice the community by armed resistance.[49] At the very least, it seems that there are two very different ways of assessing the ethics of the situation, and no apparent way to show conclusively that one of them is correct and the other mistaken.

Another important reason for being skeptical about blaming ghetto Jews (or German Jews, for that matter) is the fact that by and large other groups of Nazi victims who were similarly disarmed, defenseless, imprisoned, starved, immobilized, and often surrounded by a generally hostile community, also failed to engage in forceful resistance or armed rebellion against their German tormentors. Huge numbers of non-Jewish Poles, Soviet prisoners of war, Ukrainians, Gypsies, concentration camp prisoners, and slave workers were killed by the Germans in the "other Holocaust." When these groups engaged in resistance or armed rebellion at all, it was only sporadic and, most of the time, came only at the last moment when nothing remained to be lost.[50] The similar responses that these disparate groups made to German force and exploitation suggest that a factor like Jewish ghetto culture, though it certainly did not make resistance more likely, was neither a necessary nor a sufficient condition for the failure of Jews to resist early or "in time" during the destruction process. All of the groups mentioned subjected to overpowering German military force, imprisonment, continual violence, fear, starvation, and general deprivation reacted similarly; they all became comparatively passive, fatalistic, and socially disorganized. In many ways, the failure of Soviet prisoners of war to engage in any meaningful resistance until the very end of the war is the most telling, since they were preponderantly young, trained in the use of arms, and experienced in combat.[51]

Once a group is subjected to such debilitating conditions, individual characteristics become the most important variable in predicting behavior and the likelihood of survival. Those who survived these most extreme conditions were an exceedingly small minority. In a later work, Hilberg himself identified the individual characteristics shared by nearly all survivors of the destruction process. First, they had the favorable physical characteristics of being "relatively young, concentrated in the age group from the teens to the thirties," and they "had good health at the start of the ordeal." Second, they tended to have a favorable vocation or profession, such as carpentry or medicine. Third, they had favorable psychological characteristics. "Most critical, however, was the psychological profile of the survivors. In this respect, they differed completely from the great mass of their fellow victims. The contrast may be glimpsed in three important traits: realism, rapid decision making, and tenacious holding on to life."[52]

Hilberg does not point out the moral irrelevance of possessing these traits while being unlucky enough to fall into the hands of the Germans was itself largely a matter of luck. The person who possessed these traits as a matter of luck did not deserve any moral credit for having them, and, correspondingly, the one who lacked these traits due to bad luck did not deserve any blame either. Being young is not under personal control and is not a culturally induced characteristic. Being healthy, especially for someone who is also young, is in most cases also pure luck. Having a favorable occupation or profession is to some degree under one's control, but it was purely accidental that some victims of the Germans happened to have these favorable characteristics; it was clearly not a result of their having foresight about the Final Solution.

Thus, the psychological traits that Hilberg cites raise some basic issues of responsibility that I have already discussed. For example, in chapter 5 I argued that most people actively construct their sense of personal identity and that they often use self-deception to maintain it in the face of contrary evidence. When Hilberg refers to the trait of realism, he may have in mind a tendency to avoid self-deception. However, even if such realism is sometimes brought about in the course of active self-construction (as I am inclined to argue), those victims fortunate enough to have developed it before they were confronted with the Final Solution almost certainly cannot claim to have done so as the result of foresight or practical wisdom. On the other hand, what Hilberg calls realism may in many cases just be the effect of genetically inherited aptitude or intelligence in which active self-construction plays no part. If so, it is again a matter of luck. The trait of rapid decision making is also to a great extent an aspect of basic intelligence, and, as such, is in part due to genetic endowment, hence, in good part due to luck. Moreover, whether one evinces a "tenacious holding on to life" is itself often causally dependent on one's possessing the other favorable characteristics.

Many survivors have acknowledged the large role that luck played. One of the most acute of these, Primo Levi, admitted that being a professional chemist and understanding German were among the things that saved him; these advantages gained him an indoor job in a laboratory in the Auschwitz Buna plant during much of his imprisonment, which in turn helped save his life.[53] He was also young (twenty-five) and healthy when he was arrested. In her book, *Into That Darkness,* Gitta Sereny quotes Richard Glazer, who managed to escape from Treblinka, as saying, "If I speak of a thirst, a talent for life as the qualities most needed for survival . . . I don't mean to say that these were deliberate acts, or even feelings. They were, in fact, largely unconscious qualities." She follows this with her own interpretation of what Glazer had said: "It was clear that Richard did not mean to say that people died because they didn't have these qualities. To be chosen to live even for an extra day was nothing but luck, one chance in a thousand: it was only that if they had this incredible luck, then these qualities, he thought, gave them a chance to survive longer."[54]

In conclusion, then, Jews as a group are not blameworthy for not having engaged in resistance or armed rebellion early in the destruction process, or for failing to sacrifice themselves in a desperate symbolic act of defiance at the end.

A Brief Overview of the Nature and Scope of Jewish Resistance

In view of the great obstacles faced by Jews who attempted to engage in resistance of any kind, especially the lack of arms and the general indifference or hostility of the surrounding Polish community, the nature and scope of Jewish resistance activities is impressive. The brief overview that follows is derived from a study by Yehuda Bauer that has already been cited.[55] Bauer makes a distinction between armed and unarmed resistance. He argues that not only was there more armed resistance than writers like Hilberg are inclined to admit but also that Jewish unarmed resistance was equally important in the Holocaust.

Resistance by Jews in Eastern Europe

Most of the Jews in eastern Europe who came under the control of the Germans resided in Poland, Lithuania, and Byelorussia. Compared to western Europe, the Jewish population in eastern Europe was very large; for example, in 1939 there were about 3 million Jews living in Poland, but only 525,000 in Germany. Jewish resistance activities occurred in three main locations: the ghettos, the forests, and the concentration camps and death camps.

The Ghettos

Bauer admits that Hilberg is essentially correct about the reluctance of ghetto Jews to engage in armed resistance as long as there was some hope of surviving the Nazis and the war; they prepared for armed conflict only after a majority of the community had already been killed. Nonetheless, there were three armed rebellions in ghettos, one in Czestochowa, one in Tarnow, and one in Warsaw; these were "the first urban struggles against the Germans anywhere in Europe."[56] The revolt in Warsaw was especially hard fought. The 750 Jewish fighters were outnumbered by 3,000 German SS troops, yet it took the Germans almost a month to subdue the revolt.[57] There were four attempted rebellions in other Polish towns (Kielce, Opatow, Pilica, and Tomaszow Lubleski), and seventeen towns from which armed groups escaped to the forests to engage in partisan activity. There were seventeen wholly Jewish partisan detachments in central Poland; in addition, twenty-one partisan detachments had memberships that were 30 percent or more Jewish.

The Forests

The thick forests in which Jewish partisans could operate were located in eastern Poland, eastern Lithuania, and western Byelorussia. Bauer estimates that there were between 6,000 and 10,000 Jewish partisans in these forests, with about 5,000 surviving the war. There were also 5,000 Jewish fighters in the Generalgouvernement (the central section of occupied Poland). Some of these took part in the Warsaw ghetto revolt, and about 1,000 took part in the Warsaw uprising in 1944 just before the arrival of the Soviet troops. Most of the fighters in these two operations were killed.

The Camps

Six rebellions took place despite the tight security and secrecy surrounding concentration camps and killing centers. Three occurred in concentration camps (Kruszyna, Krychow, and "Kopernik") and three in killing centers (Sobibor, Treblinka, and Auschwitz). The rebellion at Auschwitz actually took place in the gas chambers and involved the Jewish Sonderkommando, eight hundred members of special squads who removed the bodies of the dead.[58]

Resistance by Western European Jews

Jews in the West were a much smaller minority than in the East, and they were not confined to ghettos, although German Jews were trapped in a system of social death that almost functioned as the equivalent of ghettos. Nevertheless, anti-Semitism was not as strong as in the East and Jews were more assimilated, which meant that many Jews participated as individuals in non-Jewish resistance organizations. However, there were some Jewish resistance organizations in Germany, France, and Belgium, with thousands of members altogether.

Moreover, the Jews were usually the first to act—for example, the first urban guer-
rillas fighting against the Nazis in Paris during the spring of 1942 were members
of a Jewish unit of the pro-communist MOI. The Guttfreund group in Belgium
took up arms as early as September 1941, killing a Jewish Gestapo agent, robbing
a factory producing for the Germans, and later burning a card index of Jews at the
Judenrat office in Brussels. Finally, thousands of Jews fought in northern Italy in
1943–4, and thousands more fought with Tito's army in Jugoslavia.[59]

Even in the heart of Berlin there were small Jewish resistance groups such as
the Chug Chaluzi formed by twenty or so young men and women (sometimes
their number grew to about forty) who were in hiding to provide mutual support and engage in illegal activities. Since they had no arms, they had to confine themselves to activities such as trying to save people's lives, especially
children's.[60]

Praiseworthy Aspects of Jewish Culture and Behavior during the Holocaust

A discussion of the behavior of Jewish victims would be incomplete without
some recognition of their strong communal morality and the exemplary actions
to which it gave rise. At that time Jewish culture (similarly to non-Jewish culture) in both eastern and western Europe was quite conservative in several important ways. First, the family, which was usually patriarchal in form, was a
strong and dominant institution; although many western Jews were politically
liberal, modern individualism had not made very many inroads into Jewish life.
Indeed, among eastern Jews, liberalism and individualism were virtually
nonexistent. Second, most Jews were devout and practiced their religion conscientiously; thus the synagogue was a principal institution in every community. Third, there was a very strong sense of communal responsibility for the
well-being of all members of the Jewish community, especially children and
the poor. As a consequence of these features of their culture, Jews tended to
have very strong familial ties. They were very likely to be heavily involved with
their synagogue, and they participated in a wide variety of Jewish welfare organizations that existed in each community. For example, before World War
II, even the "dictator" of the Lodz ghetto, Chaim Rumkowski, had "involved
himself in community affairs and managed several orphanages with devo-
tion."[61]

This thickly woven social fabric of Jewish communal life led many Jews to
continue to make strenuous efforts to help each other, despite dwindling resources and constant harassment, intimidation, and deportation by the Germans, almost up to the end of the destruction process. This can be seen in the
activities of Jewish welfare organizations in Germany. For example, as the anti-
Semitic policies of the Nazi regime took effect, more and more Jews became

unemployed as they were excluded from one occupation after another. The Jewish Central Bureau for Economic Relief, among others, supported the instruction of 20,000 men and women who needed new skills to find a job, and the Winter Relief Agency helped people find clothing and ever scarcer housing.[62] As the social isolation of Jews grew greater and greater, the Jewish Cultural Association offered entertainment of all kinds in forty-six locations throughout Germany up through 1941; then it was dissolved by the Nazis. The association's activities included concerts, theater, and lectures. It often employed artists who had been fired as a result of racial decrees.[63] In general, the segregation of Jews tended to increase their sense of community and solidarity.[64] The Jewish community also displayed inventiveness and creativity in the face of severely restricted opportunities brought on by the war and the generally worsening conditions. Since Jews were forbidden to use public transportation, visit parks, or take excursions in the forests, Jewish children had no place to play or take exercise free from the harassment of German children and adults. One Jewish community came up with a unique solution: using every free spot in Jewish cemeteries as a playground complete with sand boxes for the smaller children. Older children also weeded the graves, thus saving on the cost of labor.[65]

The Jewish communities in the ghettos of Poland also had many welfare organizations that were active almost up to the end, trying to ameliorate the awful conditions in which Jews were being forced to live. As already noted, the Germans used these welfare organizations as instruments of destruction, but they nevertheless did not neglect their welfare activities. For example, the offices operated by the Welfare Division of Lodz Jewish Council included an office of relief (money and products), a nursery, two orphanages, a home for the aged, a home for invalids, a collecting point for homeless people, public kitchens, a children's colony, and a children's sanitarium.[66] The Germans wanted the Jewish councils to be able to maintain at least minimum stability in the ghettos so that they could implement the program of deportations efficiently. Since German concern for the welfare of the ghettos was purely instrumental and limited, they still pursued policies of confiscation of property, exploitation of labor, and food embargoes. These policies led inevitably to mass starvation and disease, with high mortality rates. Consequently, the Germans placed severe limits on what Jewish welfare organizations could do to help their ghetto communities fight starvation and disease.[67] However, this did not prevent them from providing other kinds of welfare for their communities. For example, although the Germans forbade any kind of education in ghettos, there were widespread clandestine study groups in many ghettos, and Warsaw had clandestine high schools. Moreover, despite a German ban on all public religious observances, there were some six hundred illegal Jewish prayer groups in Warsaw.[68]

The great majority of Jews probably came, eventually, to the realization that the Germans meant to kill them all, yet many of them carried on their lives with a measure of dignity and managed to help each other, despite the horrendous conditions in which most of them were forced to live. We will never know how many Jews engaged in self-deception in order to be able to cope with their seemingly hopeless situation, including being able to keep their self-respect and continue doing whatever good was possible. However, as long as their self-deception served primarily to allow them to cope with their desperate situation and to resist the temptation to look out only for themselves, as so many did, they deserve our respect.

There are countless examples of individual Jews who showed courage and self-control. In Germany, Jewish women often had to provide for their family because their husbands could no longer find work. Many women also discovered a hitherto unknown tenacity and assertiveness when they had to battle foreign consulates and bureaucracies in their efforts to emigrate.[69] Many elderly Jews who were too frail or too poor to emigrate showed great courage and dignity as they chose to commit suicide rather than be deported and killed by the Germans.[70] In the Warsaw ghetto, Janusz Korczack, a Jewish doctor in charge of an orphanage, chose not to take an opportunity to escape from the ghetto in order to stay with his young charges. He was deported with them to Treblinka on August 5, 1942.[71] Examples like these could be multiplied almost indefinitely.

To summarize, Jewish culture maintained a strong sense of communal responsibility for the welfare of all Jews, especially the poor and children. Thus it provided the social and institutional framework within which individual Jews could fulfill the basic duties of the core content of morality, especially the prima facie duties to help others in accordance with one's justified role responsibilities and to give aid to others in Good Samaritan situations. Given the often enormous risks and dangers that Jews faced, there is little doubt that many of these acts were supererogatory, and in cases like that of Janusz Korczak, even heroic and saintly.

Notes

1. Bohdan Wytwycky, *The Other Holocaust: The Many Circles of Hell* (Washington, D.C.: Novak Report on the New Ethnicity, 1980).

2. Phillip Hallie, *Lest Innocent Blood Be Shed* (New York: Harper & Row, 1979).

3. John Sabini and Maury Silver, *Moralities of Everyday Life* (New York: Oxford University Press, 1982). The title of chapter 4.

4. Raul Hilberg, *TheDestruction of the European Jews,* vol. 3 (New York: Holmes & Meier, 1985), chap. 10; Hannah Arendt, *Eichmann in Jerusalem: A Report on the Banality of Evil* (New York: Penguin, 1977), 117–118.

5. Lucy S. Dawidowicz, ed., *A Holocaust Reader* (New York: Behrman, 1976), 330.

6. Jackson J. Spielvogel, *Hitler and Nazi Germany: A History* (Englewood Cliffs, N.J.: Prentice-Hall, 1992), 294.

7. Marion Kaplan, *Between Dignity and Despair: Jewish Life in Nazi Germany* (New

York: Oxford University Press, 1998), 232; Michael Berenbaum, *A Mosaic of Victims: Non-Jews Persecuted and Murdered by the Nazis* (New York: New York University Press, 1990), 113.

8. Berenbaum, *A Mosaic of Victims.*

9. Kaplan, *Between Dignity and Despair,* 10–12.

10. Spielvogel, *Hitler and Nazi Germany,* 270–274.

11. Spielvogel, *Hitler and Nazi Germany,* 285–286.

12. Kaplan, *Between Dignity and Despair,* 231–232.

13. Spielvogel, *Hitler and Nazi Germany,* 285–286.

14. Hilberg, *Destruction of the European Jews,* vol. 3, chap. 9, esp. 875–879.

15. Kaplan, *Between Dignity and Despair,* 162.

16. Kaplan, *Between Dignity and Despair,* 157–160, chap. 6.

17. Kaplan, *Between Dignity and Despair,* 187–200.

18. Hilberg, *Destruction of the European Jews,* 3:22–28, 1030–1044.

19. Hilberg, *Destruction of the European Jews,* 1:22.

20. Hilberg, *Destruction of the European Jews,* 1:22–27.

21. Hilberg, *Destruction of the European Jews,* 3:1038–1039.

22. David Biale, *Power and Powerlessness in Jewish History* (New York: Schocken, 1987), chap. 4; Paul Johnson, *A History of the Jews* (New York: Harper & Row, 1987), chaps. 4–5.

23. Hilberg, *Destruction of the European Jews,* 2:495.

24. Hilberg, *Destruction of the European Jews,* 3:1039.

25. Arendt, *Eichmann in Jerusalem,* 117–118.

26. Hilberg, *Destruction of the European Jews,* 2:493–494.

27. Hilberg, *Destruction of the European Jews,* 1:217–218.

28. Yehuda Bauer, "Forms of Jewish Resistance during the Holocaust," in *Holocaust: Religious and Philosophical Implications,* ed. John K. Roth and Michael Berenbaum (New York: Paragon, 1989), 149.

29. Bauer, "Forms of Jewish Resistance," 150.

30. Bauer, "Forms of Jewish Resistance," 150.

31. Hilberg, *Destruction of the European Jews,* 2:495.

32. Raul Hilberg, *Perpetrators, Victims, Bystanders: The Jewish Catastrophe, 1933–1945* (New York: HarperCollins, 1992), 109.

33. Hilberg, *Destruction of the European Jews,* 2:223, 515–518.

34. Hilberg, *Perpetrators,* 147.

35. Hilberg, *Destruction of the European Jews,* 2:517–518; Primo Levi, *The Drowned and the Saved* (New York: Summit, 1986), 60–87 for a survivor's assessment of Rumkowski.

36. Hilberg, *Destruction of the European Jews,* 1:218.

37. Hilberg, *Destruction of the European Jews,* 2:502.

38. Hilberg, *Perpetrators,* 161.

39. Hilberg, *Perpetrators,* 162.

40. Bauer, "Forms of Jewish Resistance," 147.

41. Calel Perechodnik, *Am I a Murderer? Testament of a Jewish Ghetto Policeman* (Boulder, Colo.: Westview, 1996).

42. Dawidowicz, *Holocaust Reader,* 334–335.

43. Dawidowicz, *Holocaust Reader,* 335.

44. Dawidowicz, *Holocaust Reader,* 329–330: Hilberg, *Destruction of the European Jews,* 499–509, on the Warsaw ghetto.

45. Bauer, "Forms of Jewish Resistance." See pp. 140–141 on arms.

46. Hilberg, *Destruction of the European Jews,* 2:509–510.

47. Hilberg, *Destruction of the European Jews,* 2:489.

48. Hilberg, *Destruction of the European Jews,* 3:1031.

49. Bauer, "Forms of Jewish Resistance." See page 153 for an example of admirable sacrifice by four members of the Kosow Judenrat.

50. Berenbaum, *A Mosaic of Victims,* passim.

51. Bauer, "Forms of Jewish Resistance," 143.

52. Hilberg, *Perpetrators,* 188.

53. Primo Levi, *Survival in Auschwitz* (New York: Collier, 1993), chap. 15.

54. Gitta Sereny, *Into That Darkness* (New York: Vintage, 1974), 186–187.

55. Bauer, "Forms of Jewish Resistance."

56. Bauer, "Forms of Jewish Resistance," 145.

57. Hilberg, *Destruction of the European Jews,* 2:511–513.

58. Bauer, "Forms of Jewish Resistance," 143; Filip Mueller, *Eyewitness Auschwitz: Three Years in the Gas Chambers* (New York: Stein & Day, 1979), 145–160.

59. Bauer, "Forms of Jewish Resistance," 145.

60. Kaplan, *Between Dignity and Despair,* 212–214.

61. Hilberg, *Perpetrators,* 109.

62. Kaplan, *Between Dignity and Despair,* 29–33.

63. Kaplan, *Between Dignity and Despair,* 46–47.

64. Kaplan, *Between Dignity and Despair,* 155.

65. Kaplan, *Between Dignity and Despair,* 163.

66. Hilberg, *The Destruction of the European Jews,* 1:232.

67. Hilberg, *The Destruction of the European Jews,* 1:239–269.

68. Bauer, "Forms of Jewish Resistance," 147.

69. Kaplan, *Between Dignity and Despair,* 60.

70. Kaplan, *Between Dignity and Despair,* 179–184.

71. Hilberg, *Destruction of the European Jews,* 2:504.

Suggestions for Further Reading

Ainsztein, Reuben. *Jewish Resistance in Nazi-Occupied Eastern Europe.* New York: Barnes & Noble, 1975. A standard work.

Arad, Yitzak. *Belzec, Sobibor, Treblinka: The Operation Reinhard Death Camps.* Bloomington: Indiana University Press, 1987. Pt. 3, "Escape and Resistance."

Bauer, Yehuda. "Forms of Jewish Resistance during the Holocaust." In *Holocaust: Religious and Philosophical Questions.* Edited by John K. Roth and Michael Berenbaum. New York: Paragon, 1989.

Berenbaum, Michael, ed. *A Mosaic of Victims: Non-Jews Persecuted and Murdered by the Nazis.* New York: New York University Press, 1990. An excellent, balanced account by a number of individual scholars on a wide variety of victims. Available in paperback.

Frank, Anne. *The Diary of a Young Girl*. New York: Bantam, 1997. Perhaps the best-known work by a victim, this book chronicles the two years that Anne and her family spent in hiding. Paperback.

Hilberg, Raul. *The Destruction of the European Jews*. New York: Holmes & Meier, 1985. See the chapter entitled "Victims," pages 1030–1044. An influential critical account by a historian.

————. *Perpetrators, Victims, Bystanders: The Jewish Catastrophe, 1933–1945*. New York: HarperCollins, 1992, pt. 2, "Victims." Contains many excellent portraits of individuals, so it serves as a good complement to Hilberg's discussion in *The Destruction of the European Jews*.

Kaplan, Marion A. *Between Dignity and Despair: Jewish Life in Nazi Germany*. New York : Oxford University Press, 1998. Excellent account, based largely on memoirs and diaries of Jews who lived through the years of anti-Semitic policies leading to "social death," as well as the years of the Final Solution.

Rosenthal, Abigail L. "The Right Way to Act: Indicting the Victims." In *Echoes from the Holocaust: Philosophical Reflections on a Dark Time*. Edited By Alan Rosenberg and Gerald E. Myers. Philadelphia: Temple University Press, 1988. An excellent critical examination of some of the main criticisms directed at the victims' behavior.

Suhl, Yuri, ed. *They Fought Back: The Story of Jewish Resistance in Nazi Europe*. New York: Schocken, 1975. Good collection of brief accounts of a wide range of resistance activities, most of them written by actual participants. It suffers from a lack of balance, however, since it focuses almost exclusively on the positive aspects of Jewish resistance. Available in paperback.

Wyman, David. *The Abandonment of the Jews: America and the Holocaust*. New York: Pantheon, 1984. Good account of the failure of the United States to help Jewish victims of the Holocaust from 1933 to 1945.

Wytwycky, Bohden. *The Other Holocaust: The Many Circles of Hell*. Washington, D.C.: Novak Report on the New Ethnicity, 1980. A study of non-Jewish victims of German aggression and racial policies.

Chapter 9

Helpers, Rescuers, and Bystanders

Some Basic Questions

The admirable degree of self-help and courage shown by Jewish communities described in chapter 8 is not the only morally rewarding story to be found in the midst of all of the evil that occurred during the Holocaust. There is also the remarkable story of the thousands of people throughout Germany and the rest of German-occupied Europe who helped fugitive Jews and other refugees hide, survive, and escape from Nazi oppression and extermination. Helpers and rescuers stand out in sharp contrast to the great majority of people in all countries, who were either perpetrators or bystanders. The phenomenon of helpers and rescuers raises several important factual and psychological questions that are addressed in this chapter. How many helpers and rescuers were there? How many victims did they succeed in rescuing from the Germans? What explains their choosing to give help and engage in rescue? To remain a bystander? In addition to these factual and psychological questions, I discuss several basic ethical questions. Were the acts of help and rescue supererogatory, that is, did they go above and beyond what could reasonably be expected as a matter of duty? Were helpers and rescuers extraordinarily virtuous and courageous moral exemplars who should be admired as heroic or saintly? Or were acts of help and rescue something that was their actual duty to do, all things considered? Was the failure of bystanders to render help wrong, all things considered; that is, did they have an actual duty to help victims? If it was wrong not to help, were they blameworthy for their failure, and if so, why? There is no single correct answer to any of these questions, since it is not possible to make generalizations, either about the psychology or the ethics of help and rescue, that accurately fit all individuals.

Although the numbers of non-Jewish helpers and rescuers tended to be fairly small in every country, collectively they saved thousands of victims from extermination. There are no exact figures on the number of Jews saved by individual helpers and rescuers, but in one recent study the estimates given for each of the countries in which the Germans perpetrated the Final Solution taken together total nearly 300,000. In addition to Jews helped by individual rescuers (either working alone or in clandestine networks), approximately 600,000 more Jews were saved by official actions, such as the refusal by the collaborationist governments of France, Bulgaria, and Romania to deport their Jewish citizens.[1] Thus, help and rescue by non-Jews, acting as individuals or through their governments, saved close to a million potential victims of genocide.

The number of individual non-Jews who engaged in help and rescue is unknown. As of 1994, Yad Vashem (Israel's Holocaust Memorial Authority) had honored 11,000 rescuers; however, this figure is almost surely too small. For one thing, Yad Vashem employs a very strict set of criteria in identifying those to be honored, which excludes some rescuers who probably deserve recognition. Although people who helped only for pay are properly excluded, Yad Vashem also refuses to recognize police rescuers because they were also involved in repression.[2] Many rescuers will most likely remain unidentified because they had to work in secret; any who were killed or died before they could be properly identified will perhaps never be known. Moreover, the Yad Vashem total does not include the thousands of people who rendered various kinds of help that fell short of actual rescue, such as giving food to fugitive Jews.[3] Even though the exact number of rescuers remains unknown, some estimates have been made based on memoirs, autobiographies, and interviews with survivors. The data in one such study indicate that about three hundred Germans were needed to hide sixty-five Jews because virtually all fugitives stayed with more than one rescuer, usually many more.[4] This conclusion is supported by another finding: 28 percent of all rescuers in one study were "Judeophiles," that is, people who were motivated primarily by love and friendship with Jews they knew personally or by an appreciation for Jewish religion and culture. Of these, 71 percent rescued more than one person.[5] Nevertheless, because the number of Jews who were successfully rescued is comparatively small, it must be inferred that the number of rescuers was also small. For example, even if all of the estimated 12,000 German Jews who went into hiding were taken in and helped by non-Jewish Germans (an assumption that is almost certainly too high), there would still have been only about 55,000 helpers and rescuers out of a total German population of 65 million. In most western European countries the ratio of the number of helpers and rescuers to the number of Jews hidden would probably have been even smaller. Thus, one fact seems inescapable: A relatively small number of individual helpers and rescuers throughout Europe saved the lives of approximately 300,000 Jews. It is impossible not to wonder how many more victims might have been saved if, instead of the millions of bystanders, there had also been, say, several million helpers and rescuers.

There are different explanations for the choices people made to remain by-standers. Some people were bystanders because they had to take care of elderly parents, which often prevented them from helping or rescuing Jews. Others became bystanders because they were afraid to help or because they were indifferent to the fate of Jews. As these examples illustrate, explanations can differ greatly in their moral implications. It will be argued that many bystanders had a prima facie duty to render at least some kind of help to victims, so unless they had a justification or a valid excuse, they were blameworthy for failing to give it. They had an actual duty, all things considered. Taking care of elderly parents, especially if they were frail or ill, would probably constitute a justification in many situations, but failing to help out of indifference makes one blameworthy.

The reasons for individuals' choosing to become helpers or rescuers vary. For example, some people engaged in helping and rescue because they believed (correctly, I shall argue) that it was their duty; in the particular set of circumstances in which they found themselves, they could render help without sacrificing their lives or taking unreasonable risks. Many churchmen and churchwomen in Italy had access to good hiding places in convents and monasteries in which the Jews would be difficult to find, and they had a large network of companions to draw on for financial and logistical support.[6] Nevertheless, giving such help always involved some degree of risk and demanded time and effort, and thus such helpers were praiseworthy. Other people became rescuers because they had a deep personal concern to alleviate the plight of victims; they were essentially responding out of benevolence; moreover, saving the lives of Jews gave them a great sense of satisfaction that they were helping to resist Nazism and the values it represented.[7] Some benevolent rescuers in Poland went far beyond duty to rescue Jews, despite the great risk of being betrayed by their anti-Semitic neighbors and summarily executed if caught.[8] The actions of such rescuers were clearly supererogatory and highly admirable. Clearly, explanations of the choices people made to become helpers and rescuers also differ in their moral implications. The ethics of help and rescue must be brought to bear in order to properly assess the implications of the various explanations that will be encountered in this discussion.

In general, the literature on rescuers does not support the view that men were more likely to engage in help and rescue than women; neither does it support the opposite view that women were more disposed to help than men. Reliable data are lacking on how many rescuers were men and how many were women. However, the rescue studies that have been done make it clear that there were many men and many women involved in every country. Granted, traditional gender roles often resulted in men's having most of the leadership roles in rescue networks and resistance organizations. Nevertheless as the examples in this chapter confirm, they had no monopoly on courage (physical or moral), high risk taking, resourcefulness, or quick-wittedness. There was also a tendency for women to be more involved in saving children than men, but men saved children too (as demonstrated by the example of Antonin Kalina, described later in this chapter). Neither do studies of rescuers confirm the view, defended at one time by the psychologist Carol Gilligan, that women are more likely to be motivated by "care" (what I call benevolence), whereas men are more likely to be motivated by "justice" (what I call conscientiousness, especially with regard to respecting people's rights).[9] One author summarizes her findings this way: "Both men and women showed morality based on caring and attachment. Both men and women had emotional responses to the plight of the Jews. Both men and women came to the aid of victims through an outraged sense of justice."[10] In other words, both men and women rescuers possessed moral character that exhibits the principal virtues: benevolence, conscientiousness, courage and self-control, and, of course, practical wisdom.[11]

Another popular explanation for people's engaging in rescue is that they were motivated by their religious beliefs. There are two main reasons to doubt this explanation for the helping activity of all, or even most, rescuers. First, rescuers did not differ significantly from bystanders or nonrescuers in religious identification, religious education, their own religiosity, or that of their parents. Second, only 15 percent of rescuers mentioned at least one religious reason for rescuing Jews. Moreover, rescuers' interpretations of religious teachings and commitments differed from those of nonrescuers, stressing the common humanity of all people and supporting help for Jews.[12]

Perhaps the most significant finding of recent research into the psychology of rescuers is that they differed markedly from nonrescuers in the degree to which they possessed the characteristic of "extensivity," what I have called universal (unlimited scope) benevolence and conscientiousness. Helpers and rescuers saw Jewish victims of the Final Solution as fellow human beings who were as deserving as anyone else of their benevolent concern and conscientious fulfillment of basic moral duties.[13]

The Ethics of Help and Rescue

Duty versus Supererogatory Acts

Acts of help and rescue relevant to this discussion can be divided into two main categories: acts that are one's duty (either prima facie or actual, all things considered) and acts that are supererogatory (above and beyond duty). With respect to acts that are one's duty, there are two kinds of prima facie duty to do good for others in the core content of morality (the basic moral rules). The first is the prima facie duty to do good for others in accordance with one's justified role responsibilities; for example, a doctor should provide medical treatment to someone who is critically injured. The second is the prima facie duty of mutual aid; in emergency situations if there is no one present with a relevant role responsibility, one should render aid unless doing so would involve unreasonable cost or sacrifice. For example, someone who does not know how to swim cannot reasonably be required to jump into a turbulent river to save someone from drowning. However, the duty of mutual aid may reasonably involve some sacrifice and risk, so expert swimmers may well have a duty to try to rescue someone in these circumstances. The main point is that it is not right to stand by and do nothing.

A third prima facie duty is the duty to prevent others from harming third parties. This prima facie duty is actually a corollary of the prima facie duty of mutual aid; just as we cannot stand by and watch someone drown, we cannot stand by and watch someone being attacked by others. In the context of the Holocaust this corollary duty takes on added significance, since the state-sponsored discrimination, killing, enslavement, and exploitation directed against Jews, Gypsies, Jehovah's Witnesses, all Slavic peoples, the mentally ill, as well as countless others, represented an all-out assault on the basic duty not to harm others and the principle of equal consideration that underlies it.

In particular situations, each of these three kinds of prima facie duty may also constitute one's actual duty, all things considered; indeed, most of the time, this is what happens. To say that performing some act is a prima facie duty implies that there is a very strong presumption that one ought to do it; consequently, in a particular situation, a prima facie duty becomes one's actual duty unless there are clear and weighty reasons for overriding it. Moreover, in the great preponderance of situations, there are in fact no overriding reasons. Thus a doctor's prima facie role responsibility to give medical treatment to someone who is critically injured becomes his or her actual duty, all things considered, in the great preponderance of cases. Indeed, this is the reason why treating critically injured people in emergencies is a *rule* of role responsibility for doctors; one could say that it is among their "duties of office." Similarly, the prima facie duty to render mutual aid in an emergency is, in effect, a moral rule that every person should take very seriously; in practice, in situations in which this prima facie duty is relevant, it is very likely to be one's actual duty, all things considered. Since I am primarily concerned with what individual people ought to do in particular situations, this discussion of the ethics of help and rescue will focus on *actual duty, all things considered.*

Supererogatory acts are best defined by contrasting them with acts that are one's actual duty, all things considered. This can be done by providing a logically exhaustive classification of the status of acts, all things considered, as the following outline demonstrates.

I. Actual duties
   A. Negative duties are *prohibitions:* acts that are one's actual duty not to
      do; refraining from doing them is right and doing them is wrong, all
      things considered (e.g., most acts of harming others).
   B. Positive duties are *requirements:* acts that are one's actual duty to do;
      refraining from them is wrong and doing them is right, all things con-
      sidered (e.g., most acts of giving aid in an emergency).
II. Nonduties or optional acts (acts that are not matters of duty at all; they are
    neither prohibited nor required, all things considered; however, there are
    important differences in the reasons why some acts are optional, all things
    considered).
   A. Some optional acts are *morally neutral;* they are neither right nor wrong,
      good nor bad, all things considered (e.g., many purely "self-regarding"
      acts that do not affect others one way or the other).
   B. Some optional acts are *permissible;* although they are prima facie wrong,
      they are neither right nor wrong, good nor bad, all things considered;
      rather, they are "all right" to do (e.g., killing someone in self-defense).
   C. Some optional acts are *supererogatory;* they are good to do, but (since
      they are not duties) they are *not wrong not to do,* all things considered,
      even though refraining may deprive someone of a benefit (for example,
      many acts of kindness).

Regarding the last category, acts that are optional because they are
supererogatory, it is important to note that although every act in this category
is a good act, the degree of goodness can vary greatly. Risking one's own life
to save someone else is usually supererogatory, but so is doing a small favor
like giving directions to a tourist lost in a large city. Small acts of kindness and
generosity have ethical significance, but the concern in this discussion lies with
acts of help and rescue in the Holocaust that conferred vital benefits on victims
facing isolation, starvation, and death. My purpose is (1) to explain why, in general, some acts of help and rescue are properly deemed supererogatory, (2) to
give examples of acts of help and rescue during the Holocaust that are clearly
supererogatory, and (3) to defend the conclusion that some acts of help and rescue during the Holocaust were *not supererogatory* but rather actual duties, all
things considered.

First, some acts of help and rescue are clearly supererogatory because, for
one thing (as I have already argued), people in general do not have a prima facie duty to deliberately sacrifice their own lives in order to help or rescue others. Policemen and policewomen, members of the Secret Service, and others
who have role responsibilities to risk their lives on behalf of someone else are
not really exceptions because they have voluntarily joined public institutions
charged with these responsibilities, and they have knowingly assumed their
special duties. Leaving aside people like these who have special role responsi-

bilities, any particular act of intentional self-sacrifice, such as using one's body to shield someone from rifle fire, is supererogatory; it goes beyond what can reasonably be required as a duty. Of course, such self-sacrifice is very good and praiseworthy and warrants our admiration, but it is not wrong to refrain from doing it.

Second, some acts of help and rescue during the Holocaust were clearly supererogatory. Sofia Baniecka was a twenty-two-year-old Polish woman when the Germans invaded in 1939. She became actively engaged in a network that was buying guns for the underground in Warsaw, and in the course of this work she and her mother began to hide Jewish families, including some with children. They hid some of the families in the house in which they were staying, and when they ran out of room, they would take additional Jewish families to other safe houses. "We had at least fifty Jews during the war—friends, strangers, acquaintances, or someone who heard about me from someone else. Anyone was taken in." Because she and her mother were engaged in obtaining and storing guns for the underground as well as in rescuing Jews, they were in constant danger. If the Germans had raided the house and had found either guns or Jews (or both), it would have "meant a death sentence."[14] She and her mother also had many anti-Semitic neighbors to contend with who would have betrayed them if they had suspected what they were doing.

There is no doubt that they were in objective danger because in fact large numbers of Poles who were caught helping the underground or hiding Jews were executed.[15] Helpers and rescuers in different countries encountered significantly different degrees of difficulty and danger. Among the most important variables were the degree of German political control and the Germans' use of force, as well as the degree of anti-Semitism among the general population. In Poland all three of these variables were at their maximum strength, and, consequently, there were proportionally fewer helpers and rescuers than there were in Italy, for example. Given all these relevant facts, the acts of Sofia Baniecka and her mother clearly went beyond duty; "all things considered," they had no duty to act as they did.

Third, virtually all studies of rescuers find that they tend to deny that they did anything heroic or extraordinary. Many of them explicitly state that they only did what anyone should have done, that they only did their duty.[16] Of course, people are inclined to disagree with these rather matter-of-fact self-assessments, in part because some rescuers' acts, like those of Sofia Baniecka and her mother, *were* truly supererogatory. However, there are good reasons for thinking that often the rescuers were correct; they were only doing what anyone should have done, namely, give help where it was sorely needed, when doing so did not involve unreasonable risks to oneself. All things considered, they had an actual duty. The extremely adverse conditions for rendering help and engaging in rescue that existed in Poland were also generally present in Greater Germany (Germany and Austria) and in all of the territories of the Soviet Union invaded by the Germans (e.g., the former Baltic countries, Byelorussia, and the Ukraine). However, this was not so in most of occupied western Europe or in Italy. Italy is in many ways a special case, since it was an ally of Germany and retained its political sovereignty until September 1943 when the Germans occupied the northern half of the country. There was little anti-Semitism among the Italian people. Although Italy adopted a set of stringent anti-Semitic laws in 1938, they were not very vigorously enforced. Even during the war, Italians dragged their heels when pressured by the Germans to implement the Final Solution in their country. Even the Italian military, from enlisted men up through the top levels of the officer corps, subverted the Final Solution in areas under their control in southern France, Yugoslavia, and Greece, thereby saving thousands of Jews (albeit some only temporarily).[17] The Italians' relative lack of anti-Semitism and the fact that the Germans did not intervene directly in Italian affairs until 1943 meant that, at least until the German occupation began, there were many more acts of help and rescue that could be performed without the high degree of danger and risk found in Poland and other eastern European areas.

In addition to Italy, other western countries such as France and Belgium presented more favorable conditions for helping and rescuing Jews, primarily because there was less anti-Semitism among the French and Belgians and because the Germans played a more restrained role than they did in Poland and in the East generally. This is not to say that giving help and engaging in rescue in western occupied countries was without risk or that all acts of help and rescue were actual duties. Rather, there were many more opportunities for help and rescue with less risk in those countries. Consequently, in many instances when helpers and rescuers maintain that they were only doing what anyone ought to have done (i.e., their duty), they were not only expressing their own sincere beliefs, but (I shall argue) those beliefs were also correct. An equally important implication is that many people who were bystanders and failed to give help or engage in rescue in these circumstances were blameworthy for having failed to fulfill what was in fact an actual duty for them.

Evaluative Criteria for Deciding Whether a Particular Act of Help or Rescue Is One's Actual Duty, All Things Considered

How do people make justified judgments that someone did or did not have an actual duty to render help or engage in rescue in a particular situation? Evaluative criteria identify relevant reasons that *justify* a decision (judgment) to give help or engage in rescue, as a matter of actual duty, all things considered. Getting clear about what these reasons are will provide substantiation for the claim that there were many kinds of help that bystanders could have given to victims without unreasonable risk or sacrifice, much of it being help that was essential to victims for survival or escape. It this is true, then many bystanders were blameworthy for failing to fulfill actual duties. These reasons will serve as guidelines for assessing the actions of helpers and rescuers, as well as the inaction of bystanders.

The inquiry into justification belongs to ethics and must be kept distinct from the psychological inquiry into motivation. The ethically relevant reasons that justify doing an act because it is the right thing to do in a particular situation, all things considered, may or may not be the same as the psychological reasons that in fact prompt a person to do it. Thus, this section should not be viewed as a study of the actual psychology of helpers and rescuers, but primarily as a rational analysis of the relevant reasons that, ideally, *ought* to have informed their decisions. Although I give examples of some of the motives that prompted some people to give help or engage in rescue, I am postponing a full discussion of the psychology of actual helpers and rescuers, especially the variety of their motives, characters, and personalities.

This discussion includes only criteria that are relevant for making decisions about help and rescue in the kinds of situations that were encountered in the Holocaust. The principal criteria for making a decision (judgment) in a particular situation that an act of help or rescue is one's actual duty, all things considered, are (1) the relative value of the benefit to the victim, (2) the value of the help or rescue as an act of resistance to Nazi oppression and values, and (3) the ability and opportunity of the actor to perform the act. The first conclusion to be established is that there were many possible acts of help or rescue that had the following characteristics when evaluated by these three criteria: either (a) they would provide an extremely valuable benefit such as survival or rescue to a victim or victims or (b) they had great value as acts of resistance to Nazi oppression and values, or both; and (c) not only helpers and rescuers, but also many bystanders, had both the ability and the opportunity to perform these possible acts. I shall argue that this conclusion, in conjunction with the basic rules of prima facie duty that belong to the core content of morality (already mentioned above), justifies an inference to a second conclusion: Any person (helper, rescuer, or bystander) who had both the ability and opportunity to perform a particular act, A, which had either characteristic (a) or (b), or both, had an actual duty to perform A. I shall then show that in fact many bystanders had actual duties to give help and engage in rescue.

The Relative Value of the Benefit to the Victim

What guidelines should have been used to make decisions about whether or not to perform some act in a particular situation, as a matter of actual duty? Fortunately, there are good grounds for making these guidelines fairly simple and practical to use. First, the judgments that are made to assign the relative values that various kinds of benefits have for beneficiaries are based primarily on the principle of equal consideration, the rebuttable presumption that every person's interests should be given equal consideration. The salient example of how the principle works in the context of helping and rescue in the Holocaust is the assumption that staying alive had the same value for each person threatened with extermination. Not only does this judgment seem morally correct, but it also simplifies the reasoning on which the guidelines are based. Second, the guidelines must reflect real-life constraints on time and relevant information; obviously helpers and rescuers were not omniscient and often had to act quickly in order to take advantage of opportunities as they emerged. Consequently, relative values may be assigned to different kinds of benefits based on the value they are likely to have had for most victims. For example, everything else being equal, getting a false passport or identity card had extremely high value for most fugitive Jews. In addition to this kind of instrumental value, most acts of help and rescue also had a distinct value as expressions of respect for, and solidarity with, victims. What follows is a partial list of the most important benefits that could often be made available to victims, grouped into three categories: rescue, help, and kindness.

Rescue.   Rescue had the highest relative value for victims. Only acts done intentionally for the purpose of rescue belong in this category. Presumably most helpers and rescuers intended their acts to either contribute to or directly achieve the rescue of the victims they helped. However, it appears that quite often those who gave help were moved only by pity aroused by the present plight of a victim; such people can be described as "situational responders." For example, many people responded to desperate requests from starving Jews by giving them some food, but they were often unwilling to get further involved in full-scale rescue.[18] Pity does not always translate into sustained helping because it is too often a purely emotional response that can be easily assuaged by some minimal gesture. It is likely that some victims survived in part because they received occasional help from such situational responders acting only out of pity. However, unintentionally contributing to someone's survival does not count as an act of rescue on the part of the situational responders; indeed, it does not belong in the category of rescue at all. By contrast, acts of help performed by people who intended to contribute to the rescue of the victims they helped belong in the category of rescue (even if the acts proved to be ineffective in achieving that result).

There were essentially three ways to rescue a victim: help in escaping from German-controlled territory, concealment, or the creation of a false identity. Which method was actually used depended mainly on the circumstances. For example, rescue networks in France tended to organize escape routes to neighboring neutral countries like Switzerland and Spain.[19] By contrast, escape was virtually impossible in Germany and Poland, so most rescuers had to hide victims or find a false identity for them.

There is no doubt that hiding a victim in a country that was under tight German control, such as Germany itself or Poland, was the most difficult method of rescue, both for the rescuer and for the victim. The rescuer had not only to find a secure hiding place (often in his or her own home) but also had to supply food and, in most cases, dispose of bodily waste, often under the watchful eyes of suspicious neighbors, police, and German occupation authorities. The victims could only rarely be allowed to come and go as they pleased, and often they had to remain almost constantly hidden.[20]

Escape and false identity, on the other hand, tended to present a different set of difficulties. False identification papers of all kinds were needed, such as passports, visas, and work permits. Many victims had to change their appearance to avoid drawing attention in public. Victims who did not know the local language were particularly vulnerable, so often it was necessary for a helper to accompany them in public to ward off potentially dangerous confrontations. In Poland many Jewish children were saved by living with Catholic families; these children often had to be given a new religious identity, including being baptized (if necessary), learning to pray and to take part in the Mass.[21] Escape usually required that victims be escorted to the border of a country such as Switzerland or Spain, often over rugged mountain passes.[22] The relative value of any one of these benefits to victims was almost always very great because having them was necessary for survival itself or as a means to escape.

Help. The distinction made here between help and rescue depends on the intention of the actor. Any action that provided a victim with one or more of the kinds of benefits discussed so far and was done with the intention of contributing to or directly achieving rescue (whether by hiding, escape, or false identity) counts as an act of rescue. However, it was possible to engage in many of these very same kinds of actions without intending to be involved in rescue, much less actively involved in an organized rescue network. There is little doubt that victims benefited from many such isolated acts of help from individuals who were not merely situational responders; many were motivated by genuine benevolence and solidarity with victims, which prompted them to act in ways that went beyond relieving immediate needs, however valuable such help might be. Other kinds of helping activities included giving temporary shelter or allowing a victim to rest; providing clothes, shoes, and so on, and providing escort or giving directions to safe places. One especially valuable, and surprisingly frequent, form of help consisted of advance warnings of impending searches, raids, and roundups. These warnings, which saved countless lives, were often given by sympathetic policemen or government bureaucrats who were not directly involved with rescue networks but were privy to official plans.[23] Help often took the form of *not* doing something that would harm a victim; acts of omission could be just as valuable as positive help. For example, an Italian Fascist militiaman, who realized that three young men were Jewish refugees with false identity papers, did not betray them to the German SS conducting an identity check aboard a train.[24] Another unexpected form of help came from many Germans who worked for Jewish families; some of them remained loyal to their former employers even after anti-Semitic laws forced termination of their employment. One elderly German woman who had worked for a Jewish family for over forty years continued to bring food from her own family's allotment until the Jewish family emigrated in 1941, even though she knew her husband could lose his job if she were caught.[25]

These examples, and countless others that could be cited, show how relatively easy it would have been for a great many bystanders to give victims all kinds of help if they had been so inclined. This was true even in the heart of the destruction process itself. Primo Levi, a survivor of Auschwitz, recounts an extraordinary example of attempted help from a German who headed up the chemical laboratory in which Levi worked while in Auschwitz. When the alarm for an Allied air raid sounded, the German unexpectedly took Levi and two other Jewish prisoners with him to the bomb shelter, even though it was off-limits to all prisoners. When he was told by the guard blocking the shelter door that he could enter but the prisoners had to stay outside, the German tried to force his way inside and became involved in a fist fight with the guard. Suddenly, the all-clear signal sounded (the Allied planes had flown past Auschwitz without dropping any bombs), so the altercation ended. Levi uses this example to raise the tantalizing possibility that "if anomalous Germans, capable of such modest courage, had been more numerous," history might have taken a very different turn.[26]

Kindness.   The various kinds of help and rescue discussed so far were valuable primarily because they contributed to, or actually achieved, the rescue of victims. This instrumental value of help and rescue was very likely uppermost in the minds of victims as well, both before rescue (causing anxiety over how much was at stake) and after (manifested in happiness at the realization of what had been achieved). However, there is another very significant and distinct dimension of value inherent in most acts of help and rescue. In addition to contributing to (or achieving) the physical survival of victims, they also represented a recognition (by the helpers and rescuers) of the humanity and individual personhood of each victim. These acts showed the victims that they were still cared for and respected as members of the human community. Moreover, this recognition and respect had profound moral meaning and value for victims, many of whom had experienced nothing but hostility and indifference from most people for months or years. Most studies of Holocaust victims emphasize that the psychological suffering caused by the humiliation, stigmatization, and social isolation of victims was just as devastating as physical deprivation and harm. For example, many German Jews suffered from depression, loss of self-respect, and feelings of shame during the years of anti-Semitic legislation that preceded the Final Solution.[27] The most profoundly devastating effect, however, came with the recognition that the Germans truly meant to kill each and every Jewish person they could get their hands on, including children.

The distinct value of acts of help and rescue that comes from their being an expression of solidarity with and respect for victims can be most readily recognized in what I call acts of kindness (for want of a better term). Many acts were performed that may well have benefited a victim in one of the ways discussed so far but were performed primarily as an expression of sympathy and respect for victims. This is especially clear when there was no possibility that what was done could in any way lead to rescue. For example, Polish peasants gave water to desperately thirsty Jewish victims waiting in a death train in the station outside Treblinka.[28] Acts of kindness could also be used discretely to express sympathy. For example, in September 1941, as the Final Solution was about to get under way in Germany, Jews were required to wear a star on their clothing in public. The reactions of Germans differed. "Some strangers stuck cigarettes, fruit, or other tokens of sympathy into the pockets of Jews, while others moved away from them, shouted at them, or looked through them."[29] Finally, there is a large class of miscellaneous acts whose salient feature is the respect shown for the individuality of the victim. A local commander of the Fascist militia regularly played poker with an elderly Jewish grandmother who had been left behind by her family because she was too frail to withstand the hardships of flight. "The commander, addressing her as Signora Levi, told her when the order came for her deportation, he would give her plenty of time to hide."[30] Catholic monks in Assisi, Italy, arranged kosher meals for some of the Jews they were hiding and also "set up a school for Jewish children to study their own religion and cultural heritage."[31]

The Relative Value of the Act as Resistance to Nazi Oppression and Values

Every act of help or rescue was in principle capable of having some degree of value as an act of resistance to Nazi oppression and values. The ethical basis for this value has already been mentioned, namely, the corollary to the duty of mutual aid: Everyone has a prima facie duty to prevent others from harming third parties. Still, this understanding of the corollary does not account for the distinctive value that most acts of help and rescue had as acts of resistance to evil, especially the evil of genocide; from this perspective help and rescue are still being viewed only as duties that were owed to individuals who had a right to assistance when they were threatened with harm from others. However, this corollary had an additional significance in the context of the Holocaust because the genocide against the Jews was a salient aspect of the broader Nazi assault on the core content of morality and the principle of equal consideration that underlies it. Consequently, each act of help or rescue was also potentially an act of resistance to this onslaught and an expression of protest against the immoral ideology upon which it was based. Lawrence Blum has expressed the distinction very clearly:

Resistance to evil is morally distinct from altruism itself. The perspective of altruism sees the persecuted Jew as a person in need, whose life is under threat of death. . . . But to help, or to save the life of, someone who is persecuted is to do more than just to save life, as in a flood or accident. It is to recognize a further evil—the evil of persecution (by which I refer here to state-sponsored persecution)—and to resist that evil by saying that one will not let persecution be successful in the case of this particular individual. . . . For the fact that Jews were being persecuted was known to virtually everyone in the Nazi-occupied countries, and certainly to all rescuers. Thus rescuers were aware that in saving a Jewish life they were also saving the life of a persecuted person, and so were resisting or in a sense protesting against persecution. They can be presumed to have understood that saving a Jew from the Nazis was in this regard not simply like helping the victims of natural or technological disasters.[32]

In addition, Blum argues, some actual rescuers appear to have had only a motive of resistance without altruistic concern. Help and rescue, whether undertaken in part or entirely as an act of resistance, is *political* in nature; this is especially clear in the many acts of help and rescue by members of resistance organizations and networks that were also active in a wide range of other activities such as espionage and sabotage. The purpose of such activity goes far beyond giving help to individual victims to include the eventual overthrow of the oppressive German political system. Clearly, the core content of morality does not just concern how individuals are supposed to treat each other; it also has quite specific and far-reaching implications for political action.

The distinctive value of many acts of resistance and protest under discussion does not derive entirely from their instrumental value in helping to hasten or actually bring about the end of the German occupation or the defeat of Germany; it also derives from the recognition on the part of the actors that they were engaged in an historical struggle to vindicate the basic values on which human life in political communities should be predicated. Just as the value of help and rescue to individual victims cannot be reduced to the value of physical survival alone (because they were also expressions of recognition and respect for the victims), so too the value of help and rescue as political acts does not rest on their efficacy in defeating Nazism alone because they were also expressions of convictions about basic political principles and a repudiation of persecution and genocide. One way of bringing the noninstrumental values of kindness and resistance into sharp relief is to view them in light of the not inconsiderable number of people who rescued victims only for pay. (These purely mercenary rescuers must be kept distinct from those who asked the Jews whom they hid for money because they were so poor that they could not have afforded to keep them otherwise.) Acts of rescue that were motivated only by monetary reward would nevertheless have very great instrumental value for victims, of course, but they had no value to them either as expressions of respect, recognition, and human solidarity, or as acts expressing protest against Nazi oppression. The contrast is even greater in some cases because rescuers not only took money from victims but also resorted to repeated blackmail in order to extort more and more money. When the victims finally ran out of money, the blackmailers turned them in to the Germans anyway.[33]

The Ability and Opportunity of the Actor to Perform the Act

This criterion identifies a necessary condition for an act's being someone's actual duty in a particular situation. Any act of help or rescue would be an actual duty for an individual in a particular situation if it had either one, or both, of the two characteristics already discussed: it would provide a benefit with great value to a victim (or victims) or it would have great value as an act of resistance to Nazism, or both; *provided*, of course, that the person "could have done it," that is, had both the ability and the opportunity to do it. This qualification is ethically necessary, since it makes no practical or moral sense to assert that an individual has an actual duty to do something, all things considered, when it is impossible for him or her to fulfill it because of a (nonculpable) lack of ability or opportunity. Ought implies can.

Consider an example. A helper in a particular situation has a prima facie duty to get false papers for a fugitive victim who is in hiding. If the helper succeeds in getting false papers, the victim can be escorted by train to safety in a neutral country. Thus the act of help would have enormous value for the victim. However, the helper does not have either the skill (a lack of ability) or the materials (a lack of opportunity) to provide the false papers, and there is no one else available from whom they could be acquired (again, lack of opportunity). Consequently, despite the prima facie duty, the helper does not have an actual duty, all things considered. If the helper should happen to be faulted for failing to get the false papers in these circumstances, he or she could properly block blame as unjustified on the grounds that the failure could not be helped.

This survey of the various ways to help and rescue victims leaves little room for doubt about the great number of possible acts of help and rescue that were not performed but would either have provided Jewish victims with very great benefits such as continued survival and rescue or would have been valuable acts of resistance (or both) if they had been performed. Although there was much that needed to be done for victims, the great majority of people were bystanders; they did nothing to help.

Assessing the Blameworthiness of Bystanders

If my analysis of the ethics of help and rescue is correct, all bystanders had at least a prima facie duty to render help to victims. Some of them (perhaps a majority) had actual duties, all things considered, in particular situations. In this section I sort through at least some of the principal explanations for not help-ing. I identify and distinguish explanations that constitute a justification or an excuse (thereby blocking blame altogether), explanations that mitigate blame, and explanations that bring discredit on the bystander and result in blamewor-thiness.

Bystanders with Justifications for Not Helping

A fairly large number of people had an ethical justification for not helping be-cause of conflict with a serious role responsibility. For example, a married cou-ple with several children and frail, elderly parents to take care of could reason-ably refrain from attempting rescue, since it was usually very dangerous, depending on the level of anti-Semitism among neighbors and the vigilance of local police and German occupation forces. This is not to deny that in some cases even a family with heavy role responsibilities could engage in modest acts of help falling short of rescue. Nevertheless, the extent of help that could be given was often limited; many families had little or no food to spare and lived in already cramped quarters. It seems only fair to give parents with these kinds of heavy family obligations the benefit of the doubt if they chose not to help victims at all. It is also seems quite probable that in many cases they had a sufficient justification for not helping, namely, that they had a conflicting and overriding obligation to care for their families. Consequently, they acted rightly and were not blameworthy.

There is some evidence to support this conclusion. One study found that a quar-ter of rescuers had children who were put at risk, and many of these rescuers re-port that they were criticized for it. Even some of the rescuers' children themselves came to have feelings of resentment for the risk their parents took with their well-being.[34] It is possible that some of these feelings of disapproval and resentment were not justified. However, it is likely that some rescuers who were parents did not give sufficient weight to their role responsibilities to their children.

Bystanders with Valid Excuses for Not Helping

Having a valid excuse for not helping must not be confused with having a jus-tification. Parents who did not help victims because they had an obligation to care for their family and provided the care out of benevolence and conscien-tiousness acted rightly and were not blameworthy. By contrast, persons who failed to give help to victims because they lacked the ability or opportunity to do so are not properly described as having done the right thing; to the contrary, they were not able to do the right thing. However, since the explanation why they failed is a (nonculpable) lack of ability or opportunity, they were not blameworthy. People who had a valid excuse for not fulfilling a prima facie duty could not help failing.

Lacking the skill to produce false identification papers is one example of a valid excuse. There are many other ways in which persons might (nonculpably) lack some personal ability, skill, or knowledge needed in order to give help. Examples include not knowing a language (for example, German), being unfamiliar with a large city, not knowing how to use weapons, and being ill or handicapped. However, some explanations for not giving help that appeal to personal shortcomings, far from constituting a valid excuse, are actually incriminating and bring discredit on the person. For example, many bystanders were quite understandably afraid of the risk and danger that giving help would entail, but their objectively based fear all too often became an exaggerated and cowardly preoccupation with their own safety that led to callous disregard for the dire straits in which the victims whom they could have helped found themselves. Moreover, many bystanders engaged in systematic self-deception in order to keep from accurately assessing the risks to themselves and from seeing that, in reality, they had a choice whether to help or not. Lack of courage and engaging in self-deception are both character defects and in many cases are manifestations of full-blown vices; these explanations for the inaction of some bystanders make them to some extent blameworthy.

Most bystanders who had valid excuses for not helping were prevented from acting by a lack of opportunity, primarily brought about by the activity of the military, the police, and the surrounding populace, which in most cases was unsympathetic to helping or rescuing Jews. It should be noted that in large part such lack of opportunity did not consist of being physically prevented from helping Jews (though this could happen, of course; one could be unlucky enough to be arrested, for example) but rather in being successfully deterred by the ever present threat of discovery and severe punishment. This is a good example of the moral/normative sense of not having an opportunity to help; one is not physically prevented from acting but one does not have a reasonable chance to act without incurring very severe punishment, even death. This was especially true in Germany and Austria, where anti-Semitic policies had been in place for years before the Final Solution was even begun; consequently the number of helpers and rescuers in those parts of the Third Reich was comparatively small. Elsewhere in Europe, the degree of danger and difficulty varied, depending on the level of activity by the German occupation forces and collaborationist local police, as well as the degree of anti-Semitism in the population.

The principal features of these obstacles have been alluded to in some examples, and so they can be briefly summarized. The activities of German occupation forces that made it extremely dangerous, and in some situations virtually impossible, to render help or engage in rescue included frequent raids on suspected hiding places, road blocks and identity checks on trains and buses, street patrols, coupled with summary public executions when helpers and rescuers were caught with Jews, and confinement in concentration camps for lesser acts of help. The local police were used to complement and support the German efforts; in addition, they expanded their normal police duties to include gathering information from sympathetic collaborators, many of whom were personally known to them. Finally, the local population in some countries often looked for hidden Jews and then betrayed them to the authorities. This was especially true in Germany,[35] Poland, and Holland.[36] In Germany, the Gestapo (which, contrary to popular myth, was greatly undermanned) depended heavily on information volunteered by the general citizenry to enforce racial laws and regulations.[37]

Bystanders with Mitigating Circumstances for Not Helping

Since the level of antirescue activity by the Germans, their police collaborators, and the general population varied greatly from country to country, many bystanders did not face the high-level of risk of being discovered and punished or executed that rescuers in Germany, Poland, and Holland faced. Some bystanders lived in fairly remote areas that were hardly policed at all, making it comparatively easy for them to hide fugitives successfully. Despite this, in all regions of Europe bystanders greatly outnumbered helpers and rescuers, even though many of them had some opportunities to act without great risk. It seems reasonable to conclude that remaining a bystander in such circumstances was often wrong and blameworthy. However, since these bystanders still faced some not inconsiderable risks, they were not as blameworthy as they might otherwise have been had they not faced those risks. The adverse conditions, while they were not bad enough to excuse them, constituted mitigating circumstances.

Bystanders Who Were Fully Blameworthy for Not Helping

The great majority of bystanders probably fall into this last category, especially those in western Europe where the level of German control tended to be lower than it was in Germany itself and in eastern occupied areas. Most bystanders in western Europe had the ability and at least some opportunity to help victims and engage in rescue activity. Consequently, given the vital benefits that their help and rescue could have provided to Jewish victims, they had actual duties to help and rescue that they failed to fulfill. An additional dimension of the blameworthiness of all bystanders, regardless of where they lived, does not derive from their failure to engage in help that would contribute to or achieve rescue, but in the fact that so many of them failed even to show any kindness or sympathy when it would have been very easy to do so. The principal explanations for their failures are both predictable and depressing. In Germany itself, there were fanatical Nazis, of course, who believed in the correctness of the Final Solution along with other bystanders who were traditional religious anti-Semites glad to see the Jews "disappear." However, it seems very likely that just as many, if not more, German bystanders were motivated by what I have termed triumphant nationalism, a misguided pride and satisfaction in the Nazi regime's domestic and foreign policy successes, including territorial expansion and military conquest, which at its worst translated into support for the drastic measures taken against the Jews. At the very least this nationalistic pride brought with it a willingness to look the other way. Still other bystanders, both inside Germany and throughout German-occupied Europe, were morally indifferent, callous, or selfish; and, of course, there were people everywhere who disapproved of or were horrified by what was happening but were too fearful and cowardly to act on their convictions and feelings.

Leaving aside Nazi ideologues and religious zealots, a considerable number among all of these different types were no doubt very prone to engage in self-deception in order to avoid facing the reality of what was happening to the Jews and their own failure to do anything to help. To fully appreciate the degree of wrongness of such self-deception, recall the variety of bad-making characteristics it involves (see chapter 4, "When Self-Deception Is Morally Bad"). It seems fairly clear that most bystanders who engaged in self-deception were blameworthy for doing so.

Accomplices

There were many people who, if they were not perpetrators, were far from being mere bystanders (as blameworthy as that often was); they engaged in positive acts to aid and abet the Final Solution, thus becoming accomplices. One example has already been mentioned, the many German citizens who volunteered information that enabled the Gestapo to enforce anti-Jewish laws and regulations. The most blameworthy acts of complicity, however, were those accompanied by gratuitous insult and cruelty. For example, German Jews being rounded up for deportation were taken to an "assembly point" to wait for a train to the "East." These assembly points were usually in synagogues or other Jewish communal buildings, but some were deliberately located in slaughterhouses or cattle markets in order to convey the disdain that many Germans felt toward the Jews. On top of that, the Jews were also made to sleep on straw-covered floors and were subjected to body searches; in one city "girls from the local Nazi youth organization rummaged through their luggage, stealing the last remainder of money, jewelry, food, and soap."[38]

Supererogatory Help and Rescue

Why Many Helpers and Rescuers Were Highly Praiseworthy and Morally Admirable

We can begin to gain a fuller appreciation for the reasons why so many actual helpers and rescuers truly deserve our admiration by looking at a few more people who displayed the characteristics that made their acts clearly "above and beyond duty." I refer to these people as morally committed rescuers.

Stefania Podgorska Burzminska[39]

Only seventeen years old when she first became involved in rescue, Stefania Podgorska Burzminska worked in a grocery store owned by a Jewish family named Diamant in the Polish city of Przemysl. After being occupied by the Russians from 1939 to mid-1941, the city was occupied by the invading Germans who very quickly set up a Jewish ghetto into which everyone in the Diamant family was forced to move. Stefania persuaded a Polish policeman to let her slip into the ghetto periodically to visit the Diamants to see how they were doing. Later she began helping by smuggling food to the family when she learned that they were slowly starving. Eventually it became common knowledge that the Jews in the ghetto were being sent on trains to Auschwitz to be killed. When Mr. and Mrs. Diamant were deported, Stefania decided to do everything she could to save three of their sons who were left (a fourth son had been sent earlier to the Lvov labor camp). Stefania's first attempt at rescue failed when the Diamant son she was supposed to escort to safety was shot by a policeman as he left the ghetto. The other two sons managed to escape on their own later, and she took them in when they came to her for help. Word got back to the ghetto that she was hiding Jews, so she found herself being both cajoled and blackmailed into accepting first another family, and then another individual Jew, and another, until she was hiding a total of thirteen people. These fugitives, together with a younger sister, lived with her in a small cottage that used to belong to Jews before the ghetto was established. Years later, Stefania would express her belief that she had found the cottage by heeding an inner voice that gave her instructions. She did not consider herself particularly religious at the time, but she became convinced that she had been helped by a genuine miracle. Joseph, one of the Diamant sons, with the help of others, built a false wall in the attic of the cottage so that the Jews could be hidden if there was a raid.

Stefania and her hidden charges spent over two years together in the cottage. She was able to get a job in a factory and so there was some money, but it took extraordinary ingenuity and courage for her to care for all of these utterly dependent people. Fear of discovery had been constant from the beginning, but matters got much worse toward the end of the war when the Germans, reeling from the heavy casualties that were being inflicted on them by the advancing Soviet armies, set up a field hospital in an abandoned building directly across the street. Now Stefania's quiet neighborhood was swarming with German soldiers, wounded, doctors, and nurses. In fact, two SS soldiers knocked on her door and ordered her to vacate the cottage in two hours, since it was being officially commandeered by the German government. If she did not comply, she would be shot.

At that crucial moment Stefania again heard the voice that previously had guided her to the abandoned cottage, now telling her not to leave but to stay and wait for the Germans to come back. She followed the advice, and when the Germans returned they told her she could stay after all because they only needed one room. Stefania and her sister spent the final eight months of the war with the thirteen Jews hiding in the attic; all the while two hospital nurses and their German boyfriends slept downstairs every night. Despite these formidable dangers, Stefania kept her self-control and succeeded in saving all thirteen of the Jews. Nevertheless, at least two thousand Polish rescuers were put to death by the Germans.[40]

Father Maria Benedetto[41]

At least 170 Italian priests who helped or rescued anti-Fascists and Jews lost their lives in reprisal killings, and hundreds more were deported during the German occupation. It is all the more remarkable, then, that so many Italian priests and nuns were active in helping and rescue. Father Maria Benedetto was one of the most active and successful of these, beginning his rescue work during the Italian occupation in southern France, where he turned his monastery into a center that helped hundreds of Jewish and anti-Nazi refugees hide or escape the country. After the Germans occupied southern France, Father Benedetto was forced to continue his work back in Italy, which later was also occupied by the Germans. Working in Rome, Father Benedetto and his network of assistants (usually other priests) processed refugees, directed them to rented rooms in hotels and boardinghouses, and supplied them with identification papers. "Most dangerous of all, they visited them often to bring food, clothing, money, and moral support. In a city crawling with SS troops and Fascist spies, no one was safe. Couriers in every conceivable disguise dodged pursuers and had many narrow escapes."[42] Altogether, Father Benedetto and his network supported 4,000 Jews; of these, 1,500 were foreigners and 2,500 were Italian.

Louisa and Albert Steenstra[43]

Many rescuers were married couples with children and thus faced special dilemmas. Louisa and Albert Steenstra lived in Groningen, Holland. They became involved in anti-Nazi activity almost immediately after the Germans invaded, but before they had any children. Albert became a commander of a resistance group at the wine factory where he was a supervisor; Louisa had been a secretary and bookkeeper for a business owned by Jews, but she quit when the Germans took over all Jewish businesses and put Nazi sympathizers in charge, vowing that she would rather die than work for the Germans. The event that precipitated her becoming such an ardent foe of the Germans was her rage at the bombing of Rotterdam, which took 30,000 Dutch lives. She had worked for and with Jews all of her life; thus she was not merely not anti-Semitic, she knew and liked Jews. She and Albert rented rooms to Jews and this was the beginning of their rescue activity. The first Jew they hid, Emmanuel Marcus, was the nephew of her former boss; later they also took in his brother, Carl. Eventually they would hide five Jews in their home. Louisa had a friend who was a carpenter construct an emergency hideout in a bedroom closet; it held five people and was almost undetectable.

In 1941 Louisa gave birth to a daughter, Beatrix, but continued to engage in rescue activity. She had developed an almost foolhardy sense of confidence even before getting involved in rescue, regularly visiting a Jewish friend who was the sister-in-law of Emmanuel Marcus. The friend had two young children, and her husband had already been deported to a Dutch labor camp. One evening when Louisa was visiting, the police raided her friend's home. They ordered her to dress her children and go with them to Westerbork, the camp near Groningen from which Jews were transported to Auschwitz. Merely because she had been found in the home of a Jew, Louisa was also taken to the police station and interrogated by a Gestapo officer. After being detained for two days and two nights, she got word to Albert, who managed to have her released.

Far from being deterred, Louisa became even bolder and more defiant. She was determined to go inside Westerbork and take some clothes for her friend's children, although she was warned that she probably would not be able to get back out. After getting official permission from the Gestapo, she went inside Westerbork, delivered the clothes to her friend, and talked her way back out. When she saw the horrendous conditions inside the camp, she was even more enraged about what the Germans were doing. For three years, Louisa and her husband remained active in help and rescue, with at least two fugitives in their home at any one time. They both realized the danger they were in and lived with the constant threat of death, yet they persisted because they could not refuse to help.

Toward the end of the war, the Steenstras were forced by the government to take in an elderly couple who had been displaced from their own home; this proved to be disastrous. The wife of the couple did not approve of hiding Jews, so one day, after Emmanuel Marcus had angered her with a sarcastic remark, she reported him to the police, after foolishly accepting their promise that nothing would happen to the Steenstras. Two weeks later three Gestapo officers with a German shepherd on a leash raided the Steenstra house. When Albert denied that there were any Jews in the house, the Gestapo unleashed the German shepherd on him. In a few short minutes the dog bit deeply into his hand and tore off one ear, leaving Albert bleeding profusely. The dog also discovered Emmanuel's hideout. Both Albert and Emmanuel were shot to death on the spot.

While all of this furious activity was taking place, mainly upstairs, Louisa had the presence of mind to grab Beatrix and run across the street to her mother-in-law's house. Leaving Beatrix there, Louisa ran next door to the house of a neighbor (a member of the underground) who hid her in the basement. From there she was eventually smuggled out of the city to a safe place where she spent the remaining months of the war in hiding with five other refugees. The underground was also able to get Beatrix from her mother-in-law and bring her to Louisa. When she was three and a half years old, Beatrix was tormented with a recurring nightmare about a dog that was trying to kill her, and she did not eat well for months afterward. Mother and daughter emigrated to Canada after the war because they could not bear to stay in Groningen with all of its bad memories.

Antonin Kalina[44]

If engaging in successful rescue was often extremely difficult and dangerous for people like the Steenstras who lived in their own home, it was virtually impossible for prisoners inside a German concentration camp. Prisoners were routinely killed by guards for the slightest provocation or for no reason at all. Anyone caught helping Jews in any way courted death, and getting caught actually trying to rescue them meant an automatic death sentence. Yet Antonin Kalina, a prisoner in the concentration camp at Buchenwald, saved 1,300 boys (1,200 of them Jewish) from being killed in the very last weeks of the war. Antonin was born in Moravia (later a part of Czechoslovakia) to a family of Social Democrats in 1902. When he was twenty-one, he joined the Communist party and remained a Communist for the rest of his life. He was arrested as a political prisoner and sent to Germany in 1939 and spent the entire war until the liberation in 1945 in a series of German concentration camps, including Dachau.

His rescue activity took place in Buchenwald. Consistent with their general practice, the Germans used prisoners to help run the camp, and Antonin was the head prisoner in charge of some barracks. As the Soviet front moved westward, more and more camps in the East had to be shut down, and the inmates were marched or transported back into Germany. Many camps throughout Europe were being closed as the war wound down. Buchenwald was one of the main collection centers for these thousands of refugee prisoners, many of them Jews slated for extermination. Antonin began to notice that incoming transport trains each carried from twenty to fifty children, mostly boys ranging in age from three and a half to sixteen, so he decided to keep them all together in his barracks for safety. There was some opposition to his plan from members of the prisoner underground, since they worried that having all of the boys gathered together would make it very easy for the SS to seize them and send them to the gas chambers. The SS did make some attempts to start the liquidation of the boys, but Antonin kept sabotaging the system by pretending that he could not find the particular boys whose names were on their lists. Finally, Antonin devised a scheme to fool the Germans. He created a fake quarantine for the boys by posting an official-looking sign that warned of a deadly typhus outbreak in the barracks and therefore prohibited entry to all. This was a very credible warning, since thousands were dying from typhus in the

camps due to crowding, starvation, and unsanitary conditions. When Buchenwald was liberated by the Americans in April 1945, all 1,300 boys were still
alive. Antonin lived to tell the tale, and in 1948 he had a reunion with some of
the boys he had saved.

Ethical Assessment of These Morally Committed Rescuers

The actions of these morally committed rescuers were clearly supererogatory.
First, they had no actual duty to put their own lives at great risk in order to help
Jewish fugitives; it would not have been wrong for them to refrain from rescuing. It might be thought that the people who gave the benefit could not have justified withholding it because the value of the benefit to the victims was so great
(saving their very lives). However, this argument neglects the principle of equal
consideration, according to which the rescuer's life is just as valuable as the life
of a fugitive. Matters would have been quite different in situations with a low
risk of death, but these rescuers, like Albert Steenstra, faced an extremely high
risk of getting caught and shot on the spot. One false step during the eight
months that Stefania Podgorska Burzminska kept her thirteen Jews hidden from
the Germans sleeping in her house would have meant her death. In fact, her secret was nearly discovered once when a German boyfriend of one of the nurses
searched the upstairs area.[45] The salient feature common to all of the situations
in which these rescuers acted was the lack of opportunity in the moral/norma-
tive sense: They did not have a reasonable or fair chance to rescue victims without the risk of great sacrifice or death. (Obviously, since in fact they succeeded
in rescuing victims, it was not physically impossible for them to do so.)

Second, even though they had no actual duty to engage in rescue (it would
not have been wrong to refrain), doing so was, nonetheless, a good thing to do.
Indeed, given the extremely high value of rescue to the victims, it was a wonderful and excellent thing to do.

Third, because the rescuers risked their lives by acting in the face of great danger, their actions bring credit to them; they are praiseworthy and admirable. With
regard to the people described in this chapter, this last judgment can be made
without qualification because the motives that prompted their rescue activities
are known. Stefania Podgorska Burzminska was motivated by her affection for
the Diamant family and benevolent concern for any Jew who was suffering under the Germans. She was aided by her conviction that an inner voice had given
her miraculous advice, and Father Benedetto believed that he had a Christian
duty to help refugees.[46] Two of the four persons described had distinct political
motives for rescuing in addition to benevolent concern for victims. Louisa
Steenstra's actions were motivated both by affection for her Jewish friends and
by her strong desire to resist the Germans because of her outrage over the bombing of Rotterdam. Antonin Kalina was motivated by benevolent concern for the
Jewish boys he saved; he also believed he, as a Communist, had a political duty

to fight fascism. All of these motives reflect good character traits such as universal (unlimited scope) benevolence and conscientiousness, practical wisdom, and an absence of self-deception about what was happening to the Jews. In addition, these rescuers all had enormous self-control and courage.

Finally, and perhaps most importantly, these morally committed rescuers had a sense of personal identity that made it psychologically impossible for them *not* to render help and engage in rescue, even though in doing so they faced such grave risks to their own lives that they did not have an actual duty to help. Individual rescuers had differing conceptions of themselves, of course, but they all had one or more of the following characteristics: (1) a conception of themselves as caring and compassionate persons together with an especially strong universal form of the virtue of benevolence, including a disposition to act out of care and concern despite great risk or danger, which would have manifested itself in deep remorse and a sense of shame if they had failed to help victims whose lives were at risk; (2) a conception of themselves as just and honorable persons together with an especially strong universal form of the virtue of conscientiousness, particularly concerning the duty of mutual aid, which would have manifested itself in feelings of guilt and shame if they had failed to fulfill that duty with regard to victims whose lives were at risk; or (3) a conception of themselves as independent and rational persons together with especially strong forms of the virtues of practical wisdom and autonomy, which would have manifested themselves in feelings of guilt and shame if they had failed to follow their own conscience, had engaged in self-deception, or had become bystanders out of fear. People who have a sense of personal identity consisting of commitments and values like these, and have developed the moral character to exemplify it, are very likely to find it psychologically impossible to act contrary to it. Their sense of integrity will not allow it.

Again and again rescuers make statements like "I really had no choice; I couldn't refuse to help" and "if I had not helped, I wouldn't have been able to live with myself."[47] The rescuers' statements seem to mean that, from their point of view, or given the way they felt at that moment, they could not see any other way to act. They did not see their inability to act other than the way they did as in any way a limitation or defect on their part. And they were surely right about that. To be psychologically unable *not* to help victims is not a character defect or a vice; it is a state of virtue or excellence. After all, what is personal integrity except the inability to bring oneself to do things that one sincerely believes are wrong or bad and the inability not to try one's utmost to do things that one sincerely believes are right or good. For committed rescuers, giving help to victims whose lives were in jeopardy fell in this latter category. It may be objected that committed rescuers were not really free in the sense that they could not help themselves, and therefore (so the reasoning goes), they were not really praiseworthy for rescuing victims. This objection, though it has a specious kind of plausibility, really rests on a confusion about the role played by the plea "I could not do otherwise." In its primary use it claims an excuse,

such as lack of ability or lack of opportunity, that blocks blame for wrongdoing. But excuses are not needed for doing something good, much less doing
something wonderful and extraordinary like saving someone's life in the face
of great risk and danger to oneself. It is just a mistake to view rescuers' avowals
like "I really had no choice; I couldn't refuse to help" as making an excuse;
there was nothing to excuse.

Organized Rescue in Networks

Some rescuers such as Father Maria Benedetto were active in networks. But this
discussion, for the most part, has considered individuals who acted alone or
within a small group such as a family. Many of these individual rescuers saved
a handful of victims, not hundreds or thousands. This individual focus partly cor-
rects a stereotype of the rescuer that has emerged as a result of the great attention given to a few somewhat larger-than-life figures like Oskar Schindler. I
chose to focus on individual efforts first primarily because moral praiseworthiness for help and rescue does not require either success or large numbers. The
example of the Steenstras is instructive. It was not unusual for helpers, who
made extreme sacrifices and courted great danger while trying to save a particular victim, to lose the battle through no fault of their own. Nevertheless, it is
very gratifying to be reminded of the many successful, well-organized rescue
networks that came into existence to try to save as many Jews as possible.

Andre and Magda Trocme and the Huguenot Community of
Le-Chambon-sur-Lignon, France[48]

Andre Trocme and his wife Magda were the nucleus of a rescue network consisting of themselves and other members of the Huguenot church that Andre
served as pastor. There was no single motive or reason for these French peasants' involvement in rescue; among the reasons were Christian love, a sense of
duty, and a spirit of resistance to both Nazi Germany and Vichy France that reflected the community's own experience with past persecution as a minority religion. Whatever the reasons, they saved several thousand Jews, many of them
children, whom they hid in their homes and other safe places in the countryside. Many were escorted across the border into Switzerland.

Irena Sandlerova and the Clandestine Warsaw Ghetto Network[49]

When the Germans invaded Poland, Christians and Jews working in the social
welfare department of the city of Warsaw organized a special program to help
young people traumatized by the bombing and dislocation of the war. Later,
when the Jewish ghetto was established, Irena Sandlerova transformed the pro-

gram for young people into a clandestine network to supply forged documents that Jews could use to get badly needed food, medicine, and clothing. Her network was especially successful because it used people who had been working together already. Perhaps their most significant accomplishment was smuggling 2,500 children out of the Warsaw ghetto and hiding them in homes in the non-Jewish part of the city.

The Organized Rescue of Virtually All Danish Jews, October 1943

What Raul Hilberg describes as "one of the most remarkable rescue operations in history" was the result of "an uncooperative Danish administration and a local population unanimous in its resolve to save its Jews."[50] In late September 1943, after nearly two years of stalling by the Danes, Hitler ordered the immediate deportation of all Danish Jews. However, the secret deportation plan was leaked by a sympathetic German official to a prominent Dane who immediately notified Danish officials and the leaders of the Jewish community. In the course of a few days a daring plan emerged to take all of Denmark's Jews by boat across the sea to safety in Sweden, which had guaranteed sanctuary to all who could be ferried over. Over the next few weeks thousands of Danes hid Jews in their homes, escorted them to waiting boats disguised as working fishing vessels, loaded them aboard, and sailed the vessels or acted as lookouts. Hilberg's summary says it all: "When the operation was over, 5,919 full Jews, 1,301 part Jews, and 686 non-Jews who were married to Jews had been brought ashore in Sweden."[51] The Germans managed to deport only 477 Danish Jews to the ghetto in Theresienstadt.

Rescuers with Special Opportunities

Individuals working in networks were not the only rescuers who succeeded in saving large numbers of victims. There were some rescuers who were able to save many victims primarily because they happened to be in a position with special opportunities denied to most people. For example, some were diplomats or officials of foreign countries that were neutral in the war; others were international businessmen who traveled extensively and had foreign contacts. One important factor in the success of these kinds of rescuers is somewhat surprising, given the fact that the Germans were very brutal in dealing with attempts to sabotage the Final Solution. The Germans were generally sticklers for observing diplomatic correctness and legal regulations. For example, if a foreign diplomat issued exit visas to Jews, the Germans were more likely to lodge a protest with the diplomat's government than they were to arrest him. Any brief list of rescuers with special opportunities would very likely include certain people.

Oskar Schindler was a German businessman who operated a factory in Poland using Jewish slave labor, saved over 1,100 of his workers by using his considerable talents as a con-man to bribe and hoodwink German military officers and occupation officials.[52] Raoul Wallenberg, a Swedish diplomat in Hungary in 1944, saved tens of thousands of Jews from deportation to Auschwitz by forging Swedish passports that were honored by the Germans. He also helped many of them find them safe houses in Budapest.[53] Sempo Sugihara, a Japanese diplomat in Kovno, Lithuania, saved 4,500–10,000 Jews by issuing them visas in 1941.[54] Giorgio Perlasca, an Italian businessman in Budapest, helped save 5,200 Jews in 1944 by volunteering his services to the Spanish legation under Angel San-Briz, who was himself busily handing out thousands of letters of protection to Jews. For several months Perlasca found housing and food for Jewish refugees, who were under the protection of the Spanish flag. When San-Briz was recalled by Franco's government, Perlasca masqueraded as the new Spanish diplomat in charge of the legation, which he managed to keep open.[55]

Notes

1. *Rescuers: Portraits of Moral Courage in the Holocaust,* ed. Gay Block and Malka Drucker (New York: Holmes & Meier, 1992); Jackson J. Spielvogel, *Hitler and Nazi Germany: A History* (Englewood Cliffs, N.J.: Prentice-Hall, 1992), 286, 291–294.

2. Eva Fogelman, *Conscience and Courage: Rescuers of Jews During the Holocaust* (New York: Doubleday-Anchor, 1994), 12–18.

3. Fogelman, *Conscience and Courage,* 13–15.

4. Marion Kaplan, *Between Dignity and Despair: Jewish Life in Nazi Germany* (New York: Oxford University Press, 1998), 205.

5. Fogelman, *Conscience and Courage,* 336 nn. 4, 7.

6. Susan Zuccotti, *The Italians and the Holocaust: Persecution, Rescue, and Survival* (New York: Basic Books, 1987), 201–217.

7. Lawrence A. Blum, "Altruism and the Moral Value of Rescue: Resisting Persecution, Racism, and Genocide," in *Embracing the Other,* ed. Pearl M. Oliner et al. (New York: New York University Press, 1992), 35–38.

8. Nechama Tec, *When Light Pierced the Darkness: Christian Rescue of Jews in Nazi-Occupied Poland* (New York: Oxford University Press, 1986), chap. 3.

9. Carol Gilligan, *In a Different Voice: Psychological Theory and Women's Development* (Cambridge: Harvard University Press, 1981).

10. Fogelman, *Conscience and Courage,* 240.

11. Fogelman, *Conscience and Courage,* chap. 13, "Men and Women Rescuers," gives a good overview of the issues and the evidence.

12. Samuel P. Oliner, *The Altruistic Personality: Rescuers of Jews in Nazi Germany* (New York: Free Press, 1988), 155–156.

13. Oliner, *Altruistic Personality,* chap. 10.

14. Block and Drucker, *Rescuers,* 164.

15. Block and Drucker, *Rescuers,* 162.

16. Fogelman, *Conscience and Courage,* 158; Tec, *When Light Pierced the Dark-*

ness, 188–190; Carol Rittner and Sondra Myers, *The Courage to Care: Rescuers of Jews during the Holocaust* (New York: New York University Press, 1986), 102; Block and Drucker, *Rescuers,* xiv, 9.

17. Zuccotti, *The Italians and the Holocaust,* chaps. 3–5.

18. Tec, *When Light Pierced the Darkness,* 75, 88, 182.

19. Block and Drucker, *Rescuers,* 112.

20. Fogelman, *Conscience and Courage,* chap. 6; Kaplan, *Between Dignity and Despair,* 201–212.

21. Tec, *When Light Pierced the Darkness,* chap. 1.

22. Fogelman, *Conscience and Courage,* 32–33, 208, 211–212.

23. Kaplan, *Between Dignity and Despair,* 202; Zuccotti, *The Italians and the Holocaust,* 203, 218–219.

24. Zuccotti, *The Italians and the Holocaust,* 223.

25. Kaplan, *Between Dignity and Despair,* 40.

26. Primo Levi, *The Drowned and the Saved* (New York: Summit, 1988), 169–170.

27. Kaplan, *Between Dignity and Despair,* chap. 1.

28. Gitta Sereny, *Into That Darkness* (New York: Vintage, 1974), 153–155.

29. Kaplan, *Between Dignity and Despair,* 158.

30. Zuccotti, *The Italians and the Holocaust,* 223.

31. Fogelman, *Conscience and Courage,* 172.

32. Blum, "Altruism and the Moral Value of Rescue," 36.

33. Tec, *When Light Pierced the Darkness,* chap. 5, "The Issue of Money."

34. Fogelman, *Conscience and Courage,* chap. 12.

35. Kaplan, *Between Dignity and Despair,* 203–205.

36. Fogelman, *Conscience and Courage,* 71–72.

37. Daniel Jonah Goldhagen, *Hitler's Willing Executioners: Ordinary Germans and the Holocaust* (New York: Knopf, 1996), 117.

38. Kaplan, *Between Dignity and Despair,* 187.

39. Fogelman, *Conscience and Courage,* 87–104; *Rescuers: Portraits of Moral Courage in the Holocaust,* 180–185.

40. Blum, "Altruism and the Moral Value of Rescue," 34.

41. Zuccotti, *The Italians and the Holocaust,* 208–210.

42. Zuccotti, *The Italians and the Holocaust,* 210.

43. Fogelman, *Conscience and Courage,* 118–133; *Rescuers: Portraits of Moral Courage in the Holocaust,* 58–61.

44. Block and Drucker, *Rescuers,* 204–207.

45. Fogelman, *Conscience and Courage,* 102–103.

46. Zuccotti, *The Italians and the Holocaust,* 217.

47. Fogelman, *Conscience and Courage,* 161, 168, 178 for some examples.

48. Phillip Hallie, *Lest Innocent Blood Be Shed* (New York: Harper & Row, 1979); Rittner and Myers, *Courage to Care,* 99–119.

49. Fogelman, *Conscience and Courage,* 197.

50. Raul Hilberg, *The Destruction of the European Jews* (New York: Holmes & Meier, 1985), 3:560, 566.

51. Hilberg, *Destruction of the European Jews,* 3:568.

52. Thomas Keneally, *Schindler's List* (New York: Simon & Schuster, 1982).

53. Randolph L. Braham, *The Politics of Genocide: The Holocaust in Hungary* (New

York: Columbia University Press, 1981), 1083–1091; Fogelman, *Conscience and Courage,* 8–9.

    54. Fogelman, *Conscience and Courage,* 199–200.

    55. Fogelman, *Conscience and Courage,* 198–199.

Suggestions for Further Reading

Becker, Lawrence C., ed. *Encyclopedia of Ethics.* New York: Garland, 1992. See the articles on acts and omissions, benevolence, care, charity, courage, love, and supererogation, among others.

Block, Gay, and Malka Drucker, eds. *Rescuers: Portraits of Moral Courage in the Holocaust.* New York: Holmes & Meier, 1992. The excellent introduction provides a succinct overview; most of the book consists of interviews with rescuers together with color photographic portraits. Available in paperback.

Blum, Lawrence A. "Moral Exemplars: Reflections on Schindler, the Trocmes, and Others." In *Moral Perception and Particularity.* New York: Cambridge University Press, 1994. An insightful study of the motivation, thought, and character of several well-known rescuers. Available in paperback.

Fogelman, Eva. *Conscience and Courage: Rescuers of the Jews during the Holocaust.* New York: Doubleday-Anchor, 1994. One of the best studies of rescuers currently available. Contains a wealth of detailed information about individual rescuers, networks, and various professional helpers. Also provides psychological theory and analysis. Available in paperback.

Hallie, Philip. *Lest Innocent Blood Be Shed.* New York: Harper & Row, 1979. A study of the rescue network operated in Le Chambon-sur-Lignon, France, by Andre and Magda Trocme. Available in paperback.

Kaplan, Marion A. *Between Dignity and Despair: Jewish Life in Nazi Germany.* New York: Oxford University Press, 1998. For the role of German rescuers, see chapter 8, "Life Underground."

Keneally, Thomas. *Schindler's List.* New York: Simon & Schuster, 1982. A study of Oskar Schindler in the form of a true-to-life novel. Available in paperback.

Oliner, Samuel P., and Pearl M. Oliner. *The Altruistic Personality: Rescuers of Jews in Nazi Europe.* New York: Free Press, 1988. The most ambitious scientific study of rescuers.

Rittner, Carol, and Sondra Myers, eds. *The Courage to Care: Rescuers of Jews during the Holocaust.* New York: New York University Press, 1986. A good study of some rescuers with photographs.

Tec, Nechama. *When Light Pierced the Darkness: Christian Rescue of Jews in Nazi-Occupied Poland.* New York: Oxford University Press, 1986. A sociological study of Polish Christian rescuers; especially good for material from interviews with both rescuers and Jews who were helped or hidden. Available in paperback.

Urmson, J. O. "Saints and Heroes." In *Essays in Moral Philosophy.* Edited by A. I. Melden. Seattle: University of Washington Press, 1958. A classic study of the ethics of supererogatory acts; widely anthologized in ethics readings.

Zuccotti, Susan. *The Italians and the Holocaust: Persecution, Rescue, and Survival.* New York: Basic, 1987. An excellent study, especially for comparative purposes; see especially chapters 4–7, 10, 12.

Conclusion

A Summary of the Moral Assessments Made in This Study

What lessons can be learned from a study of moral responsibility in the Holocaust? This concluding chapter summarizes the ethical judgments that were justified in each chapter. I am acutely aware that many may disagree with my assessment of the historical and psychological evidence on the basis of which I have reached the judgments I make. However, I hope that even those who disagree with my conclusions will find the theory of responsibility I have used a helpful framework within which to discuss the ethical issues.

Jewish Victims

Three questions are often raised about the behavior of Jews in the face of the German genocidal onslaught: Why did the Jews not realize the true intentions of the Germans before it was too late? Why did the Jews not refuse to collaborate with the Germans? Why did the Jews not resist? Each question implicitly blames Jews for doing things they should not have done or for failing to take actions that they ought to have taken, for lacking certain virtues like practical wisdom and courage, and for possessing vices like self-deception and cowardice. I concluded, however, that in general Jews were not guilty of self-deception and that their confidence in culturally transmitted traditional responses to threats to the community were rationally justified by centuries of successful experience. Moreover, most Jews were segregated in a state of social death and did not have adequate opportunities to learn the truth about the genocide until after it had begun. The relative lack of armed resistance is explained mainly by the fact that Jews usually could not get arms. Nevertheless, there were a number of revolts in death camps, concentration camps, and ghettos, as well as escapes to the forests in which Jews carried on partisan activities. Indeed, the level of Jewish resistance compares very favorably with that of other populations subjected to German imprisonment, torture, starvation, and slave labor, such as Slavs, Gypsies, and Soviet prisoners of war. Although some Jews were blameworthy for their complicity with the Germans (most notably some leaders who served in the Jewish councils and members of the Jewish ghetto police), the Jewish community as a whole acted in a highly praiseworthy manner, engaging in a wide range of self-help that included taking care of children, the poor, the ill, and the elderly as long as it was humanly possible for them to do so, usually in conditions that were appalling.

Helpers and Rescuers

A relatively small number of non-Jews throughout Europe helped and rescued Jews. One estimate is that almost 300,000 Jews were saved by non-Jewish helpers and rescuers. Much of this activity was supererogatory and called for extraordinary altruism, courage, and practical wisdom, particularly in Germany proper and in occupied countries in eastern Europe like Poland. Virtually all people who helped and rescued in these circumstances were highly praiseworthy and admirable. Indeed, many of these exemplary rescuers were heroic and even saintly. In many particular situations helpers and rescuers had an actual duty, all things considered, to give help and engage in rescue. This was particularly true in western European countries in which the Germans often exercised less power and control and the populace itself was relatively less anti-Semitic. Consequently, the great majority of bystanders in these circumstances were blameworthy for not helping and rescuing. There can be little doubt that a great many more victims could have been saved if more people had chosen to help and rescue instead of remaining bystanders. Recognition of this possibility underlies a great deal of the post-Holocaust interest in the psychology of rescuers. It has also prompted some people to draw what they feel is an important lesson from the Holocaust about the role of individual virtue as a means of preventing future genocides that I discuss later in the chapter.

Perpetrators

When we turn our attention away from the behavior of both Jewish victims and non-Jewish helpers and rescuers, we find almost nothing but varying degrees of moral failure, ranging all the way from the culpably self-induced ignorance, cruelty, and fanaticism of Adolf Hitler, the principal perpetrator, to the cowardice, indifference, and petty venality of most bystanders. There is every reason to think that the vast majority of perpetrators, accomplices, and bystanders were competent moral agents with sufficient powers of agency to be held accountable for their choices and actions. It is reasonable to recognize the existence of a small minority of psychologically disturbed individuals, but psychopathology cannot be used to explain or excuse the participation of all perpetrators in the genocide. Extensive psychological testing and interviewing of perpetrators after the war failed to uncover any evidence that they all shared a so-called Nazi personality that explained their aberrant behavior.[1] Moreover, there is no reason to suppose that being socialized into a bad political culture left most Germans with a diminished capacity to tell right from wrong that rendered them blameless (or less blameworthy) for their wrong choices and actions. This means that if some individuals were in fact not blameworthy for their wrong acts or omissions, it would be on account of their having been in some other way objectively justified or validly excused for the manner in which they exercised their powers of agency.

Adolf Hitler

There is no good reason to think that Hitler suffered from mental illness (caused by, say, abuse from his father) or diminished capacity (due to having been socialized in Austrian anti-Semitic culture). Rather, the evidence strongly suggests that from an early age Hitler was a virtuoso active constructor of his own sense of personal identity, rejecting his father's wishes that he become a respectable member of the Austrian middle class. Unfortunately, none of his successive identities, as an artist, a soldier, or a politician with a mission, enabled him to face harsh realities or to avoid massive self-deception. Consequently, he developed into an exceedingly evil person filled with hatred and cruelty who used his considerable political talent to perpetrate horrendous mass murder and genocide. Blaming Hitler both for becoming the moral monster that he was and for the central role he played in the Holocaust is fully justified. Very similar assessments can be made of many other members of the Nazi leadership and other high-level perpetrators of genocide and mass murder.

The Men in Police Battalions

Most of the men who served in the police battalions and participated in the mass killings in Poland and the Soviet Union were to varying degrees blameworthy for their actions. I considered and rejected a number of situational explanations that would have provided an excuse or served to mitigate their blame. These men had not been given intense ideological indoctrination, they had not been brutalized by prior combat, there was no diffusion of responsibility brought about by bureaucratic segmentation of their task, and (perhaps most significantly) they were not coerced into participating. Indeed, most of the killing was done by men who volunteered for the operations. The evidence shows that only a small percentage of men in the police battalions took advantage of the officially sanctioned opportunity to choose not to participate in the killing. The most likely explanation for most men's willing participation in the gruesome killing was a combination of having been socialized into German political culture (with its salient features of anti-Semitism, authoritarianism, and nationalism), responding to the deep kind of peer pressure that characterizes comradeship, and a feeling of triumphant nationalism and patriotic pride brought about by the years of spectacular success of Hitler and the Nazi regime. Unfortunately, instead of providing an excuse or mitigating their blame, this explanation actually incriminates them and makes them to one degree or another blameworthy. It is very likely that only a small minority of these men would have developed with diminished cognitive and deliberative capacities as the result of socialization into German political culture. Consequently, most of them either knew that it was wrong to participate in the killings or, if they believed it was permissible or right, they had the capacity to correct their mistaken belief. In addition, many of these men were especially reprehensible not only for the unprovoked killing of unarmed men, women, and children in a gruesome manner but also for systematically using humiliation, cruelty, and torture before they killed them.

Other Perpetrators

Evidence of similar behavior by men in the SS, Einsatzgruppen, or the regular army was not considered, but there is no reason to believe that they would have been entirely blameless for their participation in mass killings of Jews and other victims solely because they had been subjected to intense indoctrination in Nazi ideology or had been brutalized by combat. At most, these factors might have mitigated the blame that some individual men deserved. Most so-called desk murderers were to some degree blameworthy because either they knew (or suspected) that all Jews were being killed or they could have found out. Very few had a justified excuse for their participation, and most of them either acted from reprehensible motives (triumphant nationalism, Nazi ideology, anti-Semitism, conformity, deferential obedience, or cowardice) or engaged in self-deception to evade feeling guilty about what they were doing.

Accomplices and Bystanders

In addition to the perpetrators (those who knowingly participated directly in one of the institutions that carried out the Final Solution), many people in Germany and throughout German-occupied Europe played an indirect role by their complicitous support of the Nazi regime, the occupying German authorities, or their own collaborationist governments. By constant surveillance of their neighborhoods, informing to the Gestapo, denouncing Jews in hiding, and countless other ways, they aided and abetted the genocide. It hardly needs arguing that many accomplices were to some extent blameworthy for their positive acts of support. By contrast, bystanders did nothing. Bystanders had at least a prima facie duty to give some help to victims and in many situations had an actual duty to help, all things considered. Consequently, most bystanders were to some extent blameworthy for their failure to help.

Nevertheless, millions of Germans opposed the Nazi regime in 1933 and continued to oppose it for the entire twelve years that it was in power. Composed mostly of Communists and Social Democrats, this political opposition was effectively neutralized through murder, terror, intimidation, and imprisonment of its leadership in concentration camps. There were also countless nonpolitical opponents who realized how immoral the regime was. But such opponents (like Jewish victims) were not exempted from moral obligations merely because they were victims. The relatively few helpers and rescuers probably came disproportionately from these groups.

Resisting the Temptations of "Relativism" and "Tolerance"

Many of us who teach courses on the Holocaust have learned from hard experience that some students balk at blaming the perpetrators or holding them responsible for their wrongdoing, although virtually all students wholeheartedly agree that the genocide against the Jews was profoundly immoral. The reasons they give for their reluctance to judge perpetrators (which in some cases rises to the level of a principled objection) can be reduced to two: "relativism" and "tolerance."[2] The quotation marks indicate that the words, as used here, refer to a set of loosely connected ideas expressed in discussion rather than to carefully worked out conceptions or theories in ethics.

"Relativism"

The nearly universal consensus that the mass killings of the Holocaust were gravely immoral does not by itself justify an ethical judgment that they really were wrong. The fact that people agree that acting in some particular way is right (or wrong) is not sufficient to show that it is really right (or wrong), all things considered. At the very least, people have to know *why* they agree— what the reasons were that led them to adopt this opinion. My own argument justifying the correctness of the consensus is nonrelativist; it appeals to the basic rules of prima facie duty that constitute the core content of morality, especially the universal prohibition against harming others. By contrast, one popular version of ethical relativism denies that these rules are universally valid and binding. According to this relativist position, a necessary and sufficient condition for a rule to be valid and binding on someone is that it be a part of the conventional morality of an actual society that socializes its members to believe in and obey it. Clearly, German society (or at least Nazi society) did not include a general prohibition against killing others, especially not Jews, Gypsies, Slavs, and so on. Therefore (so the relativist reasoning goes), German perpetrators were not blameworthy, since *for them* it was not wrong to kill Jews.

In my experience, hardly any students are relativists in this sense; on the contrary, they *agree* that it was wrong to kill the Jews, and they do *not* justify their own agreement merely by the fact that they themselves have been socialized to believe that it is wrong (as a consistent relativist would do). Rather, students resist the ethical implications of their own (correct) nonrelativist judgment that the Holocaust was deeply immoral. These ethical implications include (1) adopting an attitude of strong disapproval of the killing actions and feelings of condemnation for perpetrators who were blameworthy for them (judgmental blame), (2) overtly blaming perpetrators who deserve it (obviously, this cannot be face-to-face condemnation), and (3) agreeing that most perpetrators deserved to be "held accountable" in one or more of the ways discussed in chapter 1 (being confronted with legitimate demands for an accounting of their behavior; being subjected to informal moral sanctions such as loss of love and affection or social ostracism; or being held liable to criminal punishment, as the particular case warrants).

Some student "relativists" resist these ethical implications because they think that the perpetrators were not blameworthy, their actions only reflected what their society had taught them, although the actions themselves were immoral. In their thinking, it was not the Germans' fault that they happened to be reared in an anti-Semitic and authoritarian society; they could not help having the beliefs that they had. Indeed, some students insist, anyone who had been socialized in the very same way would have turned into a convinced perpetrator. I respond to this kind of "relativism" by pointing out that either it is based on false assumptions about the social facts (e.g., it assumes that all perpetrators were in fact subjected to intense socialization that rendered them unable to realize that genocide was immoral) or it employs an inadequate "passive learner" model of the process by which socialization takes place. As I pointed out in chapter 5, most people actively construct their own sense of personal identity on the basis of which they make their moral choices. Thus they must accept (at least some) responsibility for the kind of person they have become as well as for the actions they perform. Thus this kind of "relativist" argument does not furnish any good reasons to reject the view that many, perhaps most, perpetrators were blameworthy for their participation in the Holocaust and deserved to be held accountable for it.

"Tolerance"

Other reasons given for the reluctance to blame perpetrators or to hold them accountable have nothing directly to do with "relativism." Rather, blaming and holding others responsible is itself judged to be a symptom of arrogance, self-righteousness, or hypocrisy. However, it is not at all clear why arrogance, self-righteousness, or hypocrisy must necessarily be involved in blaming perpetrators. Merely making the logically prior (and correct) judgment that the perpetrators' killing actions were wrong (a judgment that virtually all student "relativists" agree with anyway) would not involve these faults. Nor would they be involved in making the additional judgment that (some) perpetrators are blameworthy, since such judgmental blame is distinct from, and does not automatically justify, such other actions as overt blaming, demanding an account, imposing moral sanctions, or holding perpetrators liable to legal punishment. I have given detailed reasons to justify the judgment that many (perhaps most) perpetrators were blameworthy for their wrong acts; if these reasons are good ones, then there is nothing arrogant, self-righteous, or hypocritical about accepting that judgment.

If arrogance, self-righteousness, or hypocrisy were to come into play at all, they would have to be at work in the manner in which some people engage in the additional and distinct actions of overt blaming, demanding an account, imposing moral sanctions, or holding perpetrators liable to legal punishment. There can be no doubt that some people who engage in these activities do so arrogantly, self-righteously, or hypocritically. But there is nothing inevitable about this; surely some people are not arrogant, self-righteous, and hypocritical when they engage in such activities of holding others responsible. However, even when people act in these questionable ways, their behavior does not in any way detract from the correctness of the prior judgments that ostensibly justify them, namely, that the perpetrators' actions were wrong and that they were blameworthy for having done them.

Some may object to blaming perpetrators because they have an overly skeptical view of the possibility of making justified moral judgments in the first place, joined with an exceedingly broad interpretation of the virtue of tolerance. I consider this particular kind of skepticism facile and artificial because it stems from an insistence that one is justified in judging someone else only if one is absolutely certain that one's own judgment is absolutely correct and infallible. This goes far beyond the sensible warning against judging the blameworthiness of individuals without adequate knowledge of the relevant facts. The virtue of modesty in moral judgment does not require absolute certainty of one's own infallibility; in fact, insisting on such an unattainable ideal would render all moral judgment impermissible.

Tolerance, when it is relevant at all, is more properly defended by appeal to the principle of equal consideration than by an unjustified skepticism about one's own judgment. The paradigm case of justified tolerance is the political right to religious freedom, since for most people religious beliefs are among the most personal and inviolable beliefs they have, and we simply have no way to ascertain which beliefs (if any) are the correct ones. In this case, equal respect dictates tolerance. This is not so where basic moral principles are concerned. Consequently, tolerance of moral beliefs must be constrained by practical wisdom; this guarantees that tolerance will not become so indiscriminate as to condone the opinion that there is, after all, something to be said even for the Nazi point of view on the morality of genocide. It will be recalled that practical wisdom includes knowledge of basic moral principles and rules of prima facie duty and an inclination to become well-informed about relevant facts in any situation in which a moral judgment is to be made (chap. 2). The ideological beliefs at the heart of the Nazi justification for the Final Solution about Jewish blood and the alleged worldwide Jewish-Bolshevik conspiracy could not be accepted by a person of practical wisdom; they are inconsistent with the core content of morality and are not supported either by ordinary observation or by scientific knowledge. Not only are these beliefs false and immoral, but one can also be to blame for holding them if they were acquired by engaging in self-deception.

Some Possible Lessons to Be Drawn from the Study of the Holocaust

Three lessons can be drawn from this study of the Holocaust, all of them having to do with the prevention of future genocide through means other than outside intervention, for example, by the United Nations or a coalition of individual states.[3] The first lesson focuses on the need for higher levels of individual virtues, especially universal benevolence and conscientiousness; the second identifies the need for the kinds of institutions associated with political liberalism; and the third points to the need for a good political culture. I shall critically evaluate each of these possible lessons in turn in order to arrive at what seems to be the most plausible interpretation of each one. Using the results of my critical analysis, I shall defend the view that (1) when suitably qualified and interpreted, each of these lessons in fact identifies a necessary but not sufficient condition for preventing future genocides but (2) they are jointly sufficient for preventing genocide, or at least for making it very unlikely to occur.

Increasing the Level of Universal Benevolence and Conscientiousness in Society

One lesson that some have drawn from the study of the Holocaust is that bringing about an increase in the level of the individual virtues in society is perhaps the most effective way to prevent future genocides. For example, in the preface to his book *The Altruistic Personality* Samuel P. Oliner states, "If we are to live in a world free from the threat of Holocausts, we need to create it. If we can understand some of the attributes that distinguish rescuers from others, perhaps we can deliberately cultivate them."[4] In the conclusion of his book, Oliner claims that his scientific study of rescuers succeeded in identifying a trait, which he called extensivity, as statistically the most significant difference between rescuers and others. Oliner's discussion of the trait he refers to as extensivity makes clear that it includes two familiar moral virtues, universal benevolence and universal conscientiousness. "What distinguished rescuers was not their lack of concern with self, external approval, or achievements, but rather their capacity for extensive relationships—their stronger sense of attachment to others and their feeling of responsibility for the welfare of others, including those outside their immediate familial and communal circles."[5]

Moreover, the fact that a comparatively small number of rescuers saved almost 300,000 Jews from being killed in the Holocaust (see chap. 9) suggests that Oliner's conclusion has validity: An increase in the level of the individual virtues of universal benevolence and conscientiousness may be the most effective way to prevent future genocides. Thus it may seem imperative that society give the highest priority to inculcating these virtues in its citizens, assuming that there are ways to "deliberately cultivate" them (e.g., through child-rearing techniques, moral development, education, participation in community and volunteer work, etc.).[6]

Since Oliner does not spell out the details of his view in the passage quoted, I shall look at some alternative ways of construing it, first, as the very strong claim that an increase in the strength of these individual virtues in society would be sufficient to prevent future genocides. (In order to avoid tiresome repetition, the terms "these virtues" and "virtue" are used to refer to universal benevolence and conscientiousness.) There are several objections to Oliner's thesis in this strong form. First, the evidence from which it is ostensibly derived is not sufficient to establish this strong conclusion; indeed, it seems to be irrelevant. The fact that rescuers saved nearly 300,000 lives during the ongoing Holocaust does not confirm the view that the presence of these virtues (either at the same or a greater level) would *prevent* a future genocide like it altogether. All we know (or have good reason to expect) is that the same or a greater level of these virtues would prevent the completion of a future genocide once it had already started, and (perhaps), everything else being equal, that the higher the level of individual virtue, the greater the level of prevention (e.g., the greater the number of potential victims who would be saved). But as I have repeatedly stressed, in the perpetration of the Holocaust, things were not always equal. The level of German force used to carry out the genocide varied greatly from country to country; consequently, the percentage of potential victims rescued varied greatly as well.

Second, although the actual level of these virtues in Germany and elsewhere in 1941–1945 was sufficient to rescue 300,000 potential victims, thus preventing the completion of that genocide, that level of virtue was not sufficient to prevent the Holocaust from occurring in the first place. Thus the evidence does not indicate whether a greater degree of individual virtue would be sufficient to prevent a future genocide from being implemented or not, and, if so, how much more would be required. In short we do not know whether an increase in these virtues would be sufficient to prevent future genocides from being implemented. However, a high level of universal benevolence and conscientiousness among individual citizens is very likely a necessary condition for the prevention of genocide in the way that is suggested in the next two lessons to be drawn, namely, by the establishment of liberal political institutions characteristic of constitutional democracies together with a good political culture. I shall argue that each of these individual components is necessary but not sufficient to prevent genocide; it is the conjunction of all three that is sufficient to prevent genocide or make it very unlikely. However, matters are quite different where authoritarian regimes are concerned.

Third, even if an increase in these virtues turned out to be sufficient to prevent genocide (something we do not yet know), we know that individual virtue among the citizenry is not universally necessary for prevention anyway. As opposed to democracies, an authoritarian regime has much more freedom to act against the wishes of the populace. For example, in order to explain why German anti-Semitism did not lead to genocide before the Nazis came to power, Goldhagen makes the very sensible observation that the German government would not allow it to happen.[7] Indeed, action by constituted governments is by far the most effective means to prevent genocide that has been found so far. This is confirmed even in the actions taken by collaborationist governments in France, Romania, and Bulgaria to protect their own citizens from deportation; in fact, these governmental actions were twice as effective as all of the individual rescuers and rescue networks combined, saving about 600,000 potential victims. These particular examples are not the best evidence to use to support the main thesis, however, because these governments were allowed to act as they did only because it was expedient for the Germans to do so. Furthermore, each of these collaborationist governments *failed* to help other Jews who were not citizens, and Romania actively participated in killing thousands of them.[8]

A much more relevant piece of evidence is the fact that no government of a constitutional democracy has ever perpetrated a genocide, either against its own people or against foreigners. (This should not be overstated; for example, some aspects of U.S. policy in regard to Native Americans had genocidal implications.) Therefore, might not the best method for preventing future genocides be found in paying close attention to how past genocides actually got started and were carried out? In other words, should we not pay attention to the political origins of official, state-sponsored genocide?

Establishing a Set of Institutions Characteristic of Political Liberalism

What is missing from the first lesson to be drawn is a recognition of the crucial role played by the unconstrained use of the power of the state in implementing genocide. Spontaneous violence and short-lived pogroms can occur without official sanction, but genocide requires the resources that only the institutions of the state can mobilize. Consequently, if there is an effective way to constrain the use of state power, there is also a way to prevent genocide. It certainly seems plausible to argue that in fact such an effective constraint has long been recognized and used, namely, the familiar set of liberal political institutions found, for example, in constitutional democracies.[9] These institutions include the rule of law, equality of citizenship, an independent judiciary, protection of civil liberties, a free press, and electoral accountability of the government. When these institutions are in place, it should be virtually impossible for a genocidal program to get started, much less be successfully carried out.

If this second lesson to be drawn is interpreted to mean that the formal establishment of liberal political institutions alone is sufficient to prevent genocide, then it is almost certainly false. The Weimar Republic was established on the basis of a very liberal constitution that provided for most of the institutional features under discussion, but this did not prevent the breakdown of parliamentary government and the quasi-legal Nazi assumption of power. Even though this particular failure was only an indirect cause of the Holocaust, it illustrates the main point I want to make: It is not enough to have the political institutions formally in place; they must also be working well, if genocide is to be prevented. As I argued in chapter 5, this was decidedly not the case in Weimar Germany because of the bad political culture that existed. Thus the second lesson to be drawn from this study must be revised to acknowledge that establishing a set of liberal political institutions, just like the presence of high levels of individual virtue, is necessary but is not sufficient for preventing future genocides.

Developing a Good Political Culture to Complement Liberal Political Institutions

In chapter 5 I identified five good-making characteristics that a political culture ought to have: (1) citizens have respect for the rule of law, including a strong disposition to refrain from using violence, (2) citizens strongly value and support the institutions of constitutional democracy, (3) citizens have mutual respect and tolerance toward each other, (4) citizens are disposed to actively participate in government and civic affairs, and (5) political parties have a commitment to the common good. Characteristics 1, 2, and 3 are the ones most directly relevant for enabling liberal institutions to work well in the prevention of genocide. Notice that each of them identifies a civic virtue, that is, an individual trait of character that it is good for citizens to have, all things considered.[10] I shall argue that these civic virtues have an equally important role in the prevention of genocide, alongside universal benevolence and conscientiousness. Each of these civic virtues deserves some comment. The lack of these virtues is illustrated by examples from Germany under the Nazi dictatorship. In making the point that citizens of actual constitutional democracies are sometimes far from being exemplars of these civic virtues, I draw examples from U.S. history.

Respect for the Rule of Law[11]

Clearly, the rule of law is not a feature unique to constitutional democracies; it is virtually a defining feature of legality itself. The legal concept of the rule of law is actually quite complex, but it suffices here to mention a few of its main features and the justification for them in order to appreciate why it is so important for citizens generally, and government officials in particular, to have the virtue of respect for the rule of law. The first thing to note is that the rule of law is the denial of autocratic or dictatorial rule; the precept "no one is above the law" is meant to express this idea, which is fundamental to the very conception of a legal system as opposed to personal rule. All persons who hold a public office, no matter how high or low it may be, are restricted in what they can do by the legally defined powers of their particular office. Furthermore, wherever the powers of office include the direct use of force or coercion (e.g., police, prisons, and the military) there are significant limits to the discretion allowed in its use. The second thing to note is that, with only a few exceptions such as self-defense, all citizens are forbidden to use force or violence; correspondingly, one of the most stringent duties of public officials is to vigorously enforce this aspect of the rule of law. These first two features of the rule of law clearly reflect the basic prima facie duty not to harm others that forms part of the core content of morality. The third feature to note is that no one can be legally deprived of their liberty (arrested, detained, imprisoned, etc.) or their property, except through due process of law. For example, no one can be imprisoned or punished in any way without being convicted in a duly constituted court of law for having committed a crime, and a crime has been committed only if there has been a violation of a valid public law duly enacted by the legislature and signed by the executive.

Examples of violations of the rule of law are far too easy to find. During the very first months of Nazi rule in 1933, police killed hundreds of the regime's political opponents and summarily arrested thousands more and threw them into the newly established concentration camps. Of course, these actions were legal, having been authorized by a presidential decree of February 28 (prompted by the Reichstag fire) that suspended some basic civil liberties and authorized the Nazi central government to take over local police powers if they deemed it necessary. These gross violations of the rule of law were not protested because the great majority of Germans approved of the use of force as long as it was directed primarily against people on the political left (Communists and Social Democrats), Jews, Gypsies, and homosexuals.[12] In 1942, just a few months after the Japanese attack on Pearl Harbor, the government of the United States forcibly removed nearly 107,000 Japanese-Americans from their homes and imprisoned them in concentration camps (euphemistically called "relocation centers") until just before the end of the war in 1945. Many of them lost jobs, homes, and property without any compensation. Seventy percent of these people were citizens who had been born in the United States. They had not committed a crime; they were "guilty" of Japanese ancestry and thus, deemed to be security risks.[13] The American people did not protest this gross violation of the rule of law. (This example throws doubt on the assertion that genocide would be impossible in a constitutional democracy. Most Americans had no way of knowing for sure what was happening to the Japanese who had been "relocated.")

Support for the Institutions of Constitutional Democracy

In addition to the rule of law, central features of constitutional democracies include such institutions as an independent judiciary, individual civil liberties, a free press, and equality of citizenship. Equality of citizenship, an institution that clearly reflects the principle of equal consideration underlying the core content of morality, shows that the legal system is intended to give equal protection to all members of the political community. The Nuremberg Laws of 1935 stripped Jews of their citizenship and clearly signaled the intention of the Nazi regime to treat Jews in a fundamentally different and harmful way than it treated other members of German society. Nevertheless, Germans generally welcomed the Nuremberg Laws because they seemed preferable to the recent upsurge of pogromlike violence.[14] Likewise, the Constitution of the United States initially denied citizenship to African-American slaves, thus legally justifying the American system of slavery that had already existed for over 150 years. This violation of equality was not protested by Americans until the rise of the abolitionist movement in the nineteenth century. Even after slavery was ended, most Americans continued to accept serious violations of equal citizenship for African Americans. In addition to the wide-ranging restrictions imposed by legalized segregation, they were denied the right to vote, hold office, and use public accommodations.

Mutual Respect and Tolerance among Fellow Citizens

This virtue is distinct from respect for the institution of equality of citizenship, yet it complements it in an important way. Many people accept political equality but are very prejudiced. For example, some white racists believe that blacks are inferior but tolerate political equality with them as a pragmatic necessity. They may well not want to return to legal segregation, but they are unwilling to have any associations with blacks. Racists such as these would at best be bystanders if the rights of blacks were to be jeopardized, just as many Germans stood by as the hard-won political rights of Jews were taken away.

A great deal of empirical psychological research has confirmed that prejudice is maintained by avoidance of social interaction with members of the devalued group. Correspondingly, prejudice is weakened when people have ongoing experiences of working or associating with those whom they have formerly denigrated, especially if they cooperate with them in mutually beneficial activities. Mutual respect and tolerance is not an inevitable part of human nature; it has to be acquired through direct experience.[15] Citizens who have mutual respect and tolerance are also capable of participating together in a wide range of intermediate civic associations and organizations that are essential for the exercise of political rights in the wider community.

Summary

There is a complex set of conditions (not including outside intervention) that is sufficient to prevent future genocides or at least make them less likely to occur. This complex sufficient condition consists of three elements, each of which is necessary but insufficient by itself for the prevention of genocide: (1) a high level of the individual virtues of universal benevolence and conscientiousness, (2) a set of liberal political institutions characteristic of constitutional democracy, and (3) a good political culture, including especially the civic virtues of respect for the rule of law, support for and loyalty to the other institutions of constitutional democracy, and mutual respect and tolerance among citizens. In real life these conditions are only imperfectly realized, so there is always the possibility that an actual democracy will someday resort to genocide. However, the historical record indicates that if future genocides occur, they will most probably not be perpetrated by a democracy but by an undemocratic, authoritarian, or dictatorial regime.

Notes

1. Eric A. Zillmer et al., *The Quest for the Nazi Personality: A Psychological Investigation of Nazi War Criminals* (Hillsdale, N.J.: Erlbaum, 1995), 194.

2. Berel Lang, *Act and Idea in the Nazi Genocide* (Chicago: University of Chicago Press, 1990), 234–240, "Teaching the Holocaust," Lang's discussion of his own experience with this phenomenon.

3. Pursuing the topic of outside intervention as a way to prevent genocide within a country would take us too far afield into areas such as international law.

4. Samuel P. Oliner, *The Altruistic Personality: Rescuers of Jews in Nazi Germany* (New York: Free Press, 1988), xviii.

5. Oliner, *Altruistic Personality,* 249.

6. Morton Hunt, *The Compassionate Beast: The Scientific Inquiry into Human Altruism* (New York: Anchor, 1990), 209–224.

7. Daniel Jonah Goldhagen, *Hitler's Willing Executioners: Ordinary Germans and the Holocaust* (New York: Knopf, 1996), 72.

8. Raul Hilberg, *The Destruction of the European Jews* (New York: Holmes & Meier, 1985), 759.

9. Judith N. Sklar, "The Liberalism of Fear," in *Political Thought and Political Thinkers,* ed. Stanley Hoffmann (Chicago: University of Chicago Press, 1998), chap. 1.

10. David H. Jones, "A Pragmatic Defense of Some Liberal Civic Virtues," *Southern Journal of Philosophy* 30, no. 2 (1992): 77–92.

11. John Rawls, *A Theory of Justice* (Cambridge: Harvard University Press, 1971), 235–243.

12. Jackson J. Spielvogel, *Hitler and Nazi Germany: A History* (Englewood Cliffs, N.J.: Prentice-Hall, 1992), 70–73.

13. John Armour and Peter Wright, *Manzanar* (New York: Vintage, 1988), 3–10.

14. Spielvogel, *Hitler and Nazi Germany,* 271–273.

15. Ervin Staub, *The Root of Evil: The Origins of Genocide and Other Group Violence* (New York: Cambridge University Press, 1989), chap. 18.

Suggestions for Further Reading

Chalk, Frank, and Kurt Johanssohn. *The History and Sociology of Genocide.* New Haven: Yale University Press, 1990. Part 1, "The Conceptual Framework," provides a definition of genocide and a discussion of preconditions.

Fein, Helen, ed. *Genocide Watch.* New Haven: Yale University Press, 1992. An excellent anthology of articles primarily by activists with practical experience with recently threatened genocides (e.g., in Iraq against the Kurds and in Iran against adherents of the Baha'i religion).

Hunt, Morton. *The Compassionate Beast: The Scientific Study into Human Altruism.* New York: Anchor, 1990. A very readable but sophisticated presentation of recent research into altruism in general. Chapter 10 is devoted to Samuel Oliner and his study of rescuers.

Staub, Ervin. *The Roots of Evil: The Origins of Genocide and Other Group Violence.* New York: Cambridge University Press, 1989. See especially chapters 2 and 15 on the origins of genocide and chapters 17–18 on ways to prevent genocide.

INDEX

About the Author

David H. Jones is Professor of Philosophy Emeritus at The College of William and Mary, where he continues to teach a course on the Holocaust. He received his B.A. in philosophy from the University of Kansas City (now the University of Missouri–Kansas City) in 1958, and his M.A. and Ph.D. in philosophy from Harvard University in 1960 and 1963, respectively. He taught at the University of Kansas before joining the faculty at William and Mary in 1967. He has published articles in professional philosophy journals on a variety of topics in ethics, philosophy of mind, and the psychology of morals. His article "Freud's Theory of Moral Conscience" has been anthologized in the United States and Britain.